By the Same Author

THE

POWER

OF

FAITH

THE

ROAD

TO

SUCCESSFUL

LIVING

by Louis Binstock

SIMON AND SCHUSTER

NEW YORK

1958

LIBRARY OF CONGRESS CATALOG CARD NUMBER: 58–7511
MANUFACTURED IN THE UNITED STATES OF AMERICA
BY KINGSPORT PRESS, INC., KINGSPORT, TENN.

TO RUTH

My wonderful, wonderful wife

ACKNOWLEDGMENTS

To Stephen Becker, for editorial suggestions and technical skills; to Bernard Geis, for continuing counsel and kindness; to Helen Bagden, for secretarial interest and industry.

L. B.

CONTENTS

ix

THE

MAN

WITHOUT

A SHIRT

Chapter One

> *If fortune wishes to make a man*
> *estimable, she gives him virtue; if*
> *she wishes to make him esteemed,*
> *she gives him success.*
> —JOSEPH JOUBERT

The most conspicuous failure in our time is success. No age
in man's history has been so feverishly preoccupied with success;
no age has been so noisily boastful of it. The reality or the promise
of "good things" pervades our view of the world; almost everywhere plenty has replaced, or has begun to replace, poverty. We
are aware of paradoxes, of course, and some of them are witty
proofs of our successes: able to gorge at will, many of us diet; able
to cover our nakedness, many of us choose to expose more and
more of it; as the work-week is reduced, many of us bring our
most concentrated efforts to leisure activities. These are frivolous
paradoxes, not dangerous in themselves. But they spring from one

1

of humanity's recurrent disillusionments, one of the great un-learned lessons of history: Success does not create happiness.

The statement is not original. There have been many "Golden Ages"; each believed that ultimate human happiness was near at hand. Each declined, lost its hold on humanity, and left only the bitterness and chaos of failure. And each was succeeded, sooner or later, by another which made the same mistakes: which built its hopes, laws, and traditions on men or ideas, but not both; on the flesh or the spirit, but not both; on power or humility, but not both.

A cardinal error—seemingly simple, actually complex—lay in man's definitions, written or unwritten, of success. Success has generally been defined in terms of goods rather than needs, fixed doctrines rather than the dynamics of life, and groups of men rather than the individual.

This book is an examination of success and failure. The theme of the book is self-fulfillment. Its hero is man; its villains are the false gods he worships. And the uses of this book are many: to erect signposts, to fix landmarks, to hack our way through the tangled brush of success and failure—to clear the path to happiness.

The United States in particular has been and is a nation of success. We have certainly been the most successful of all peoples in developing a prosperous economy and a powerful community. We are the traditional haven of the oppressed; we are the land of opportunity; we are now, willy-nilly, the guardians of a whole culture, the ultimate defenders of two thousand years of history. Our own tradition of success (backed by a pride in liberty and a vigor in its defense) has carried us to this pre-eminence.

But we—all of us to some extent—are beginning to wonder whether the glow of health has become the flush of fever; whether the strains and tensions of worldly success have induced a fatigue; whether decades of producing most and advancing fastest have left us depleted; whether the cultural Benzedrine of our philosophy of success is leaving us with a national hangover. We

2

have, in short, begun to question seriously our own ideas of success; and in the process we must question the very tradition of success.

At the turn of the century Arnold Bennett, in a book called *How to Live,* set down the average man's definition of success, dividing it into four categories:

(1) Distinction in pure or applied science, which may be achieved without accumulating much money or great fame.

(2) Distinction in the arts, usually accompanied by great fame and not much money.

(3) Distinction in power and prestige over other men, usually accompanied by much money and great fame.

(4) Distinction in amassing money.

We may set against this definition all the great civilizations that have flourished over the last thirty centuries. By and large the definition holds good. There are shifts in emphasis, and occasionally new values or rewards may be added, but material success has had much the same meaning for three thousand years. There was always distinction, either by accomplishment or acquisition. And distinction brought with it, to a greater or a lesser degree, fame or money or both.

In antiquity the Jews emphasized religious learning and righteous living: they honored the sage and the saint. The Greeks emphasized power of thought and beauty of form: they honored the philosopher and the artist. The Romans emphasized conquest and government: they honored the warrior and the legislator. In the Middle Ages there were two heroes: the chivalrous knight and the priest of piety. During the Renaissance, poets and painters restored light and laughter to the grim darkness of Europe. With the Reformation, ministers insisted upon the dignity of labor and the honor of trade. With the cataclysmic revolutions of the eighteenth, nineteenth, and twentieth centuries—political, industrial, racial— political philosophers, visionaries, inventors, tycoons, and nationalist leaders became the idols, and often the dictators, of the modern world.

The era, the form of government, may change the emphasis;

but in ancient Israel (a democracy with strong overtones of theocracy), in ancient Greece (a democracy with strong overtones of autocracy), in the feudal systems of the Middle Ages and the Renaissance, in the later and purer democracies (the United States and Great Britain), in still later dictatorships (Soviet Russia and Red China), the concept of success remains the same. In patriotism, religion, education, art, science, business, in a free or a slave group, in a church-controlled or a state-dominated nation, success was distinction, and distinction usually led to fame or money or both.

Man had to distinguish himself in the eyes of others. He had to be *something more than himself*. It was not enough simply to be; it was necessary to surpass what he already was.

And in time man, the individual, himself a miracle surpassing all other miracles, ceased to be valued for himself. He was measured against the traditional notions of distinction, fame, and wealth. He was inevitably found wanting. No one thought of reversing the process: of measuring the notion of success against man, who had created it. We have begun to do that now; and it is this notion of success which is found wanting.

Primitive societies are often invoked—nostalgically and mistakenly—as examples of cultures in which happiness is attained in the absence of traditional success drives. (This is a very natural and normal reaction to the civilization in which we live. Most primitive cultures are tropical, and most observers live and work in more hostile climates. This page is being written in Chicago, in January; the wind pierces to the bone; and my vision of happiness tends more and more to take on the outlines of Tahiti.) Yet in Margaret Mead's first classic study of a primitive society, *Coming of Age in Samoa*, we note that success drives similar to our own were just as strong among simple and "backward" Polynesians as they are among ourselves. Samoa is a land where neither tragic poverty nor great natural disaster threatens society. No one is hurried through life or punished for slow development. On the

4

contrary, the gifted, the precocious, are held back until the slow among them have come level. No one plays for high stakes; no one pays exorbitant social prices; no one suffers for his convictions or fights to the death for special ends. But Margaret Mead goes on to say:

At seventeen or eighteen a boy is thrust into the Aumaga, a group of young men and older men without titles, called the strength of the Village. Here he is badgered into efficiency by rivalry, precept, and example. The older chiefs who supervise the activities of the Aumaga gaze eagerly, sternly upon any backsliding and any undue precocity. The prestige of his group is ever being called into account by the Aumaga of the neighboring village. His fellows ridicule and punish the boy who fails to appear when any group activity is on foot. . . . He hopes that some day he will hold a *matai* name, a name which will make him a member of the assembly of head-men, which will give him the right to work with chiefs rather than with young men. . . . Proficiency in some techniques will set him off a little from his fellows; fishing prowess means immediate rewards in the shape of food, gifts to offer to his sweetheart. Without such gifts, his advances will be scorned.*

Furthermore, in the same author's penetrating analysis of American culture, *Male and Female*, we find this:

The American child drinks in the admonition to succeed, to be the right weight, to learn to walk at the right time, to go up grade by grade in school with good marks, to make the team, to make the sorority or clique, to be the one acclaimed by others for success. . . . A man in America should be, first of all, a success in his business; he should advance, make money, go up fast, and if possible he should also be likable, attractive and well-groomed, a mixer, and informed,

---

* From *Coming of Age in Samoa* by Margaret Mead; published by William Morrow & Company, Inc.; copyright 1928 by Margaret Mead.

good in the leisure-time activities of his class, should provide well for his home. . . . A woman, to receive equal recognition, should be intelligent, attractive, know how to make the best of herself in dress and manner, be successful in attracting and keeping first, several men, finally, one, run her home and family efficiently, so that her husband stays devoted and her children surmount the nutritional, physical, and ethical hazards of maturation and are successful too.*

We may grant, then, that the notion of success is fairly constant; but we realize that emphases differ, that the specific outward form of success may depend on the age, the nation, or the culture. In an industrial age it is perhaps natural to find a widespread conviction that the hunger for success, in particular the average American's, is a new phenomenon. Success, it is said, is the child of the nineteenth century, conceived in the union of two rebellious and progressive forces, Individualism and Industrialism, both of which were most vigorous in America. Born in a time of violent change, success became an end in itself; and, like youth, it was equated with happiness. More important, perhaps: it was ever more easily attainable. The country was growing; there was land, there were jobs, there was the desire, there was pride. In the bright lexicon of youth there was no such word as fail; Horatio Alger was a household name, and *Rags to Riches,* one of his titles, became a part of the language. Novels and plays used the Cinderella myth, in different settings and with different casts, but always with the same beginning (poverty) and the same ending (prosperity); they were best-sellers and Broadway hits. An Al Smith, rising from the slums to political power, honor, and prestige; a Babe Ruth, pitching and batting his way out of an orphanage to stardom and idolization; a Charles Lindbergh, flying out of obscurity into the sun: these were the heroes acclaimed and adored by America. These were the success stories; they were the

* From *Male and Female* by Margaret Mead; published by William Morrow & Company, Inc.; copyright 1949 by Margaret Mead.

hope of—and the example for—those who were left behind.

For half a century the American child has been taught by both precept and example that material success—distinction in the aquisition of fame and money, position and power—is the most important goal of life. He has been taught other things—trust in God; honor; love for his fellow man—by precept but rarely by example. He is urged to eat certain products for greater strength; to study diligently for greater keenness; to attend Sunday School for moral edification. Why? Because, the answer comes, these are necessary to success. To be healthy, wealthy, and wise is good; but, we are told, to put the health and wisdom at the service of the wealth is better. The taste of a good meal, the power of a book, the strength we derive from morality: these are joys in themselves. But they have been made tools; we have been told too often that their value lies only in their contribution to our climb toward material success.

A churchman has written in *Why Jesus Died*, "Instead of good and bad, just and unjust, the new values are efficiency and success. Everything is measured by success, even the churches. Today goodness is measured by the amount of success it contains. The morality of success is enthroned in our midst and the new ethics of success apply to all the manifestations of life." *

One unblushing manifestation of American life is Miss America: presumably not the typical, but the ideal American girl. Some time ago one of the candidates for this title, asked whether the man she hoped to marry would necessarily be rich, replied winsomely, "No. I will never marry a man for his money. But, of course, if he didn't have a lot of money he'd be very unhappy, and since I'd want him to be a happy man, I'd . . ."

The Roaring Twenties really began in 1923: the market was bullish, and Roar was at first a gentle lowing. Six years later it was

---

* From *Why Jesus Died* by Pierre van Paassen. Copyright 1949 by the author. Used by permission of the publisher, The Dial Press, Inc.

a magnificent, infernal bellowing—and six months after that it trailed off to a tragic whimper, echoing in the groans of the survivors.

In that great winter of discontent—1929—an important meeting was held at Chicago's Edgewater Beach Hotel. Around the conference table sat nine tycoons. They were not, as the phrase goes, ordinary tycoons. These were without question the world's nine most successful industrialists. Their desires and decisions determined the fortunes of half the world's population. Their distinction, fame, and wealth seemed forever secure. They were:

The president of the world's largest steel agglomeration.

The president of the world's largest public utilities agglomeration.

The president of the world's largest gas company.

The world's most powerful wheat speculator.

The shaggiest bear in Wall Street.

The director of the world's largest monopoly.

A member of the Cabinet of the United States.

The president of the New York Stock Exchange.

The president of the Bank of International Settlements.

O tempora, o morituri! Twenty-five years later Charles Schwab was dead, a bankrupt. Samuel Insull was a penniless fugitive from justice. Howard Hopson was insane. Arthur Cutten died insolvent abroad. Jesse Livermore was a suicide. Ivar Kreuger was a suicide. Albert Fall was released from prison that he might die at home. Richard Whitney had just completed a term at Sing Sing. Leon Fraser was a suicide.

None of these men was a success. *True success is indestructible:* at no point in their lives had any of these men attained it.

Neither had Edwin Arlington Robinson's Richard Cory:

> *Whenever Richard Cory went down town*
> *We people on the pavement looked at him;*
> *He was a gentleman from sole to crown,*
> *Clean favored, and imperially slim.*

8

And he was always quietly arrayed,
   And he was always human when he talked;
But still he fluttered pulses when he said,
   "Good-morning," and he glittered when he walked.

And he was rich—yes, richer than a king—
   And admirably schooled in every grace:
In fine, we thought that he was everything
   To make us wish that we were in his place.

So on we worked, and waited for the light,
   And went without the meat, and cursed the bread; ,
And Richard Cory, one calm summer night,
   *Went home and put a bullet through his head.**

The problem had been posed dramatically: public, or outer, success, which we call material, was no index of private, or inner, success, which we shall call spiritual. Material success is what a man has; spiritual success is what he is; and we had tended to lump them together, to assume that happiness was the product of wealth. We had been proved wrong.

But the lesson was wasted. Americans are a resilient people: over and over we can be stunned by the truth, but we always recover; we never quite lose that fine and hardy capacity to regulate our lives by solid, realistic, businesslike wishful thinking.

On February 1, 1956, under the heading "Business Is Good But the Boss Is Sick," a Chicago newspaper sounded the alarm: "If you're a successful executive, you may be sick and not know it." The point was supported by the results of a study conducted by the School and Institute of Industrial Health at the University of Michigan. Among 500 business executives who underwent

* From *The Children of the Night* by Edwin Arlington Robinson. Reprinted by permission of Charles Scribner's Sons.

physical examination, 41 per cent showed major symptoms of bad health.

At about the same time, a medical journal made public a survey of 600 upper-bracket executives. The purpose of the survey was to find out why executive ranks are unconscionably thinned by premature death. The survey indicated that 55.8 per cent of the men and 64 per cent of the women had serious diseases. About twenty-five separate unhealthy conditions were found—*and none of them had been known to the subjects before the examination.* Some of them were important enough to be definite hazards to normal longevity.

Speaking before the American Association's Personnel Conference, two eminent physicians pointed out that in today's industrial and business world, being an executive has a specific, and rather poignant, psychological meaning: the lucky one feels that he is sniffing the rarefied atmosphere of management—that he has arrived. Why, then, the doctors asked, do executives become troubled—harassed, angry, grumpy, depressed; why do they develop physical, mental, and emotional diseases and imbalances? Among the twenty-seven answers they offered, the three most serious were frustration, fear of failure, and feelings of insecurity.

Dr. Kardiner, in *The Psychological Frontiers of Society,* devotes many pages to an analysis of the "drive for success," which he insists is the source of many breakdowns and premature cardiac deaths in the relentless race for power and place. Some years ago, Dr. Russell L. Cecil, a renowned authority on arthritis, asserted that four prime causes of this crippling disease are marital shipwreck, financial disaster, loneliness and worry, and long-cherished resentments. He observed that the first three are connected with failure, and that the fourth may be a result of failure. He went on to a doubtful conclusion: Since we know, he said, that failure can thus upset the balance of nature, our first duty is to realize that success is not the basic aim of nature.

Well, success may not be *the* basic aim of nature, but human nature as we have known it includes a strong success drive. Man is a success-seeking animal. His idea of success may be distorted; but on the conscious level his urge to success is often as strong as his sexual drive. It is as unremitting in its demands. Its satisfaction is requisite to the well-being of the individual. Part of man's spirit subsists on his successes; without a sufficiently steady supply, his spirit may wither.

And yet material success, which we have tried to define, can also bring death to the spirit; it can become dust and ashes in a man's hands. It can cause a man to cry out with King Solomon: "I gathered me silver and gold and the peculiar treasures of kings and of the provinces. . . . the delights of the sons of man; concubines very many. So I was great and increased more than all that were before me in Jerusalem. . . . And whatsoever my eyes desired I kept not from them. . . . And this was my portion from all my labors. Then I looked on all the works that my hands had wrought and on the labor that I had labored to do; and behold, all was vanity and a striving after wind and there was no profit under the sun."

Vanity. A striving after wind. These are grave indictments. Is material success only a cardiac condition? Suicide? An arid sense of emptiness after a lifetime of work?

If man were simply the son of Heaven, we might say Yes. But man is also a child of the earth. Robinson Crusoe, alone for decades, could center his attention on his best self; but even so, he required a house, and garments, and food; even so, he raised cats for pets and goats for meat; even so, he prepared a signal fire; even so, he rejoiced to find Friday. And we, more than any generation in history, are members of a wide human society. The circles expand: family, friends, neighbors, community, nation, mankind. And these other selves are also sons and daughters of earth as well as of Heaven; they too must feed their bodies along with their souls, fulfill their complete selves. Each man must find the balance; he must serve his best self, but he must get on

11

with the selves around him. He must please himself; he must consider others. He must remain an individual, but admit the individuality of others.

And here we touch upon another significant misunderstanding. Most of us believe that we are individuals; but most of us are simply personalities. There is a difference, and too many of us are unaware of it.

The root meanings of "person" and "individual" are very suggestive. "Person" is derived from the Latin *persona*, "mask." Roman actors wore masks; the masks had mouthpieces through which the actors made their words to sound: *per sonare*. Wearing the masks, the actors were not themselves: they had become personalities *with a specific function to perform for a specific audience*. They were not, themselves, what they seemed—and only children and morons believed that they were, gasping in alarm to find that the matinee idol butchered in Seneca last week was alive in Terence this week.

But the word "individual" derives from *individe*—undivided. The whole human being, not an amalgam of parts. The individual cannot split himself, cannot present one face to the applauding public and another to his deeper self. He is natural man. He maintains natural balance. He is of society, and because he is whole he determines, in his small way, what society will be. The "personality," on the other hand, must allow society to determine what *he* will be; and in his own heart he may despise the role he has forced himself to play.

We are so busy, these days, fashioning masks that we have little time to be individuals. The masks are many, and they are all imposed on the individual from without. They are often money, power, fame, conformity, unctuous piety, compulsive generosity. They make us sound and seem good—exceptionally good—in public; they establish us as personalities. Yet behind them there is always the individual, often smothered, often dying.

Why not simply destroy the masks? Because Paradise is lost: we are no longer in the Garden of Eden. The first mask was a fig leaf,

and we have fashioned thousands since. We are no longer innocent; we know shame. For many of us shame and sin and failure are unbearable, so we fashion more masks. We are members
of a complex social order and a highly advanced technological
civilization. Our instincts are burdened daily with a multiplicity
of choices; and our choices must be at least somewhat conditioned
by the society to which we belong. Our preferences, our desires,
are often determined for us: clothes, customs, ceremonies, creeds,
possession, power, position, prestige. To destroy all the masks is
impossible; and it might well be fatal.

But we must learn to destroy many of them. We have reached
a time when each new mask is a kind of groveling, another de-
scent to self-abasement and ultimately self-destruction. We have
learned to please others as a means to material success. We think
in terms of pressures and influences, in terms of pleasing others—
praise from Caesar is praise indeed!—and we drown the individual
in a sea of social approval. We bury him under layers of masks.
We gain the world; we lose our souls; and only then do we realize
that the world is not enough.

Let it be thundered from the rooftops: *Praise from Caesar is
no praise at all!* A man must come to terms with himself. A man
must know his own soul. A man must *be*.

It is reported of Rabbi Zusya of Hanipol that he once said,
"In the coming World they will not ask me, 'Why were you not
Moses?' They will ask me, 'Why were you not Zusya?' " In the
play *Picnic*, Madge Owens pleads with Hal Carter to stop trying
to be like others, and to be himself. "Yeah," he says, in a moment
of self-recognition, "but what good is me?" The "me" he was
talking about was not the real Hal Carter. It was the personality
he had tried to project in the sight of his fellow men. When Hal
is asked to pose for a picture, Millie Owens remarks, "But he's
always posing." And Hal answers, more perceptively than he
knows: "I don't know how to act natural." The great E. Stanley
Jones has preached over and over again: "I have no obligation to

succeed. I have only the obligation to be true to the highest and best I know."

That is success, in its broadest definition: to become the highest and best we know. To be Zusya!

The Hebrew word for sin is *chautau*. It comes from a root verb which means, "to miss the mark." God has set a target for man— man in general and man in particular—on this earth. He has asked the species of man to become perfect even as He is perfect. But of the individual man He asks only that he strive to fulfill himself. To miss the mark that is within a man's reach—that alone is sin. To discover and strike the target of his best self— that is success.

In the Talmud is a searching question: "Who is rich?" And the ready response is: "He who rejoices in his portion." He, in other words, who has found his highest self and fulfilled it. He alone has found success. "What is the worst thing the Evil Urge can achieve?" asked Rabbi Shalomo B. Karlin. He answered: "To make man forget that he is the son of a King." Every human being is a child of God. We are created in God's image, but each of us is an individual; we are all unique. No man is expected to be, or to believe, or to behave, like any other man. But he must not forget that whatever he is, or thinks, or does, he is the son of the King. From His hands we have received the gift of life. Before His throne each man will account for the use of that gift. And each man should be able to say, "Oh, Lord, I have been myself. All that You gave me, I have used. No more, because I could not; no less, because I should not. All!"

The King does not indicate to His sons the nature or size of their reward for labor on earth. The Rabbis tell a parable: There was a rich man who hired laborers and brought them into his orchard. He set them to work pruning and nursing a variety of trees. Each laborer selected the tree which appealed to him. They worked hard and long. When evening came the rich man gathered them together and asked each one, "At which tree have you worked?" One pointed out a pepper tree; he was given a gold

14

piece. One who had worked on a white-blossom tree was given half a gold piece. Another who had worked on an olive tree was given 200 zuz. Thus for all; and the laborers who had received the smaller sums were perplexed and disgruntled. "If you had told us in the beginning," they complained, "for which tree there would be the higher pay, each of us might have had the opportunity to work on it." And the rich man replied: "Had I done that, would my whole orchard have been properly pruned and nursed?"

Spiritually, the parable is instructive. God does not specify the reward that will be granted each of His children for his labor. Each must choose the tree to which his spirit responds; let him work long and hard at that tree, and he will know happiness through his own strength. Spiritual treasures cannot be measured in coin.

The materialist will of course interpret the parable otherwise. "Why," he will ask, "were the men not paid the same wage? Each worked long and hard, and the rich man had no right to set a different value on each tree." And by his own terms, the materialist may be right. But this is not a parable of labor and management. It is a parable of happiness. We cannot all work the most materially profitable tree. Spiritually, only one tree—that to which we are drawn in our souls—*can* be profitable to us. In the privacy of his soul a man counts his true profits. And God does not ask whether we have been like others or done their kind of work; He will examine our souls, and not our purses. Each man knows whether he has given his best self to the work he loves.

Each man knows whether or not he will be able to say to the Master, "I did not seek to be Moses. I was Zusya."

An American parable is Nathaniel Hawthorne's "The Great Stone Face." We all know the story, of a boy named Ernest living in a valley dominated by an immense cliff which formed, when viewed at a proper distance, a noble human face. Prophecies were passed from generation to generation: some day a great man

15

would rise from the village, and the sign of his greatness would be his features: he would be twin to the Great Stone Face.

Ernest grew to manhood, living plainly and thinking high; and he searched for that great man. He thought it might be Gathergold, who having become rich had returned to live in the village; but Ernest saw the cold glint of his eyes, and turned away. He thought it might be Blood-and-Thunder, the famous general; he saw that it was not. He thought it might be Stony-Phiz, the great statesman; Ernest listened to one hollow speech and turned away. And then a renowned poet returned, but neither was it he.

By now, Ernest was an old man. The poet spent many days in the valley, and one evening he stood with the crowd listening as Ernest spoke to the people; Ernest's talks were a weekly custom. Hawthorne goes on: "The poet, as he listened, felt that the being and character of Ernest were a nobler strain of poetry than he had ever written. . . . At a distance, but directly to be seen high up in the golden light of the setting sun, appeared the Great Stone Face, with hoary mists around it. Like the white hair around the brow of Ernest! Its look of grand beneficence seemed to embrace the world. . . . The poet, by an irresistible impulse, threw his arms aloft and shouted, 'Behold! Behold! Ernest is himself the likeness of the Great Stone Face!' "

Not the tycoon, nor the warrior, nor the stateman, nor the poet—but he who, being himself at his best, seeking little in material things, searching deep for spiritual values, grew so great in soul that his life was a blessing to his fellow man. "To be what we are," Robert Louis Stevenson once said, "and to become what we are capable of becoming, is the only creed of life."

"The Beast in the Jungle" is one of Henry James's most meaningful short stories. Its hero spends his life waiting excitedly for some rare and prodigious stroke of destiny; he is sure in his bones that he has been singled out for a unique fate. And toward the end of his life he discovers that he was right: his fate was precisely to become the one man in the world to whom nothing of deep significance ever happened. He had spent his life waiting for the great event, and had been so preoccupied by his vision of glory that the one important act he might have performed—marriage to a woman who wanted him and loved him, and who saw what was happening to him—never came to pass. He had lived in fantasy; he had done little but wait, all his life, and in the end he was nothing. At the woman's grave he saw the truth; he learned, too late, that his life of anticipation, of fancy, had kept him from being himself, and had driven away the one woman who might have helped him fulfill himself. He had existed; but he had failed to *be*.

"No passion had ever touched him," James concludes. "He had survived, but where was his deep ravage? He had been outside of his life, not learning it within—what he presently stood there gazing at was the rounded void of his life. . . . The fate he had been marked for he had met with a vengeance. He had emptied the cup to the lees. He had been the man of his time, the man to whom nothing on earth was to have happened. . . . He had justified his fear and achieved his fate. He had failed with the last exactitude of all he was to fail of. . . . He saw the jungle of his life and saw the lurking beast."

He had been born with infinite possibilities, as all men are; and he had reached the end of his life without unraveling fully any of the threads of his destiny. To himself, to the world about him, to his God, he was a true failure. He had lived and died untested, untouched; he had left his gifts and talents unformed, unfelt; all of life was for him unattempted, unchallenged.

This was the meaning of failure.

They tell of a Persian king who one night dreamed of great happiness. In the morning he summoned his wisest counselors and demanded that they show him the way to make the dream reality.

Fearing punishment, even death, they offered a formula: "Find a happy man, O King, and wear his shirt. Then shall thy desire be fulfilled."

And an army of searchers was sent forth, through the length and breadth of the kingdom, and they searched for days, and then months, and then years. And their search was fruitless.

But when twenty years had passed, and they were weary with their search, they came upon a man alone in a hut, in the deep forest. He radiated a spirit of outer joy and inner peace. This man was supremely happy, and the searchers sighed and smiled. Their search was ended.

Then they looked again, and knew that they had wasted twenty years. The man was so poor that he had no shirt.

THE

SIRE

OF ALL

THE

FEARS

Chapter Two

Adversity has the effect of eliciting talents which, in prosperous circumstances, would have lain dormant.
—HORACE

In the Talmud are recorded the minutes of a long and occasionally hot debate on the proposition: Not to be born is the best for man. The affirmative wins, unanimously; it is agreed that the burdens of life overbalance its joys. But with this decision, a recommendation is handed down: as man, through no choice of his own, *is* born, then he must make the best of his life; he must make it the best life possible. His is the duty to return his best self to his Maker.

Man's struggle begins at birth. The baby's first cry, which psychiatrists say is a call for return to the security of the womb, is also its first cry for help: help in survival. It reaches for food; it reaches for love. It grows, learns to touch, to grasp, to distinguish objects, to make sense of sounds. It learns to respond, and by responding to overcome frustration. Its frustrations are its failures, and its first satisfactions begin its long training in the techniques of success. Babies frown and fawn, smile and glower, clap for joy and howl in anguish; later they laugh aloud or throw tantrums.

These are obvious techniques. As a child grows, however, he learns more subtle ways of satisfying his urges to success. Obeying and pleasing his elders; adjusting to the characters and caprices of friends; conforming to the standards of the group, the class, the club: these make life easier and happier for him. His pattern of behavior is still very predictable; he has, as it were, a "system." His requirements are modest and normal; his methods of fulfilling them are similar. Within his small orbit he demands physical survival and social approval; he can best achieve them by adapting quietly.

In adolescence the child moves into a wider, more variegated, and more complicated area of struggle. He begins to project himself into the future, to watch, and wait, and wonder. When, how soon, will he grow up, take on the characteristics and privileges of adults? Are his shoulders broadening? Is his voice changing? Will the pimples recede? Will he be sexually attractive and sexually capable? He wants to be accepted by his peers, to belong to the gang, to date successfully, to love and to be loved; vaguely, still beyond his horizon, he senses marriage and children of his own; more immediately, he must choose a career and learn to make a success of it.

He was not born complete; and growing up is, in one sense, becoming aware of and accepting that fact. Ours is a universe in which there have always been dangers: denial and defeat, disease and death. To attain our ends we have always had to run

20

those risks. The body's natural will to grow; the mind's normal will to learn; the heart's instinctive will to love; the soul's intuitive will to transcend time and space—we have always known that these were worth the braving of many dangers. They are all affirmations of the will to live, to live not only physically but also spiritually: of the will to be more than we have been.

The very process of living means growth: addition and extension. From the hour of his birth man seeks to become more than he is. Even past his prime, when his powers decline and his pursuits diminish, he sees himself as growing in esteem and honor and wisdom; he feels that even after death he will grow in bliss and beatitude.

There is another way to say all this. We may say that every living thing, *in order to become itself,* must grow. Its growth is a combination of evolution from within and acquisition from without. A plant may have air, water, sunshine, good soil; but it has not become itself until it has unfolded all the potential of its seed. So it is with man. He may be nurtured, loved, encouraged from without; but he has not fully become man until he has fulfilled his inner human capacities. He must *have more* for survival; he must *become more* for true success. One *more* must complement the other. Too often one kills the other.

The problem of balance has never been solved. The ideal balance differs for each man. But most of us are unaware of even the need for that balance. *Having more,* accumulating, is an art we exercise daily; *becoming more* is something we reserve for emergencies, not realizing that without exercise, a talent for becoming can wither as easily as a talent for accumulating.

Yet the reservoir of spiritual capacities remains intact, even if the instinct for their use has atrophied. We have within us more of strength and power and purpose, of courage and hope and faith, than we know. These virtues cannot, however, be stored away, like forests, oil fields, or bars of gold, for future generations. *Those of man's capacities which remain unfulfilled in his lifetime die with him.*

21

Often the reservoir is tapped by accident. In the journal of his trip across North America in the early part of the sixteenth century, the Spanish explorer Cabeza de Vaca noted a very personal response to the flowering of the spirit. He and his companion had stumbled across a tribe of Indians most of whom were deathly sick; their own medicine men had failed them. Convinced that the two Europeans were supermen or demiurges who had been sent to their rescue, they demanded to be cured; failure would mean death to the explorers. Sick himself, short of food, in despair because he had wandered off his course, knowing that he had no healing power, Cabeza de Vaca saw the end near. "But we had to heal them or die," he wrote, "so we prayed for strength. We prayed on bended knees and in an agony of hunger. . . . Truly, it was to our amazement that the ailing said they were well. Being Europeans, we thought we had given away to doctors and priests our ability to heal. But here it was still in our possession. . . . It was ours after all. We were more than we thought we were. . . . To be more than I thought I was—a sensation utterly new to me."

But for most of us the accident never happens. We conscientiously reduce the possibility of accident by piling comfort upon necessity and luxury upon comfort; and then we conceal ourselves from our own spiritual possibilities by adding the mask of the public personality. Whatever dissatisfactions we feel, we attribute to a lack of comfort or luxury, or to a malformation in the mask. We resent any implication of our own spiritual deficiencies; we shift the blame to salary, position, climate, bad luck in youth, the selfishness of others. There is no balance between inner and outer growth, and under stress we pay the price.

A good part of that price is dissatisfaction: a sense of failure. The Japanese have a fable about a stonecutter named Hashmu. (The fable's application is universal; an animated cartoon was made of it in this country.) Having hacked away at the same large, hard rock for weeks, Hashmu one day muttered to himself in his weariness, "Why is this my life? Why must I go on tapping,

tapping, tapping at a stubborn rock? I wish I were rich and famous; I wish I were the Emperor, and never had to touch a rock again!" He heard the sound then of a horse at the gallop; he looked up and saw a royal carriage. And a voice said to him, "Hashmu, mount this carriage; thou art now the Emperor." Hashmu rejoiced, saying, "Behold, I am the Emperor. There is none mightier than I." In high glee he rode off into the mountains. But soon he felt the heat of the sun; his coachmen were perspiring and tired; the horses slowed to a walk. Angrily, he cried out, "Then there is something stronger than an Emperor," and the voice answered, "Yes: the sun. Hashmu, thou art the sun." Hashmu sailed the skies and beamed upon the fields below— until a dark cloud cut him off from the earth below, and left him traveling in a void. "Ah," he groaned, "then there is something stronger than the sun." The voice answered, "Yes, a cloud. Hashmu, thou art a cloud." Hashmu floated lazily; he released rain upon the earth, and the rain became a brook and the brook a river and the river a flood, carrying off trees and houses. Only one thing it did not, could not carry away: the rock. "Then," Hashmu said, "there is something stronger than a cloud." And the voice answered, "Yes: a rock. Hashmu, thou art the rock." And Hashmu was the rock, and saw coming toward him a man with a mighty hammer, and the man set to work, and as the chips began to fly Hashmu called out, "Then there is something stronger than the rock." And the voice answered, "Yes: a man. Hashmu, thou art again a man."

The moral is obvious; some version of this fable exists in all mythologies. Whatever his attainments and attributes, a man must ultimately come to the question, Who am I? And in answering that question he answers all others.

The importance of simply *being*—being alive, having an identity—is often apparent in the sickroom. Here are men and women passing their last days on earth—and how they cling to life! Paralytic, cancer-ridden, wasting away, they are more pointedly and frighteningly aware of themselves as individuals than ever before. Gone are the masks, gone the preoccupation with bank-book, property, clothes, social standing, the opinions of others; we are down to bedrock humanity, to the organism struggling for one thing only: being. One more dawn is worth millions; one more word from a loved one is worth the treasures of the fabled Orient.

We are mortal. Even the human race is mortal; the universe has given us no assurance that we will survive. In his *Origin of Species,* Darwin discussed "survival of the fittest" (a doctrine much misinterpreted because of varying notions of fitness), and he left open the question whether man was fit to survive indefi-nitely. Man may already have devised his own destruction; perhaps with the creation of the hydrogen bomb organic evolution has come to the end of the line. In his fight for survival it is apparent that man's most formidable rival is himself. He is not necessarily evolution's fondest hope; nor does he have a permanent claim to existence.

Birth does not ensure life, for either the individual or the species. Millions of individuals are born every year who die of disease or starvation within a decade. In areas like our own where the survival rate is higher, masses of people and billions of dollars are devoted to keeping them alive. Yet we all die; our success in fighting for life is a matter of postponing death.

In the struggle of the species for survival, man battles not only nature, but also human nature. There seems to be incessant war between man and his fellow man, not only for possession and posi-tion, but for keeping both. Contemplating his neighbor with a justifiably jaundiced eye, Rousseau said, "We may admire human society as much as we please, it is nonetheless true that it neces-sarily leads men to hate each other in proportion as their interests clash. What can be thought of a relationship in which every man finds his profit in the misfortune of his neighbor? There is perhaps not any man in a comfortable position who has not greedy heirs and perhaps even children secretly wishing for his death; in a ship at sea of which the loss would not be good news to some merchant or other; in a house which some debtor of bad faith would not be glad to see reduced to ashes. . . ."

The way is hard. We are born with the knowledge that we will die; and yet we never seem to learn to live. We fight failure constantly; but we have never really known success.

Alexander the Great (so goes the legend), at the height of his meteoric career and with no earthly worlds left to conquer, finally stormed the gates of heaven. He rapped imperiously. The Guardian Angel answered, "Who is there?"

"Alexander."

"And who is Alexander?"

A surprised pause; then, "Alexander the Great, Conqueror of the World."

"Here we know him not," came the answer. "This is the Lord's gate, through which only the righteous may enter."

Frustrated and penitent, Alexander begged for a token to prove that he had come so far. He was thrown a small piece of human skull, with the admonition, "Weigh it."

He brought it to the wise men of his kingdom and bade them make ready a pair of scales. In one pan he set the bone; on the other he heaped silver and gold. The bone outweighed the metal. He added more silver and gold and precious stones, even his own crown jewels. It was useless.

Then one of the wise men sprinkled a few grains of dust on the bone. It flew up immediately, upsetting Alexander's treasures. They examined the bone more carefully: it was the one that surrounds the eye.

Alexander understood. "Nothing will ever satisfy the human eye," he said, "until it is covered by the dust of the grave." Only when he has ceased to exist does man abandon his feverish search for success.

Throughout our lives, whether or not we have attained our provisional goals, the fear of failure is ever with us. Have we money and goods? They are not enough; others have more. Have we security? Security against what? Starvation? War? Lightning? Have we friends, a loving family? Can we trust friendship and love? We are called a success; do we feel success? Are we individuals or personalities? Are we living a lie? These questions spare none of us.

The fear of failure haunts man all the days of his life. Its faces and forms are many, imaginary and real, confused and clear, temporary and permanent. It terrifies the baby learning to stand erect, the child placating his parents, the girl seeking a mate, the boy impressing a sweetheart. It terrorizes a man fighting to hold his job, a wife striving to save her marriage, a family working its way out of debt, a nation struggling to preserve its independence. It tortures alike prince and pauper, sage and fool.

One of Grimm's least known fairy tales is "The Story of the Youth Who Went Forth to Learn What Fear Is." A boy was born absolutely without fear. Sitting by the fireside, listening to tales that made strong men shudder, he was puzzled, and thought to himself, "They shudder, and they cry out, and I don't understand. I can't shudder. I should like to know how to shudder. I should like to understand this thing they call fear."

One day he was offered the hand of a king's beautiful daughter —the pattern of many fairy tales—on condition that he recover a rich treasure hidden in a haunted house. Boldly he entered where others feared to tread. The specters, the ghostly figures, the clank of chains, the supernatural moaning, held no terrors for him. *The only fear he knew was the fear of failure;* and it did not make him shudder. It was a fear that conquered all other fears. It drove him to success. Spurred by it, he vanquished the ghosts, found the treasure, married the girl, and lived happily ever after.

Fairy tales are, of course, symbolic, simplified, and idealized. In our world of reality, the fear of failure is the primary cause of failure and the greatest single cause of unhappiness. Even when it leads us to what is generally regarded as success, it does not leave us happy. Here, from a different kind of fiction (Cameron

26

Hawley's best-seller, *Executive Suite*), is another commentary on success:

The bigger a brass hat gets, the more of a sucker he is for some guy who comes along and calls himself an expert. You know why? Because he still gets scared. The bigger he gets, the more scared he is. When he is on the way up, he is so busy tearing the hell out of things that he never stops to worry about being wrong. Sometimes he gets knocked on his can. Does it bother him? No. He pounces back like a fighting bull. Then what happens? He gets to be a success. Why? Because that is what it takes to be a success. Then what? The first thing you know he is a tin-plated god sitting on a big throne. Now he doesn't like getting knocked on his can. It is not dignified. The stockholders wouldn't like it. He begins to get scared. So what does he do? He turns into a sucker and starts hiring experts. Why? Because they tell him they can help him from being knocked on his royal can. It's as simple as that.*

Standing on great heights, we best conquer fear by looking up, and not down. Above we see what we have not yet reached, what we may never reach. Below, we see only the long drop to the bottom. We become dizzy with the thought of failure, with the fear of those depths, that sudden destruction. And that very dizziness can sometimes pull us down and destroy us.

What is true of physical heights is also true, in this respect, of financial, social, emotional heights—even moral and spiritual heights. The higher the climb, the greater the fear of falling. During the depression those who suffered most dramatically from the fear of failure were not the workers whose meager savings had been wiped out (and who were tougher, because they were more familiar with struggle and destitution); they were the tycoons whose bank balances had been reduced to a few tens of thousands.

---

* From *Executive Suite* by Cameron Hawley; published by Houghton Mifflin Company.

Removal from the Social Register—the 400—may be more devastating than rejection by a civic club. It is the intellectual, the sensitive, who are most likely to suffer nervous breakdowns. And they whose consciences are keenest, whose souls know the greatest profundity, suffer most painfully, and are most likely to be destroyed by questions of right and wrong, faith and doubt. There is no vice without a previous glimpse of virtue; no tragedy without a previous glimpse of nobility; no failure without a previous glimpse of success; and no damnation without a previous glimpse of Heaven.

For months after I had seen Arthur Miller's *Death of a Salesman,* the story of success-driven, doomed Willy Loman lived with me. His tragic presence refused to leave me. And then one day I knew why: *Willy Loman was I*—as he was everyone else who had seen the play. We had all been weeping not for Willy but for ourselves. We had undergone a major psycho-surgical operation. In laying bare the failure-haunted life of the salesman, Mr. Miller's penetrating scalpel had probed deep into the complex anatomy of every man's fear of failure. Caught for an hour in the glare of the footlights, we saw ourselves with deadly clarity.

It was not a pretty picture. The shabbiness of what we were appeared beneath the flashiness of what we wished to believe we had become. The fat meat of power upon which we thought we had been feeding now looked like the thin fare of pretense. The house of success in which we had taken shelter revealed ugly cracks and rotten foundations. The signs on its doors read FAILURE. We wept for Willy Loman; we wept for ourselves.

We are all salesmen. We may reject the designation, but it is no less true that all our lives we offer ourselves to society as desirable commodities, *deserving of success.* As infants we cry and coo for food and attention. As young lovers we put goosegrease on our hair and make propitiatory offerings of half-melted chocolate. As married men and women we exchange flattery, good meals, paychecks, and guarded opinions on the in-laws. As parents we assume godlike attributes: here at last is a captive audience,

28

convinced that we can do no wrong. As business and professional people, we accept friends we despise; we engage in, or countenance, practices we loathe; we subordinate idealism to expediency. As citizens we follow the crowd even when conscience calls us cowards.

We become, in short, so absorbed in the art of salesmanship that we neglect a higher art which we may call soulsmanship— the art of satisfying the soul's hunger. And ultimately the realization comes to all of us—it may come as we stand on the pinnacle of public success—that we have failed in the deepest sense. We have been childish, adolescent, immature in our search. We have been led astray (much like Adam) by the treasures and trappings which this world has always offered as tokens of its approval. We have been flattered by the applause of the marketplace. We have succeeded in competition; we are admired by others. We have become attached to the masks of distinction that mark us off as personalities. And yet we are unsatisfied, unfulfilled.

We are successes in salesmanship and failures in soulsmanship. However wide the frame, however great the reward, neither is ever an end in itself, but only a means to the true end: spiritual success, inner completeness. *When we know this we have taken the first step on the road to maturity;* we have begun to grow up. We have acknowledged failure; we have admitted selling our birthright—the right to be an individual—for a mess of pottage.

Some of us are crushed by this sudden awareness: like Willy Loman, we wish for death. Many become disturbed emotionally, and evince a common sign of the knowledge of failure: neurosis.

The most dangerous, and yet the most logical, neurotic reaction to this knowledge is one of guilt: a feeling that material success is somehow sinful, that we have been led into paths of unrighteousness and immorality; that we have, like Faustus, sold our souls for material gain. Or that we have succeeded at the expense of others, sacrificing family and friends on the altar of the Golden Calf.

And there are many who, by way of quick remedy, suddenly

reject material success altogether. The pendulum of the spirit swings; if we have been vicious for the sake of material success, we shall be virtuous in renouncing it. But a new problem rises: we live in a world, in a social order, established on a material foundation. We are of flesh and blood, bound by precious ties, accustomed to pleasing comforts. For us to emulate Jesus, Augustine, Francis of Assisi, Gandhi, even Tolstoi, would be fatal. We cannot toy with absolutes; we are not saints and devils. We are people, men and women, made in the image of our Creator, but made flesh by Him. Material success alone is not enough; but spiritual success alone is for the one man in a hundred million who can live upon the mountaintop. The need of our time is balance: the beast and the angel must be reconciled in man.

We need a closer look at the mechanics of failure. Doctors of the spirit, like doctors of the flesh, cannot treat symptoms alone; we must examine causes. And as a clergyman, interested in the guidance of the young, I have seen those causes at work early in life.

We can never accurately measure the damage done to a child's spirit when a sense of failure is instilled. I have seen many children put on bright faces, make friends, do brilliantly at school, all the while hiding a grievous hurt, like the absence of parental love. And I have seen them crushed by bafflement at a failure to "make good" when their parents or their community had demanded success.

Many years ago a mother came to me with her gifted twelve-year-old son. A piano prodigy at eight, he had won a prize scholarship at one of the country's leading conservatories. After a year, because of his failure to measure up under rigorous disciplines, long hours of practice, and a need for careful attention to minute details, he was dismissed. His mother begged me to help gain readmission for her son.

We were successful; the boy had his second chance. He returned, applied himself, graduated with honors. He won acclaim as one of America's most promising young pianists. But he has never fulfilled that promise. He is considered a competent, an accomplished, concert pianist. He will never reach first rank.

He still suffers from that childhood failure. He has spent his life disguising it, denying it to himself, explaining and excusing it to others. (Perhaps the most poignant note in the story is his mother's blind contribution to his failure: it was she who first wanted success for him; she who formed his first oversimplified notions of success and failure; she who established the standards by which he might measure himself, and by which he was found wanting.) The boy has never accepted that first failure as a reality, a setback he will never enjoy thinking about, but with which he must live. Beneath the balm of all his later successes, that wound has festered in his spirit; and because of it he will never achieve the success he has been taught to desire.

Much more recently a boy of eighteen was brought to me. He was mentally retarded, with a very low reading level. He had attended remedial schools, gone to special agencies, consulted child psychologists. He had tried jobs, and failed to keep them; made friends, and failed to hold them; made efforts to adjust, and failed to feel himself a part of society. Now he was completely withdrawn; he spent twelve hours a day at home, watching television and whimpering occasionally, "I want to learn to read. I want to learn to read."

His inability to read was obviously a crippling failure, a deep wound to his spirit. In general comprehension his I.Q. was not far below normal. He was presentable and well-mannered. He was industrious and reliable. He was capable of adequate performance in simple tasks. I asked him why he would not take a job that demanded no reading ability; his invariable, and pathetic, answer was: "I want a job where I *have* to know how to read. I want to read."

I tested him. At first he stumbled and stammered. Then, relaxing, responding gradually to my encouraging manner, he let the words flow; he read slowly but smoothly. There was even the

31

faint trace of a smile on his face. For a few moments the ache of years of failure had been relieved. He saw himself on the road to success.

But he could not have a guide with him always, and when he went home he fell back. Constant failure had ruined him. He took up his place before the television set, and went on whimpering, "I want to learn to read."

He will never reach the reading level of his age group. His failure has conquered him.

But the more mature among us make adjustments. We try to see failure in a new light, an altered perspective. We look back, and we find that failure has been a constant companion. And often, seeing it that way, we discover that it has not always been our enemy; it has often been a needed friend.

We learn that the fear of failure is a natural and universal human emotion. It is a prod as well as a protection. Often it pulls out of a man more than he knew he had in him; often it pushes him toward goals that once seemed unattainable. It may occasionally be a very salutary fear, shielding him from threatened harm. It is a useful emotion. It is the sire of all the fears: of insecurity, of injury, of dishonor, of death.

Failure itself, of course, is not a fault. We fail often for reasons that have little to do with our fears. We may follow the lure of ambition beyond our capacity for achievement. We may select occupations for which we are unsuited. We may lack health and strength, intelligence and knowledge, courage and self-control. There may be temporary emotional paralyses caused by unusual strains—illness, worry, great grief. But when these are not present, success is often at hand.

But many of the *causes* of failure are faults; and many of the uses of failure are deceits and hypocrisies. One may fail deliberately in order to evoke sympathy, with success as the ultimate objective. Children look lonely and forlorn to arouse greater concern and care on their parents' part. A mooning swain will proclaim that no one loves him, in an effort to provoke his beloved

32

to an open avowal. When we hear people sigh "I just can't make friends," or "I just can't remember a thing," or "I wish I knew how to take a vacation," we suspect a bid for special attention. These people most often desire to be singled out as examples of particular distinction and success.

Or failure may be an outright pretense, a pose, disguising egotism. A very distinguished speaker, a famed personality who took infinite pains to disavow any claims to greatness, once listened with his habitual modesty to the extravagant praise with which he was being introduced. "Our honored guest," the chairman boomed, "is a renowned statesman, a great scholar, an eloquent orator, a man of noble character. . . ." As the chairman concluded the speaker was overheard to whisper, "Don't forget to mention my humility."

Or failure may be a weapon. With it a child may calculatedly hurt a parent whom he resents. A parent may employ it against an unloved child. A husband may use it to make life difficult for his wife. I have known failures apparently caused by an unconscious desire to undergo the same tragic experiences of denial and defeat, and even death, as a beloved relative or friend.

And failure may be a rationalization for a number of things such as laziness or stubbornness—but we must remember that laziness and stubbornness are usually rationalizations for some other emotional problems. There are those who refuse to pay any price for success. "I am myself," they say. "Shirtless and shiftless, but myself. This is the real I: I am Zusya."

I suspect that Zusya would protest.

The Plains Indians, unable to treat frostbite, solved their problem by burning the affected area and treating the burn. Many modern thinkers, unable to accept failure for itself, insist on defining it as a kind of negative success, after which they can discuss it happily and painlessly. They point out that many of us are now relieved, rather than bitter, over past failures: that we are quite happy not to have married the woman we first so desperately desired, not to have remained in the business or profession we first entered. We find ourselves grateful for these pseudo-failures. They are, it is asserted, necessary stepping-stones to success, valuable in disciplining our character, essential preparations for mature living. Inspirational articles in praise of failure fill books and magazines. Witness Agnes de Mille, in *Rhythm in My Blood:* "Granting a modicum of true ability, one must not be afraid to fail now and then. . . . A creative life without failure is unthinkable. . . . Far better than succeeding regularly is a good tough falling short of a challenge." Statements like these are not uncommon. We may be in at the birth of a new aphorism: "In the bright lexicon of youth the first word is 'Fail.' "

This attitude is illusory. We may, by rationalizing, convert the idea of a failure to the idea of a success; but the failure itself remains a failure, and if we forget that, if we yield to the mystical alchemy that would call it a success, we will sooner or later, more or less painfully, suffer disillusionment. Failures are, in general, not helpful to us in themselves. They are discouraging, depressing, and destructive. They cause mental disturbances and emotional disorders. Failure is the most fundamental tragedy of human experience.

We cannot, in other words, know ourselves, function fully, until we recognize the reality of failure. Until we can distinguish success from failure, how can we recognize our goals? When we have accepted the reality of occasional failure we are ready to work for success.

Even in the happiest of lives, some failure is inevitable. It is not in itself indispensable to success, but *recognition* of it, *acceptance* of it as a reality, *is* indispensable to success.

The distinguished American artist James McNeill Whistler is an example of the intelligent approach. In 1854 he was a cadet at West Point, on his way to a career of soldiering. In chemistry class one afternoon he was asked to discuss silicon. He rose and began, "Silicon is a gas."

"That will do, Mr. Whistler," said his instructor.

34

A few weeks later Cadet Whistler was discharged from the Academy. Years later, when he was quite famous as a painter, he liked to say, "If silicon had been a gas, I would have been a general."

He had failed. He had recognized his failure and gone on to better things. He had not assumed that his failure was a success in disguise. He was no more a soldier than silicon was a gas— *but his failure as a soldier did not make him a great painter.* Hard work and good training made him a great painter; without them he might very well have failed there, too.

A classmate of mine at the Seminary, the late Lewis Browne, author and lecturer, used to paraphrase Whistler: "If I had not been expelled from Rabbinical College, I might never have become a writer." True. But Lewis Browne had the intelligence— the *balance*—to recognize failure and to dominate it. Granted this intelligence, this self-knowledge, there may be reason to agree with Rebecca West's epigram, "Nothing succeeds like failure."

I know a top-level executive in one of this country's largest corporations; he is dynamic, imaginative, creative; he may be characterized as an obvious success. He is more than that: he is a fulfilled man, because he has made his peace with both success and failure. He likes to tell us that it was an awareness of failure that led to his success. He had been a collegiate boxing champion and had, upon graduation, decided on professional fighting as a career. As a first step he entered the annual Golden Gloves tournament. He fought his way savagely to the finals, but on the threshold of victory he suffered a hopeless defeat: he was knocked out by his opponent's first blow. He recognized failure, abandoned his boxing career, and entered the business world.

(It may be objected that this shows a lack of persistence. But I believe that if the gentleman in question had felt that his only chance of happiness lay in boxing, he would not have looked upon one defeat as a failure. The defeat served as a catalyst: once he had recognized it as a failure, had stripped himself of delusion, he was better able to see where his happiness lay.)

35

Before we leave the prize ring, we should hear Cus D'Amato, manager of world heavyweight champion Floyd Patterson: "Whenever a new boy comes to me, I first discuss with him what might be termed the psychology of fear. I explain to him that all normal people are afraid. In fact, if a fighter didn't have fear, I'd send him to a psychiatrist. So I try to get the boy to understand himself and recognize that fear is normal. Otherwise, he guards his fear as a guilty secret as if he were the only frightened fighter in the business. I want him to see that this is nothing to be ashamed of. But once fear is controlled, it ceases to be an enemy and becomes a friend. Uncontrolled fear can destroy a man, but once it is mastered, it supplies an incentive to better performance. It makes a man more alert and helps him anticipate more readily the situation he fears."

His words make sense. All of us can remember fears and failures in our own lives. We recall obstacles and defeats that denied or delayed success. And we can interpret each of them as an early failure, awareness of which, control of which, helped us to later success.

The tendency to look upon failure as "a kind of success" is partially due to a suspicion of success. Millions of us suspect all success. It demands its price: work and worry, energy, responsibility, stomach ulcers and nervous breakdowns, marital rifts and family problems. "Success went to his head," "He couldn't stand success," "Success ruined him"—we hear those comments often. They indicate widespread distrust, a devaluation of success, and often, these days, a fear of success, of the spotlight, a fear that conspicuous success is nonconformity, or at least bad taste. In an exhaustive study made by *Fortune,* it was established that success is, as often as failure, the cause of breakdowns among the executives of large corporations. The effects of success, we begin to believe, may be as destructive as the effects of failure.

But this is worldly success, success within the chosen competitive field. The pressures are strong, and can defeat even the strongest of men. Rocky Marciano once hinted at a resolution of this paradox. Talking to friends after a fight, he said, "Know what I was thinking about? I was thinking of my first knockout of Jersey Joe Walcott. That punch made me and ruined me. It was the perfect punch. I nailed him just as he was bouncing off the ropes. His guard was down, he was coming toward me as I was coming toward him. That jaw of his—just the right size for me to hit with maximum power. The embarrassing part about it is that everyone now seems to expect that every punch I throw will be as perfect as that one. It's like expecting Ted Williams to hit a home run every time he comes to bat."

Obscurity can certainly be more comfortable. The drive to beat failure takes much out of a man; the drive to maintain success takes more out of him. The time may come when he is afraid to go on; afraid that his reputation has grown beyond his capacities, and that the next step will take him over the edge, into the dizzying chasm of failure.

And this leads us to a remarkable, paradoxical, and strange phenomenon: the conscious will to fail. Many psychologists and psychoanalysts are convinced that the will to fail is as deeply rooted in man as the will to succeed. The two wills are, theoretically, in constant tension. In the healthy individual each acts as a brake on the other. Recently a well-known psychiatrist told a meeting of grade-school teachers that courses in "How to Fail Gracefully" should be made part of the elementary school curriculum. "The American ideal of success," he said, "is producing neuroses in American children. Everybody cannot be a success. Children brought up under the slogan of 'You must and you will' are more likely to break down under the stress of having too much expected of them."

If we accept the notion that the pressure of the American success drive is responsible for a good deal of the country's mentally ill, then perhaps we can accept the idea of the will to fail, properly controlled, as an occasional brake. We know that success as measured by popular standards of approval and reward can be too much for many of us. Perhaps by fearing failure so greatly we have denied ourselves the occasional useful help of a calm and unterrified look at failure. Perhaps the will to failure, like the awareness of failure, needs to be acknowledged, brought out into the daylight, and discussed.

Certainly, when it is ignored, the will to fail can be more deadly than the will to succeed. The fear of success has been engendered and encouraged not so much by the tragic lives and ends of a few so-called great men as by an all too easy misinterpretation of the lessons taught by the world's dominant religions. Current literature, the drama of our time, much modern poetry, tend to blame many of the sins and sorrows of modern civilization on man's drive for material success; this is a reflection of certain values drawn from folklore and Scripture. In time we shall discuss the failure of religion; for the moment let us note that the fear of success runs a close second to the fear of failure in the minds and hearts of many people.

There are examples everywhere. Brilliant children turn away from their books and sneer defensively at education: they are afraid of taunts, goody-good, eager-beaver, greasy-grind. Competent young men—the hero of *The Man in the Gray Flannel Suit,* for one—turn down advancement for which they are qualified, presumably because they prefer to find happiness within themselves and their families, but actually, I suspect, because they are afraid they lack the capacity to achieve inner peace in a competitive world. Lovely women give up dazzling careers, fearful of the evils of success. Men whose success brings them money and position develop serious guilts, and try to give away the money and minimize the position; we feel that they are trying to unload a sense of sin.

These examples are important. Taught that extreme success creates devils, people turn from success, forgetting that extreme self-abnegation creates saints only where there is holiness and solitude. The man who is not a saint, and who denies himself worldly success, becomes simply a pauper, financially and emotionally;

38

and one day, when he is insignificant enough, his fear of failure will again outweigh his fear of success, and he will set out again around the vicious circle.

There are psychoanalysts who attribute the rejection of success, the will to fail, to guilts buried deep within the unconscious from the earliest days of life. The "Oedipal situation"—rivalry with each parent for the affection of the other—creates resentments and hostilities. It can create a struggle for pre-eminence into which all the dark passions of the unconscious are poured, though on the surface there may be calm. And if we admit this much of the hypothesis, we must admit, for example, that the boy's competition with his father, like his instinctive love for his mother, may, if he feels he must repress it, become morbid; may, indeed, become associated in his unconscious with that greatest and most terrible human sin—the sin of Oedipus. And if this occurs, the child may well grow up to feel uneasily—without knowing why—that all competition is sinful and all success horribly guilty. He will have no love for failure, but he will fear success. And he will therefore seek a middle ground. His success as an individual will depend on a rejection of gains and prestige, a rejection of distinction. He will be forever uneasy at worldly success.

This is a profound interpretation, and it will not be acceptable to all of us. For our purposes we may use much simpler and more manageable categories.

We may say, for example, that failure is always with us, and that fearing it is no more reasonable than fearing the air we breathe; and that an awareness of failure may lead us to success.

Success is not to be feared *unless it is permitted to become an end in itself.*

The fear of failure and the fear of success must be brought into balance; each is a means, and each can be made a valuable tool.

Success and failure in themselves are not permanent, and can never be sources of permanent pride or shame.

And all the factors which we have mentioned—ambition,

shame, greed, pride, fear—must be recognized as components of that imperfect vessel, man. This recognition, honest and unashamed, is the first step toward true maturity, true happiness. It is a step that must be taken with courage and resolution.

I have a friend whom I call truly successful and truly noble. Through his own genius and charm he has accumulated wealth, friends, admirers, and a large family bound to him by strong ties of affection, devotion, and appreciation. He is a collector of ivory figurines, and years ago he bought a small reproduction of the traditional Chinese God of Happiness. It stands now, conspicuously, in a handsome cabinet in his living room.

The figure is roly-poly and bald; a single garment drapes the loins. A wide grin lights up the face. A glint of humor shines in the half-closed eyes. The mouth is slightly open; we expect a profound and witty comment about our foolish world. The stomach is round and full. Over the shoulder is slung a knotted cloth; it contains all his worldly goods. He has the appearance of a wandering tramp. His is not material success; but he looks supremely happy.

My friend, like all of us, has problems. There are nights when his nerves tighten, when sleep is a stranger, when dark thoughts trouble his soul. He has taken to visiting the God of Happiness at those times. He fixes his gaze on the happy, roguish face. Again its meaning sinks in; peace begins to pervade his spirit. A smile comes to his own face. And he finds himself laughing off silly fears and petty frustrations. Once more he distinguishes between the means and the ends of life, between public success and happiness, between the personality and the individual.

He is Zusya; he is himself.

DEFEAT

FROM

WITHIN

Chapter Three

> *A fool often fails because he thinks what is difficult is easy, and the wise man because he thinks what is easy is difficult.*
> —CHURTON COLLINS

A modern (and yet traditional) Chinese story is a grim allegory of failure. A woman in a small upriver village lay sick, wasting away; months of care by the local herb-doctors, a stream of offerings in the Buddhist temple, had worked no cure. Desperate, her husband sold what little he had left to finance a sampan trip downriver to the foreign devil's hospital in Chinkiang. The village disapproved: it was well known that the big-nosed foreign devils practiced only black magic. But the villagers held their tongues—except for one neighbor-woman, a famed busybody with a shrewish tongue. As the husband and wife prepared to cast off, the neighbor-woman shouted her criticisms. Already on edge, the husband answered angrily. A verbal brawl developed, and a large crowd gathered, and when the husband's patience had been over-

41

strained he lost control of himself and slapped the woman. Her blistering curses followed him down the river.

At Chinkiang the wife's malady was diagnosed as advanced cancer. Her husband hurried her home; she must join her ancestors in familiar surroundings. And when they reached their hut they found the shrewish neighbor's body dangling from their lintel. She had lost face; she had been slapped in public; there was no alternative to suicide.

This is, you will say, a silly Oriental custom. Face is not what we are, nor even what others think we are, but rather what *we think* others think we are. Saving face is a matter of keeping up appearances, of observing the outer forms. And an occasional loss of face is surely not cause for suicide.

But a great many of our own most demoralizing failures are purely and simply face failures. We measure ourselves against our neighbors. Our marriage is as happy as theirs, our home as secure, our job as secure. But one of our neighbors is in television, and his name appears in newspaper columns; another has been to Africa; another is descended from a Founding Father; another is a professional football player. So we see ourselves as failures. We have not their measure of distinction, and the joys of life become as Dead Sea fruit, bitter to the taste and of no value in our sight.

It may not be simply the neighbors. Parents are haunted by obscure fears that they have failed their children. Husbands and wives who find their gregarious instincts warring with local standards of respectability, begin to feel that secretly they are failures as mates. A businessman reads a magazine article on home carpentry; he has not held a hammer for ten years, and he feels suddenly that he has failed his family, that he has lost the pioneering spirit. A wife and mother toys with the notion of tinting her hair: television commercials imply that "everybody" does it; will she alone lose face if the gray begins to show? The captain of a high-school baseball team, with three other boys, robs a candy store: his peers had set standards of loyalty and courage, and to have refused the gambit would have meant a loss of face.

A soldier comes home without medals; he has done his job well, but is morose: his sweetheart, he feels, will be dissatisfied.

The attempt to measure up to another man's standards can be suicidal. When a man takes on a job, he accepts a responsibility; presumably the job is within his capacities, and by taking it on he implies its fulfillment. Must he then come home from work and feel unsuccessful because his next-door neighbor is a jet pilot? Yet many men do; they are competent, loving, cheerful individuals, but they are too concerned with the fluctuations of public opinion, and far too seriously affected by the eternal process of competitive comparison. Their own inner security depends on the approval—and often on the envy—of others; *which means that it is no security at all.*

Most suicides in the Western world are of the spirit and not of the body. We have not reached the goals established for us by billboards, magazines, mass media. We have a five-year-old sedan, and not a new station wagon; we work for another, and do not own our own business (or, on another level, we work for a neighborhood garage and not for General Motors); we are married to an attractive, competent, loving companion, and not to the curvaceous Astarte worshiped by millions. The result? A feeling that "it isn't worth it." That we have "gone wrong somewhere." That our best efforts will never achieve for us those goals which society says are the most desirable.

Society's approval can be important. We recall de Maupassant's classic "A Piece of String." A poor, thrifty, respected old man was seen one day by his neighbors in a small French town as he bent to pick up an object from the middle of the road. The man was an inveterate string saver, and he had spotted a good length of it. But a wallet was lost that day; and the rumor spread rapidly that what the old man had so carefully picked up was actually the wallet. His denials only added to the force of the accusations. Frenzied, he pursued his fellow townsmen, proclaiming his innocence. They laughed, winked, and disbelieved. He went mad, finally, wandering the streets, stopping in doorways, mumbling over and over, "But it was only a piece of string. It was only a piece of string." He had been broken by public opinion; he had lost the approval of his fellow man.

But most of us *have* the approval of our fellow man; and what we want—what we have been taught to want—is his adulation. It is no longer enough to be respected; we must be envied. We have forgotten what spiritual security means; we have lost confidence in our own goodness. So has our fellow man, for the most part: he has accepted standards of adolescent wish fulfillment rather than of mature self-fulfillment, and because we require his approval we adopt his standards. To love thy neighbor is too difficult; it requires character and honesty and individuality. To impress thy neighbor is easier; it requires only a mask.

There was once a foolish man who owned a beautiful garden, luxuriant with lofty trees and blooming flowers. One day he trapped a hummingbird, eating and destroying his finest fruits and blossoms. The bird offered—and the man accepted—three wise teachings as the price for his release: "Don't regret the irremediable. Don't believe the impossible. Don't seek the unattainable."

Safely out of reach, the bird burst into raucous laughter. "If you had not let me go, you would have found inside me a pearl the size of a pomegranate."

Enraged, the man climbed the tree after the bird. As he came closer, the bird flew higher. With the man in frenzied pursuit, the bird hopped to the highest branch of all, and walked to its very end. The man came scrambling after; the branch snapped, the bird flew off, the man dropped with a savage thud.

Dazed and bruised, he picked himself up. He gazed ruefully at his tormentor. "Wisdom is only for the wise," the bird admonished, mocking him. "I told you not to regret the irremediable; no sooner did you let me go, than you came after me again. I told you not to believe the impossible; yet you believed, in your greed, that a bird my size could contain a pearl the size of a pomegranate. And I told you not to seek the unattainable; yet you climbed a tree to catch a bird. O fool!"

The fable illustrates three kinds of what I shall call "folly" failures. Most important to us is the failure to attain the unattainable. We consider ourselves rational beings; none of us would consider a paraplegic a failure because he was unable to play football, or a deaf mute a failure because he was unable to sing professionally. Then why do we consider a backward child, of actually inferior brain capacity, a failure if it cannot make the grade in a primary school? Why do we consider an emotional deaf mute—a man, for example, so warped emotionally by a sordid childhood that his responses to law, beauty, truth, love are inadequate—a failure? Consciously or not, we *do* look upon unfulfilled human beings as failures, so that when we ourselves feel unfulfilled a sense of inadequacy and failure pervades us. *We cannot do the impossible.* The phrase, "He did the impossible," means simply that he performed magnificently, using all the hidden reserves of untapped power and faith within him. A man's accomplishments may seem impossible to others—may, indeed, *be* impossible to others—but they were possible for him; they were part of his potential. Any man who fulfills his potential is a success. Potentials differ; the species of man is made in the image of God, but how much of His power resides in each individual, we will never know.

A second kind of folly failure results from believing the impossible. Many a success has been wrested from dreams; more often they lead to failure. The men who dreamed of flying, from the ancients until our century, were called failures in their time; the sum of their failures was our success. There is an analogy here between the species and the individual: flying was part of man's potential, but before the twentieth century it was no part of any individual's potential. If Leonardo da Vinci had wept, beat his breast, called himself a failure, and sunk into a gloomy decline, we would now know him only as a failure; but he was intelligent enough to see that his own fulfillment might take many forms, and that the day of flight was not yet possible for man. And Leonardo, who failed as a flier, is cited by many of us today as probably history's most truly successful individual.

Yet we go on: there are those who dream of acting, singing, painting, writing, and who feel that only persistence is necessary, who are never able to reconcile themselves to a lack of genius— or even talent; who will never admit that true success for them may lie in other fields. There are husbands and wives who have never yielded the fairy-tale dream of perfect wedded bliss, and who are destroyed when the reality of occasional failure breaks upon them. There are fathers and mothers who dream for their children, who fit them to a mold from infancy, and who collapse in guilt and misery when the awakening comes. How many fine musicians have been destroyed by fathers who wanted an engineer— and how many fine engineers, by fathers who wanted Menuhins!

These people are not failures. They are fools. They chase hummingbirds; they look for pearls as large as pomegranates. They reject the reality, and embrace the shadow.

The third folly failure is the expense of energy and life in vain crying over spilt milk. Yesterday's failure becomes tomorrow's obsession, with the result that success is further than ever away. Why can't we remember that one more failure behind us may mean one less failure ahead? A friend of mine, one of the most successful real-estate operators in the country, told me that his early successes, which were few and far between but were the foundation of his later successes, were built, in a way, on his failures. Every day he made seven calls on prospective clients. Whether they were good prospects or bad, in rain or in shine, sale or no sale—seven calls a day were made. There were weeks of apparent failure: not a client even interested, not a dollar made. But he kept calling, seven times a day. Perhaps it was sheer persistence, perhaps the law of averages: in the end he was successful. Each failure became a part of the past; he did not carry the sense of defeat with him; he left room for success.

We waste our lives, many of us, regretting the irremediable.

46

The opportunities lost, the orders missed, the job we couldn't handle, the friends we couldn't hold, the money we couldn't make, the fame we couldn't achieve. We are comfortable on the mourner's bench, weeping over yesterday's defeats and denials. Today's performance, tomorrow's promise, are forfeited. Emotionally, professionally, we are already dead. And death is easier than life: in death there is no struggle.

Then there is a group of "false" failures. These are not failures in the eyes of society. We understand fully that we shall be asked, not, "Why were you not Moses?" but "Why were you not Zusya?" We perceive that the measure of our success is in self-fulfillment. But we do not properly recognize and use our capacities. We overestimate them; we underestimate them; we become complacent; we allow them to decay. Occasionally we are unaware that they exist.

One of the philosopher's earliest admonitions is "Know thyself." Ultimate self-knowledge is perhaps impossible, but we can—it requires honesty and application—come to know very intimately our weaknesses and strengths, our limitations and possibilities. Self-knowledge alone, the wise men might have added, is not sufficient. "Control thyself" is another valuable precept. We must learn to keep ourselves in balance; we must learn that success and failure are personal. In his *Alone to Everest,* Earl Denman says, "I sensed that supreme elation, not of conqueror but of a privileged human being who has been permitted to worship at this shrine mountain. Personally, I felt that the only one to be conquered was myself."

We must learn the use of ourselves. It is not enough to be able to disregard the competition and, in the heat of work, even the ultimate goal; we must also keep ourselves under constant surveillance. As we grow, we change, and we must remain aware of what we are. (Occasionally, this absorption with the self is carried too far, and a man spends the better part of his life in fascinated, but unfruitful, introspection. The image here is of the

47

golfer, who, when addressing the ball, must ignore both his opponents and the pin. He must concentrate utterly on the ball. Sooner or later, however, he is expected to swing at it.)

The causes of failure, as we saw in Chapters I and II, lie within a wide and confusing area: the culture we live in, our definitions of the two words, *success* and *failure,* our personal psychological make-up. But often failure, and the approach of failure, take more common and obvious forms. We are not all scholars, we are not all godly, we are not all psychoanalysts: we must deal with the world as it presents itself to us.

There are, in terms of our everyday reactions, ten common causes of failure, ten factors that keep us from "being Zusya." These ten are basic. Know them, conquer them—even a few of them—and you will have removed the most stubborn obstacles from the path of true success. No one else can handle them for you. You must clear your own path. Others may help; but the job is really yours alone.

The first stumbling block is the age-old trick of blaming others. This is not the same as worrying about what others think (or have, or do). It is the actual fastening of responsibility onto another. (The difference between witchcraft and medicine, we are informed by a man who has spent twenty-five years as a doctor in Africa, is that when a man falls sick witchcraft makes him ask, "Who did this to me?" while medicine makes him ask, "What did this to me?") It is the primitive or juvenile mind that seeks the cause of fears and failures outside itself. And almost always the primitive mind seeks a "who"; if it suspects a "what," it believes it to be animate, to have a "who" inside it. We sometimes credit success and failure to good and bad luck, as though luck were a god or goddess intervening in the affairs of men. Rarely does the primitive mind look inside itself and ask, "What in me is responsible for this?" The more sophisticated mind, educated and civilized, learns to ask, "What is there within me that caused me to think (or not) that thought, to feel (or not) that emotion, to do (or not) that deed?"

48

But even now very few of us are ready to admit immediately, "Maybe it's my fault." Most of us respond initially in a primitive, or childish, way to any situation involving fault or failure. It is almost instinctive for the child to blame a brother or sister; "He made me do it," or even "He did it," are common reactions when punishment is in the offing. A schoolboy may blame his teacher for his own deficiencies in learning or conduct ("She's always picking on me"); the motorist claims it was "the other guy's fault"; a husband shouts at a wife, "Why do you always pick quarrels?"; the employee claims, "The company doesn't appreciate me." Mankind's great bewildered cry has always been, "Who did this to me?"

The practice of blaming others accounts not only for perhaps half our failures, but also for our failure to cash in on failures. We do not recognize failure for what it is, and consequently we cannot deal with it. Instead we set up straw men, knock them down several times, and waste days in a battle which we cannot win. The battle we ought to be fighting is within ourselves; that battle, if we bring valor to it, we cannot lose.

A second stumbling block is the opposite of the first: the ready tendency to blame oneself, in private anyway. Why was I such a fool? What an easy mark I am! Why do I always put my foot in it? Why do I always say the wrong thing? What a dope I was!

We do not believe, really, that we are fools or easy marks. This is a quick, easy way to brush off a failure that probably runs much deeper and requires more consideration than we are willing to admit to ourselves.

Instead of wrestling with the problem behind the failure and struggling to resolve it—to prevent its recurrence—we blame ourselves (as though we were congenital failures!) and let it go at that.

This is pernicious thinking and dangerous practice. It plants deep the feelings of inferiority and insecurity which will later spring up like weeds to dominate "the well-ordered garden of the mind." Abraham Lincoln, who failed in many things but was far from being a failure, once said, "My great concern is not whether

49

you have failed, but whether you are content with your failure." This contentment is paralyzing. You may see yourself as happy in failure; and you will tend to fail everywhere.

When Major General William F. Dean was released by his Communist captors, a newsman, it is reported, asked what sustained him during his three years of misery. "I never felt sorry for myself," the General replied, "and that's what licked it." Self-pity whips more people than anything else; and I would say that self-blame is even worse, because it is one of the prime causes of self-pity. Or we may proceed from self-blame to self-deprecation to self-contempt, and thence even to self-destruction.

Excessive self-blame opens the door to guilt feelings. In the habit of blaming yourself for your apparent failures, you may come in time to seek the blame for the failure of others. In my own study many a wife has cried, "It was my fault!" when clearly it was her husband's. Many a mother has wept, "Where did I fail?" when obviously a child's failure had brought destructive tension to the family.

And self-blame closes the door to self-development. Behind the closed door one's personality may withdraw permanently; it may languish in extreme melancholia. Like a deer blinded by a bright light, it may stand paralyzed in feeling and will, lacking the nerve and the drive that would carry it to safety.

It has been often observed that the Great Wall, centuries old, stretching 1800 miles across plains and deserts, is one of history's monumental structures—and a symbol of China's failure to progress as a nation. The wall was a barrier; the Chinese isolated themselves behind it and turned inward. Self-blame can be the Chinese Wall of our lives. Stone after stone of self-criticism, self-contempt, self-deprecation, falls into place; and one day we find ourselves so restricted and inhibited that we are isolated from family, friend, and community. We become companions of death.

A third stumbling block is having no goals. Dr. William Menninger opines, "A fellow must know where he wants to go, if he is going to get anywhere. It is so easy just to drift along. Some people go through school as if they thought they were doing their families a favor. On a job, they work along in a humdrum way, interested only in their salary check. They don't have a goal. When anyone crosses them up, they take their marbles and walk out. The people who go places and do things make the most of every situation. They are ready for the next thing that comes along on the road to their goal. They know what they want and are willing to go an extra mile."

William Saroyan has provided us with a character—Willy, in *The Time of Your Life*—who personifies man without a real goal. Willy has a mania for pinball. Throughout the play Willy fights the machine. In the last scene he wins a game—finally. Red and green lights flash, a bell rings six times, an American flag leaps out of the machine, Willy salutes, collects six nickels from the bartender, and says, "I knew I could do it!"

Success.

No goal is bad enough; but low goals are worse.

Probably there is no such thing as *no* goal. Willy had a goal. To beat the machine. He succeeded. But at the cost of failure in everything else. His story is like the old one of the dog who bragged that he could outrun anything on four legs. He gave chase to a rabbit soon afterward, but fell behind. The other dogs laughed derisively. He shrugged it off: "Don't forget, the rabbit was running for his life. I was just running for the fun of catching him."

We rarely see them in their pure form, but there *are* those whose only goal in life is fun; who do nothing but amuse themselves, often at the expense of others, and always at the expense of their real selves. They waste their God-given talents on worthless pleasures; they spread the salt of their energies over the meat of their life, and they find that the salt has lost its savor. Or—to change the metaphor—they aim simultaneously at a number of targets, scattering their talent like buckshot and exaggerating the value of whatever they happen to nick. The shooting and shouting are all that their hearts desire.

Then there are a few, like the protagonist of "The Beast in the Jungle," whom we have already met, whose goal is an undefined

51

"break" somewhere in the future. Like Micawber, they wait for something to turn up; meanwhile they turn everything down. It's beneath them, beyond them, not what they're suited for, they don't like it. They wait for the Fairy Prince, the Dream Boat. And their instincts for life atrophy; their minds dull and their bodies grow flabby, and when the Prince comes, when the Boat docks, they are not ready. In the end, all is vanity. "It isn't always clear," says Richard L. Evans of the Detroit *Times*, "—perhaps it's seldom clear—just what we are waiting for, but some of us persist in waiting so chronically that youth slips by, opportunities slip by, and life slips by—finding us still waiting for something that has been going on all the time. . . . But when in the world are we going to begin to live as though we understood the urgency of life? This is our time, our day, our generation . . . not some golden age of the past, not some Utopia of the future. . . . This is it . . . whether we are thrilled or disappointed, busy or bored. This is life . . . and it is passing. . . . What are we waiting for?"

Be it understood that there *are* dreams and goals, often with no immediate chance of attainment, which enable a man to fulfill himself. But these are definite; they are part of a constant and energetic search to which a whole life may be devoted. Kenneth Roberts, in the foreword to his book *Northwest Passage*, says, "On every side of us are men who hunt perpetually for their personal Northwest Passage, too often sacrificing health, strength, and life itself to the search; and who shall say that they are not happier in their vain but hopeful quest than wiser, duller folks who sit at home venturing nothing, and with sour laugh deriding the seekers for that fabled thoroughfare." * They may not find the passage; but they fulfill themselves. And they do something more: they set a heroic example for all mankind to follow—a willing-

* From the Foreword to *Northwest Passage* by Kenneth Roberts. Copyright 1936, 1937 by Kenneth Roberts. Reprinted by permission of Doubleday and Company, Inc.

ness to serve and sacrifice beyond one's self. That is success enough.

But care is needed: a fourth stumbling block is choosing the wrong goals. The Chinese tell of a man of Peiping who dreamed of gold, much gold, his heart's desire. He rose one day and when the sun was high he dressed in his finest garments and went to the crowded marketplace. He stepped directly to the booth of a gold dealer, snatched a bag full of gold coins, and walked calmly away. The officials who arrested him were puzzled: "Why did you rob the gold dealer in broad daylight?" they asked. "And in the presence of so many people?"

"I did not see any people," the man replied. "I saw only gold."

When gold or glory, power or place, become a fixed idea, we are usually blinded not only to the needs of others—in the home as well as in the marketplace—but also to our own needs, to the needs of our inner selves. I have met and talked with hundreds of men and women who were accounted great successes, but who, within the sanctity of my study, confessed to a devastating sense of failure. They had set their sights upon one goal and allowed it to represent self-fulfillment; they had attained the goal, and found that it was not what their souls required. It was often one that destroyed their souls.

This is a great sadness: to discover after many years of struggle that attaining the object of your efforts will not bring happiness. Often it is a question of professional displacement: the practice of medicine, or of the law, or of management, which once promised all success and all happiness, may leave the practitioner weary and disillusioned, empty of hope. And when he has reached his fifth or sixth decade, he knows that it is too late to turn back, to find contentment in another life. (There are rare souls who have gathered their courage, faced the truth, and turned away from a lifetime of "achievement" to a calling that brought them peace. But most of us, I am afraid, would carry dissatisfaction with us. Even Tolstoi was not entirely happy when he had renounced the life of a count and gone back to the land.) Most of us, dissatisfied

53

or not, realize that we must go on to the end of the trail. We have begun badly, and compounded the error through the years, but no further choice is possible. We may never be Zusya; but we must be responsible.

Here is a dangerous paradox: Most of our choices, vocational and domestic, are made when we are young; and yet the responsible man cannot easily take advice; he must find out for himself what life is all about. Often he is beyond the possibility of change when he comes to realize what happiness consists of. It takes great honesty and serious thought to be able to make a firm and confident choice before it is too late. Too many of us allow the choice to be made for us—by family or circumstance—and regret it later.

A great preacher, Phillips Brooks, once commented: "There is a young man droning and drowsing along at what he calls the practice of law. It amounts to nothing. The profession does not want him any more than he wants it. He is there because it is an honorable and respectable employment; because the tradition of his family or a little set of people put him there. Let him once get some moral courage; let him once briefly ask what he is really here for, what he can really do well and with love, what is his duty, and such questions would carry him perhaps to the carpenter's bench, perhaps to the blacksmith's forge."

Chuang-tzu, a disciple of Confucius, was fishing one day in the P'u River. The prince of Ch'u sent two high officials to ask him if he would take over the administration of the state of Ch'u. Chuang-tzu ignored them, and went on fishing. Pressed for an answer, he said, "I have heard that in Ch'u there is a sacred tortoise, dead now these 3,000 years. The Prince keeps this tortoise locked in a chest on the altar of his ancestral temple. I ask you: Would this tortoise rather be dead and venerated, or alive wagging its tail in the mud?"

"Alive, wagging its tail in the mud," the officials said quickly.

"Begone!" cried Chuang-tzu. "I too will wag my tail in the mud!"

A fifth stumbling block is the short cut. "Out at Forest Hills last week," reported the late sports columnist Arch Ward, "sixteen-year-old Maureen Connolly had just defeated Doris Hart in the semi-finals of the Women's National Singles. Her opponent, according to expert testimony, had never played better. But the Wimbledon champion and tournament favorite had been no match for the teen-age Californian and she went out in straight sets. Mary Hardwick Hare, former British champion and Wightman Cup veteran, rushed to the dining room to congratulate Miss Connolly. 'Mary,' said Maureen, 'if you can be ready in thirty minutes I'd like to practice!' They worked for more than an hour. The next day Maureen won the National Championship. Most of us could profit," Ward commented, "by rereading the story of the San Diego miss who, in the hour of her greatest triumph, said: 'I'd like to practice.' "

An electric current will follow the line of least resistance; but a bulb glows precisely because there *is* resistance. Many of us instinctively choose the shortest, easiest, quickest way to success, only to discover that the success was illusory; that the bulb did not glow. There have been too many platitudes about hard work; we shall try not to add to them. Hard work is only rarely pleasurable. But conquest—of matter, mind, or soul—is pleasurable; it is conducive to well-being, to happiness. And no conquest can be achieved without hard work—no conquest can give true pleasure if it has not required hard work.

Too often the short cut, the line of least resistance, is responsible for evanescent and unsatisfactory success. Too often the short cut is responsible for the choice of unsuitable goals we discussed a moment ago. I know of a man who is a magazine editor, and a good one; but he has known for fifteen years that he was born to be a teacher. Teaching meant first the acquisition of a Master's degree; then a slow start in a small school; a long period of hard work and low salary. He had a flair for writing and rewriting; it paid off quickly and opened a good future to him in magazine work. He took his choice consciously, and he is not miserable; he is a competent and respected man. But he is not entirely happy; he cannot feel successful. He is good-natured about it, and views his failure quite sensibly; but it remains a failure.

There are other short cuts. One is the refusal to observe established rules of decency and honesty. A good many of our higher-bracket businessmen might have been just as rich, just as powerful, but more respected and infinitely happier, if they had taken the slower and longer road of absolute ethical integrity and moral decency. The habit of sharp dealing, hard driving, seemed necessary to success; it was certainly quicker and more profitable. Some part of them is now forever cut off from happiness. Can this be called success? Sharp practices and immorality often "succeed"— precisely because the vast majority of mankind senses intuitively that decency and honor are necessary to happiness; they are therefore relatively innocent, and to some extent at the mercy of the liar and swindler. Barnum was right, in a way: there is a sucker born every minute. And thank God for the suckers of decency: they are the salt of the earth. They are those in whom the possibility of happiness has not been killed.

A sixth stumbling block is the exact opposite of the fifth: taking the long road. There's an old saying that the longest way round is the shortest (and sweetest) way home. That may often be true in love but not always in life. It is told that once Einstein, when asked to explain his theory of relativity, replied that perhaps the simplest example he could offer was the following: When a boy spends an hour with the girl he loves it seems like a minute, but that same boy compelled to sit on a hot stove for a minute would feel that it was an hour. We're talking, however, about reality and not relativity.

The ancient Biblical commentators in explaining why God did not lead the children of Israel to the Promised Land via the short straight route, up through the land of the Philistines, requiring only an eleven-day jaunt, but instead led them over a long circuitous route through the wilderness for forty years, said that it was in order that the slavery-conditioned people might gradually prepare themselves for the wise use and enjoyment of freedom. But we learn that they (the entire adult generation that left Egypt) died in that wilderness. They took so long in getting to the Promised Land that they never got there.

Again we are reminded of "The Beast in the Jungle." John Marcher spends his entire life waiting for some tremendous event that will shape his whole destiny into something unique. But it never happens. What was really his had been waiting for him for many years—a woman who, if he had married her, would have helped him to become his true self. He was so busy traveling the road of preparation for that vague far-off event that he was blind to the real opportunity that was close at hand.

How often have I seen young men and women already well-equipped for marriage, with more than adequate mates in prospect, wait and wait for the special person, the opportune time, the favorable situation, and end up as bachelors and spinsters. Sometimes they are too afraid to yield to the flood tide of their emotions or too calculating in their expectations of what their partners will bring to them rather than what they will be to them. And often they will allow an exaggerated conception of economic necessity, or of family obligation, to tie them up in engagements so long that even when they at last result in unions, little time is left to gather the ripe fruits of wedded bliss.

I know men and women who have spent such a long time growing up (staying childish and adolescent—frequently aided and even forced by parents—in their interests and activities, their tastes and temperaments, far beyond their teens into their twenties and thirties) that they will never be grown-up. They have never been weaned from their great concern about whether their chosen baseball or football teams win or lose; they have never gotten over their puppy-love mooning and spooning days; they become college bums remaining in academic halls of learning long after they should have been thrust into the challenging arenas of life.

From time to time, I officiate at the last rites of a man in his fifties or early sixties who has suddenly died, just as he was making plans to use his hard-earned wealth and his remaining years in the doing and enjoying of all the things of which he dreamed when he first started to carve out his career. With tears in their eyes the family tell me of the long difficult road of toil and trouble, of struggle and sacrifice, he has traveled to achieve his great success, and how their hearts ache when they realize that at the very time when he could have taken it easy and "lived it up" he was taken away. "What a pity," they cry. And I think, what a pity he hadn't stopped on the road sooner; hadn't been satisfied with less material success and fulfilled himself earlier. The longest way round is not always the shortest way home. Too often if you wait or travel too long, you never reach home.

The seventh stumbling block is neglecting little things. An anecdote about President McKinley—the story is possibly apocryphal but perfectly relevant—illustrates the point. He was in a dilemma; he had to choose one of two equally capable men for a high diplomatic post. Both were old friends. He reminisced, and recollected an incident that helped him to make his decision. One stormy night McKinley had boarded a streetcar and taken the last available seat, toward the rear, when an old washerwoman climbed aboard with a heavy basket of clothes. She stood in the aisle; despite her age and forlorn appearance, no one offered her a seat. One of McKinley's two candidates, then much younger, was seated near her; he was immersed in a newspaper, and took care to remain immersed in it so that he could ignore the old woman. McKinley went down the aisle, picked up the basket, and led the woman to his seat. The man never looked up, never knew what had happened; nor did he ever know that this act of minor selfishness later deprived him of an embassy, the crown of his ambition.

There are hundreds of stories stressing the importance of little things. A door left unopened, a document unsigned, a few live coals left upon a hearth; Edison losing a patent because of a misplaced decimal point. Vital battles have been lost for the "want of a nail." We grow sentimental over songs that tell us "It's the little things that count," but we go right on disregarding the little things.

At a prayer meeting in an old country church, a pious member was overheard imploring fervently, "Use me, O Lord, use me— but in an executive capacity." Big ideas, big money, big events, big shots: we feel we want to be in and around them; little things (so-called) are for little people (so-called). The truth is that no man, no job, is little. Men and jobs are different: easier to handle, or easier to approach, or with a less significant result. But everything that requires noticing or doing is big. "Without sharp knives," a French chef once said, "I am just another cook." It was good news to the apprentice who sharpened his knives.

The good executive keeps his finger on the little things: he knows that they may, if mishandled, become big problems. To an operating surgeon there are no little things: every slightest detail is a matter of life and death. To a lawyer, an obscure and minute legal confusion may cost a client liberty, even life. To a clergyman there are no small problems: in a human soul there is nothing unimportant.

We must appreciate the details; we must *care* for them. Oscar Hammerstein II once saw a close-up of the Statue of Liberty, taken from a helicopter. The head of the statue was revealed in fine detail, and Hammerstein noticed that the sculptor had done a painstaking job with the lady's coiffure. Every strand of hair was in its proper place. In his day he could hardly have known that anyone—save possibly a seagull—would ever see that hair. But he gave it as much care as he had the face, the arm, the torch.

And the New Testament tells the parable of a nobleman who, finding that a servant had handled a small assignment with unusual success, said to him, "Well done, thou good servant; because thou wast found faithful in a very little, have thou authority over ten cities."

The eighth stumbling block is quitting too soon. Recently I read

THE ROAD TO SUCCESSFUL LIVING

a magazine story (the author claims it to be true) called "The Pebble of Success." Discouraged, physically exhausted, Rafael Solano sat on a boulder in the dry river bed and made an announcement to his two companions. "I'm through," he said. "There's no use going on any longer. See this pebble? It makes about 999,999 I've picked up, and not a diamond so far. If I pick up another, it will be a million—but what's the use? I'm quitting."

It was 1942; the three men had spent months prospecting for diamonds in a Venezuelan watercourse. They had worked stooping, gathering pebbles, wishing and hoping for one sign of a diamond. Their clothes were ragged, their sombreros tattered; but they had never thought seriously of quitting until Solano said, "I'm through." Glumly, one of them said, "Pick up another and make it a million."

"All right," Solano said, and stooped, put his hand on a pile of pebbles, pulled one forth. It was almost the size of a hen's egg. "Here it is," he said, "the last one." But it was heavy—too heavy. He looked. "Boys, it's a diamond!" he shouted. Harry Winston, a New York jewel dealer, paid Rafael Solano $200,000 for that millionth pebble. Named the Liberator, it was the largest and purest diamond ever found.

Perhaps Rafael Solano needed no other reward; but I think he must have known a happiness that went beyond the financial. He had set his course; the odds were against him; he had persevered; he had won. He had not only done what he had set out to do—which is a reward in itself—but he had done it in the face of failure and obscurity.

An old hunter's aphorism teaches us that half the failures in life come from pulling in the horse in the midst of his leap. Elihu Root once said, "Men don't fail; they give up trying." Often it is not the wrong start but the wrong stop that makes the difference between success and failure. To quit while we're ahead would be silly; to quit when we're behind is even sillier. It requires will to hold on a little longer. It requires wit to know that the measure of success is not the luck, the breaks of the game, but the conquest of failure.

"The trouble with most of us," it has been said, "is that we stop trying in trying times." There is wisdom even in puns.

The ninth stumbling block is the burden of the past. We can never free ourselves from memories; we can only face them honestly. Somewhere I have read, and noted, this wise observation: "All our lives we have to live with our memories, and as we grow older we depend upon them more and more, until one day they may be all we have left. Either they can be depressing, embittering, humiliating, tormenting, or they can be cheering, sympathizing, self-respecting, comforting. The things that went in are the things that will come out, whether we put them there or were forced to receive them."

Memories of the past can infuse us with courage and confidence and creative power; or they can bind us in a dark shroud of dejection and defeat. Even the joys of the past can shackle us: I know men and women so proud of their ancestors' names, achievements, or accumulations, that they are unable to strike out in new directions for themselves. I know men so spoiled by one early success that there remains no further impulse to accomplishment.

But discouraging memories are more common. The memory of pain, of loss, of previous failure, can make life seem not worth the living. Often this is temporary—we see it among the bereaved, or among suddenly liberated prisoners, or among refugees who have been through all the horrors of modern life and have never known its joys. And depressing memories tend to congeal, to harden; we carry them like weights, and we lose our ability to transform them into creative energies.

A distinguished psychiatrist reports that a disturbed patient conceded, after several sessions, "It's easier to lie on a couch digging into the past than it is to sit on a chair facing the present." It is even harder to get up and walk toward the future. Preoccupation with the past is always a retreat. An old hunting joke makes the point: Two hunters on safari cornered a lion, who, instead of attacking, turned tail and disappeared into the underbrush. One terrified hunter stammered to the other, "You go ahead and see

61

where he went to. I'll go back and see where he came from."

We react often like that hunter. Tomorrow's problems are unknown; they may cause new pain. Yesterday's are over with; they are still painful, but the pain is familiar, almost comfortable. It is easier, less risky, to be static, to take what comfort we can out of our accustomed miseries. And sooner or later we find ourselves incapable of moving forward; we are trapped in the quicksand of our own regrets. David Livingstone, the great explorer, once explained: "I will go anywhere so long as it is forward." This is an ideal not always possible in practice. There are times when we must take a step or two backward to orient ourselves. But our drives should be forward, our instincts should be for advancement. Remember that life is growth, and in ceasing to grow, in fearing the new, we deny life.

The tenth stumbling block is the illusion of success. Success is a fickle goddess; we think we have her, but she knows better. One of modern literature's favorite themes is the tragedy of the easy success, the quick success, the near-success, the *ersatz* success. Many of us are deceived by an event, an accomplishment; it has all the marks of success, and others act as though it were a success, but it fails to satisfy us. We shrug off our doubts; we agree that we have arrived; we don a mask and accept the high popular opinion of ourselves.

At that point we have stopped trying to be ourselves. We have accepted praise or money, identified it with happiness, and assumed that success was ours. Further accomplishment seems unnecessary. We have abjured the right to go on to true success.

Napoleon knew this (little good it did him!); he said once, "The most dangerous moment comes with victory." The achievement of success is most precarious when it appears to be permanent. Overconfidence sets in; and when a new problem rises we are puzzled and bitter: how can I have troubles now, when I have already succeeded? The answer is that success, being fickle, must be continuously wooed; she can never be won forever and ever. Victory loses its value unless we use it as a means to even greater ends. Of itself it is only a temporary, *and essentially use-*

less, triumph. Talleyrand once commented, "A man can do everything with a sword but sit on it." The same is true of success.

And when we have lost the habit of constant striving, success can do us more harm than good when it comes to us again. Horseplayers like to tell the story of Broadway Ltd. (a son of Man o' War), who cost his owner $65,000 in 1928. Broadway Ltd. never won a race (he might have preferred hunting, we should remember, or even a milk wagon, but of course he was not consulted); his heart was not in his work. Finally, in 1930, running for a $900 purse, he rounded the stretch turn out in front. Alone and ahead for the first time in his life, he dropped dead.

We cannot suffer from illusory success unless we are so foolish as to consider public success an end in itself. The trouble is that most of us have not learned to disentangle the notions of vulgar success and personal success: we constantly aim for goals of which we think others will approve, and we are pained to find that they have little to do with true happiness.

Tolstoi has left us a striking parable, an allegory for the twentieth century, in his "How Much Land Does a Man Need?" The Russian peasant Pakhom is convinced that he will be a success when he owns as much land as that contained in the vast estates possessed by Russian noblemen. The time comes when he is offered free as much land as he himself can encircle by running at top speed from sunrise to sunset. He sacrifices all he has in order to move to the far-distant place where this generous offer has been made. After many hardships, he arrives and arranges for his great opportunity the next day. A starting point is fixed. Pakhom is off like a shot with the breaking dawn. Running with the morning sun, he looks neither to the left nor to the right; feverishly he runs into the blinding light and the burning heat. Without stopping to eat or rest, he continues his grinding, grueling round. And as the sun sets, he staggeringly completes the circle. Victory! Success! The realization of the dream of a lifetime!

But with his last step, he drops dead. All the land he will need now is six feet of earth.

℞

Chapter Four

*I am not bound to win, but I am
bound to be true. I am not bound
to succeed, but I am bound to live
up to the light I have.*
—ABRAHAM LINCOLN

"There are no such things as incurables," Bernard M. Baruch has
said. "There are only things for which man has not found a cure."
He made this assertion in praising the development, from semi-
quackery to an accredited medical science, of the rehabilitation
of the physically handicapped. Similar praise must be accorded
the extraordinary development of the science of mental and emotional rehabilitation. Spiritually as well as physically, there are no
incurables. For every ill of man a cure can be found.

Now there are general cures and specific cures, partial cures and
complete cures, temporary cures and permanent cures. The cure
we all seek—for whatever ails us—is specific, complete, and permanent. But seeking cures for failure we find nothing that is
specific, nothing that promises completeness, nothing that guarantees permanence. There are, however, precepts, rules of attitude
and of action which may, if faithfully taken in regular doses, re-
habilitate the individual, restore his purpose and pleasure in life,
and revitalize his pursuit of happiness.

Another medical parallel is instructive: antibiotics. These are
the "miracle drugs" of our day. Introduced into the body of the
patient—any patient at all, save a few with special allergies or

℞

rare diseases—they work like magic. The results are swift and sure.

But, unlike antitoxins, antibiotics are not specifics. Nor do they guarantee completeness or permanence in curing. Their help is only partial; it is supplementary. They provide the body's forces with needed auxiliaries. They prevent the bacteria from multiplying, and thus afford the body's natural defenses an opportunity to regroup effectively against the invaders. The antibiotics do not save the patient: they simply give him an opportunity to fight his battle on even terms, to use his own resources most efficiently in his fight for health. They do not destroy all the harmful bacteria, nor do they prevent a recurrence of the disease. Used widely, they restore the body to its condition previous to the attack. They cannot recreate bones or blood; they cannot reform deformities; they cannot perfect defects. *But they do offer the patient a chance to use what he has.*

What antibiotics achieve for man's body, our few rules may accomplish for his spirit. They are to be taken regularly, over a lifetime; they are not for emergencies. And here, too, there will be exceptional individuals with allergies or rare diseases, e.g., skepticism, stubbornness, or laziness (allergies), or complete submission to the unconscious fear of success (a dangerous disease). But the average person of normal instincts—allowing for the current elasticity of the words "average" and "normal"—can, by absorbing these philosophical and yet practical principles, condition his spirit against the debilitations of failure. He has, whether he knows it or not, superb natural defenses against failure; they can be made stronger, given the chance to develop fully. They can, indeed, be made so strong that a new sense of vigor will rise. The individual will liberate new energies, new confidence, new certainty of purpose. He will, in short, find himself within striking distance of true happiness.

The first—the fundamental—cure for failure is: Concentrate on what you have. Remember that what you have includes your

65

person; it is not simply your possessions and your position, but your heritage, your capacities, your desires, your temperament. However great your wealth, however exalted your position, you can enjoy only that which your mind can encompass and your soul grasp. What we have embraces not only our memories of the past and our performances in the present, but also our potential for the future. We are all in a constant process of change, and at any given moment we are moving away from what we have been and toward what we are to become. And our self-assessment at that moment often determines, in part, the direction of our growth.

Self-assessment is, of course, essentially an egoistical process. During World War II, a Bill Mauldin cartoon showed two soldiers crouching in neighboring foxholes, under withering fire from the enemy; one was saying to the other, "The hell this ain't the most important hole in the world, I'm in it." The most important point in your life is wherever you are, with whatever you have, at the given moment. A man who had for many years been the disciple of a very wise teacher, was asked, "What was most important to your teacher?" After brief consideration the man replied, "Whatever he happened to be doing at that moment." Horace Mann, founder of our American public school system, once set down in his diary, "Lost yesterday, somewhere between sunrise and sunset, two golden hours, each set with sixty diamond minutes. No reward is offered, for they are gone forever."

Place and time are as much a part of what we are and have, as possessions, position, skills and abilities. We have so many days allotted to us on earth, as a tightrope walker has so many yards of wire before him; and as he concentrates on the next few steps, so we should concentrate on here and now. The tightrope walker cannot dissipate his attention and energies; does not think back to the wire already crossed, nor does he glance carelessly to left and right. He is intensely aware of his present position, the job before him, and the steadiness of his body and sureness of his foot for the next few steps. He grapples with problems of today—of the moment—without frittering away his possibilities in idle speculation on the future or senseless regret (or rejoicing) over the past. If he concentrates fully on each step, the end will take care of itself.

La Rochefoucauld said, "There are no circumstances however unfortunate that clever people do not extract some advantage from, and none however fortunate, that the unwise cannot turn to their own disadvantage." And one of Aesop's fables tells of an ass who, during a hard, cold winter, wished for warm weather and fresh grass. When spring brought these—but with them much toil and weariness—he longed for summer. But summer meant even more drudgery; he yearned for autumn. But autumn brought the harvest, and the ass was overworked. As he completed the cycle of seasons, his final prayer was that he would soon see winter again.

André Gide, in his *The Fruits of the Earth,* set down a passage of surpassing beauty: "Nathaniel, let your waiting be not even a longing, but simply a welcoming. Welcome everything that comes to you, but do not long for anything else. Long only for what you have. Understand that at every moment of the day, God in His eternity may be yours. Let your longing be for love, and your possession of a lover's. For what is a longing that is not effectual?" *

The second step is: Stop being sorry for yourself. Stop regretting lost opportunities; give up vain desires. The capacity for happiness should lie within you, and if it does not, then no wealth, no power, no glory in the eyes of the public, will grant it to you. It follows that to envy the rich and powerful solely for their money or power is foolish; beating your breast, shedding tears over your low estate, over your "bad luck," will not improve it at all. And if you have tried to learn to rejoice over what you have— however little it may be—you may discover more personal happi-

* From *The Fruits of the Earth* by André Gide; translated by Dorothy Bussy; published by Alfred A. Knopf, Inc.

ness and peace within yourself than you suspected. An Arabian proverb says, "I cried when I had no shoes, until I met a man who had no feet."

Some time ago, Irv Kupcinet, the Chicago columnist, printed a letter sent him by a Mrs. Jack Kerns. She wrote, in part: "It is true that multiple sclerosis does strike the nervous system, but it does not result in ultimate death any sooner, barring complications, than just plain living. . . . I have had multiple sclerosis for six years. My trunk and lower limbs are paralyzed and I am blind. But I have no fear that death is waiting for me as a result of the disease, and no amount of misinformation will break down my hopes. I will walk again and I will see again."

I have learned to know Mrs. Kerns well; have visited her often. I am proud to number her in my congregation. I have been privileged to enter into the secret spaces of her soul. She has much to make her sorry for herself. Still beautiful in face and form, she is blind, and paralyzed from the waist down. I am certain that despite her brave assertion she, like other victims of multiple sclerosis whom I visit, is often sorry for herself. But I am sure, too, that whenever self-pity begins to invade her mind and heart, to push her mentally and emotionally downhill, she applies the brakes of her own courageous noble spirit, and brings the depression to a stop. This is power; this is a personal wealth that no distinction, no fame, no worldly riches, could ever bring her.

It was Boswell who said, "You can't stop the birds of sorrow from flying over your head, but you can keep them from nesting in your hair."

Romain Rolland tells us that when Beethoven first discovered that he had become deaf and could no longer hear the voice of his best friend, Nature, he gave way to despair. For very little he might have put an end to himself. By God's grace, his energies, his will to create, were too imperious; in this very hour of his deepest distress his creative impulses overflowed. They alone gave him life, and it was then that the demon of the *Eroica* cried out within him, "Forward!" Here was the true might of the spirit in action, carrying the exhausted body from an abyss of despair to the heights of glory.

None of us reaches his prime without being slowed, even stopped, even thrown back, by handicaps, hurts, hates, failures. But being sorry for ourselves does not break the chains of defeat; it only saps us of the strength we need to go on fighting. That strength—muscles and mind and heart shouting the everlasting *Yea*—can carry us through despair and into the full life. A little of the spirit of a certain Mississippi farmer is what we all need He had been driving to market, urging his sweaty horses over a rutted dirt road, moving slowly and painfully in his overloaded wagon. "How much longer does this hill last afore I get to town?" he asked a man at the roadside.

"Hill?" came the answer. "There's no hill. Your hind wheels are off."

Years ago, when Judy Garland was in a mood of terrible depression, on the verge of self-destruction, the late Fanny Brice stormed at her, "You listen to me, Judy Garland. It's time you stopped pampering yourself. Good Lord, girl, do you think you're the only person on earth who has problems? We all have things we can't face. I know every heartache in the book, but I never gave up—and you're not going to either! Now you keep your head up and your sights on tomorrow—and the h—— with yesterday!"

The third step is: Get rid of excess baggage. Arnold Toynbee tells us that a fundamental rule in the art of writing history is knowing what to leave out. He learned that truth from his mother. He watched her one day doing a water color of a ruined church. When she had finished, he pointed out that the painting was incomplete; she had drawn only the ruined church wall and a seascape visible through the glassless windows, and she had left out the beds of nettles sprouting through the cracked and shattered pavement. Quietly, his mother explained that the secret of sketching lay in knowing what to leave out.

One of the secrets of living lies in that same knowledge. The older we grow, the more important selection is. Life becomes complicated, cluttered up with mental and emotional excess baggage: memories, desires, dreams and hopes, loves and hates, unrealized ambitions, unattained goals, unhealed wounds, unassuaged sorrows, destructive passions, unthinking prejudices, old grudges, enslaving loyalties, divisive snobberies.

In the physical process of breathing, experts, oddly enough, place more emphasis on exhaling than on inhaling. The body must cleanse itself of poisonous carbon dioxide before it can beneficially absorb the fresh oxygen. The analogy is good: excess baggage, stored too long in man's spirit, may also create a poisonous mental and emotional atmosphere. In that atmosphere ugly temptations flourish, and the capacity to absorb fresh views, to act on new visions of life, diminishes. The spirit too needs regular housecleaning, a vigorous going-over with a new broom. Much outmoded emotional furniture—the equivalent of worthless antiques and trunks full of old letters—must be jettisoned cheerfully, to make room for better, fresher ideas, for nobler ideals. We are, as I have said, constantly changing, with the growth and development that life comprises; but an attic full of old furniture—or a mind full of old preoccupations—is simply a burial ground for the obsolete, and impedes change, growth, and development.

A little girl refused to go to sleep unless the door to her room was left open. She was stubbornly insistent.

"Do you want the door open to let in the light?" her mother asked.

"No, Mommy," came the answer. "To let out the dark."

For "open door," read "open mind." An ancient teacher once asked, "Why did God create forgetfulness? Because," he answered, "if there were no forgetfulness man would incessantly think of his death. He would build no house; he would launch no new enterprise. That is why God planted forgetting within him. And so if one angel is ordered to teach the child in a certain way, that it will not forget, the second angel is ordered to strike him in the mouth, to make him forget."

70

The art of forgetting can no more be perfected than the art of remembering. But both can be developed, and both are important. If you cannot, for example, clean out the attic completely, at least you can get rid of a few of the older pieces, and stack the rest in out-of-the-way corners. By ordering your mental and emotional life you can clear large areas for new growth. Remember, what you do today determines the shape of tomorrow's world: the evils and excesses that you carry with you will only mar its beauty, and destroy your own happiness.

Travel light.

The fourth step is: Don't put all your eggs in one basket. Let your interests—people and things—be many. Bertrand Russell admonishes, "To bear misfortune well when it comes, it is wise to have cultivated in happier times a certain width of interests. . . . All our affections are at the mercy of death which may strike down those we love at any moment. It is therefore necessary that our lives should not have that narrow intensity which puts the whole meaning and purpose of our life at the mercy of accident."

To stake "success" on one particular interest or ambition, on one person or possession, is to admit ignorance of the meaning of success. It is almost as dangerous as staking your entire fortune on one throw of the dice: if you win, you have doubled what you had, *which may already have been enough for happiness;* and if you lose, you lose all.

A generation ago, cotton was king in the Mississippi Delta. When the crop was large, the sharecroppers' shacks were full of food and rejoicing. When the crop was small, starvation and despair moved in. The cry of the new economy was, "Diversify your crops." And this was ultimately the salvation of the South.

Diversify your crops. Let no one thing or person become the supreme, the all-consuming, interest in your life. Cultivate all that your energy and temperament permit; you can never be sure wherein lies the richest promise for the future. And if one interest fades or dies, if a loved one is struck down, there remain others;

71

your instincts for life and activity will not all be nipped at once.

We have mentioned those whose success consists of money, power, or fame. Any one of those three—even all three—can be quickly and easily lost. No one of them—not even all three—can guarantee the success of a man's life. Often they prove to be the causes of failure, not because they are evil in themselves—they are not—but because they keep us from cultivating more fertile areas of our souls; they deprive us of still richer harvests.

There are others who see success in terms of one child (among three or four), one friend (among many), one companion, one adviser. They have narrowed their hopes for the future to a single human possibility. And if separation, or betrayal, or death, should come, all is lost. Having neglected the richness and variety of humanity in a futile concentration upon one individual, these people have forfeited all other hopes. And it goes without saying that, in the process, they have deprived themselves of many of life's most heartwarming and ennobling experiences.

The most tragic, however, is the man who puts all his eggs in *his own basket*. The egoist, the man who sees no hope of happiness but in utter concentration on his own desires and ambitions. W. Béran Wolfe reminds us, "No one can be happy in work which is centered entirely about his own person and deals exclusively with the satisfaction-relations which focus only himself and his immediate narrow sphere of influence." To find happiness, we must seek it in a focus outside of ourselves. In Dickens' *Christmas Carol*, self-centered Scrooge finds happiness only when he learns to focus on others.

"How shall a man die?" the Talmud asks.

"Live," is the answer; "live selfishly—solely for the gratification of one's own passions and ambitions."

"And how shall a man live?"

"Die. Slay himself. Destroy all that is base in one's being. And then begin to live in the noble service of God and one's fellow man."

℞

When a man lives most for others, he lives best for himself. To be a success only for oneself is to be a failure in life.

The fifth step is: Choose goals suited to your nature. In the Chinese classics there sparkles this gem of speculation: "Once upon a time, I, Chuang-tzu, dreamt I was a butterfly fluttering hither and thither, to all intents and purposes a butterfly. I was conscious only of following my fancies as a butterfly, and was unconscious of my individuality as a man. Suddenly I awakened, and there I lay, myself again. Now I do not know whether I was a man dreaming I was a butterfly, or whether I am now a butterfly dreaming I am a man."

There is no fixed rule: some of us fail because we are content to be simple men when we ought to dream of being butterflies, and others of us fail because we dream of being butterflies when we should desire only to be men. To aim low is as tragic as to aim high.

An industrial engineer has told me that factory personnel have a tendency to freeze themselves into their jobs by a process of rationalization. They cannot see themselves as potentially more capable than they are at the moment; they refuse to climb. Or, on the contrary, they refuse to admit obvious ineptitude; they cannot face stepping down to the position of the "average man." Both ways they fail to find the best within themselves; they fail to do the best for either themselves or the industry. They have rationalized themselves into accepting goals unsuited to their natures.

"Until the donkey tried to clear the fence," said Arthur Guiterman, "he thought himself a deer." Some of us are born to be deer, others donkeys: but none of us need be a jackass. A good donkey is worth a good deer. He sticks to the work he likes and does best; he wastes no time leaping fences or, to revert to the earlier image, fluttering about like a butterfly. "To find a career," Mark Sullivan advised, "to which you are adapted by nature and then to work hard at it, is about as near to a formula for success and happiness as the world provides." One of the fortunate aspects of

73

this formula is that—if the right career has been found—the hard work takes care of itself. It ceases to be oppressive; often it ceases to be work at all.

A good many failures occur because a man or woman spends a lifetime in fantasy, dreaming of becoming what he or she was never meant to be. For every Roman emperor crowned, how many young men left their native villages and found misery in Rome, striving for the mantle? And yet more than one emperor complained, late in life, that he would have been happier on the farm where he was born. Robert Louis Stevenson stated a problem: "Benjamin Franklin went through life an altered man because he once paid too dearly for a penny whistle. My concern springs usually from a deeper source—to wit, from having bought a whistle when I did not want one." He meant that his nature did not demand a whistle. It was accounted a prize possession by others, but it was not suited to his own soul.

In one of his memorable sermons Phillips Brooks said this: "I remember talking once with a brave general who had fought throughout the war. He was telling me about an officer whom he had rebuked upon the field of battle for cowardice. "I did not blame the man for being a coward," he said. "He could not help that. . . . It was no more disgrace for him to be afraid than it was credit for me not to yield to the temptation I never felt. What I blamed him for was simply that having found out that physically he was a coward, he yet allowed himself to occupy a place where cowardice could do such mischief, so I degraded him."

You know your nature. Don't put it in a position it can't effectively occupy—for your own sake as well as others'. Don't just drift into a spot in life: pick your place. There are jobs, people, towns, just right for you. They may not be the ones that your childhood friends and neighbors have. They may not be those you once envisioned; those you once hoped you would be qualified for. But with them lies your destiny. Choose them intelligently, gladly, gratefully, and success will be within your reach.

The sixth step is: Don't be too independent. One of the

proudest, and most foolish, boasts uttered by great tycoons is: "I am a self-made man." No human being is self-made. God, parents, teachers, fellow workers, fellow citizens, play vital roles in the making of a man. "The story of the self-made man," said a millionaire Kentucky lumberman, "is a myth. Those who work with a man help make him."

The fact must be acknowledged: we are dependent on those about us from birth to death. In infancy, the truth of the proposition is obvious. Without help, we would not survive. In adolescence, in maturity, it is easier for us to forget that we are formed by the humanity around us. We may decide to break our ties, make our own decisions, refuse advice or financial help, go it alone; but every step of the way we are surrounded by people whose opinions and actions affect us, whether we admit it or not.

The Prodigal Son, in the New Testament, was probably more than just a young man out sowing wild oats. He wanted to prove that he could make his way without help; that he could be a self-made man. He came home sadder and wiser, happy once again to eat at his father's table, to know the warmth of a family and to share friendships. He was not rejected. The others, who suffered under no delusion of total independence, rejoiced to receive him, and restored him to a place of honor, love, and peace.

So many of us seem to feel it a mark of disgrace if we must accept advice, or help, or even love. Children become cold to their parents. Young men and women ready for careers are contemptuous of counseling. Husbands and wives are ashamed to visit marriage counselors; they prefer to let their marriages drift recklessly. I know children who have not only defeated their own purposes, but also destroyed the lives of their parents by their too stubborn independence. I know parents who have not only denied themselves happiness, but also driven their dutiful children to fury and distraction by their pathological fear of dependence. Yet help was at hand, freely offered. Out of pride and a false sense of humiliation, these people drove themselves into situations of true humiliation.

Absolute dependence is, of course, equally crippling. But *some* dependence is recognized by every society; in a sense, the word "society" *implies* dependence, by implying the group, the interaction, the common way of life. No man is an island, Donne said; how then can he achieve that cold, total independence? He cannot; he should not. He should not, because helping one's fellow man in a time of need is one of the basic human responsibilities; *and the man who will not accept help cannot be trusted to give help.*

Shall we be prouder than God Himself? Judaism teaches that He made man His partner in the work of creation; He accepted man's help. Did He thus degrade Himself? Of course not. Yet so many of us set ourselves above help; so many of us suffer unnecessarily, add years to the struggle for comfort, by rejecting material help, advice, or leadership. Why do we resent letting others share in the fashioning of our happiness? What have we lost through their help?

The answer can only be selfishness: if we succeed alone, we can hoard the fruit of our success.

Hoard it then; it will rot, and you will learn a new kind of starvation.

The seventh step is: Convert your liabilities into assets. Once there was a king who owned a rare diamond. There was none to equal it anywhere. And then an accident marred it with a deep scratch. The diamond-cutters, the artists, agreed that it could never be restored to its former perfection. So the king took the diamond to a famous lapidary in a distant land. The master artist used the scratch as a stem, and engraved a delicate rosebud around it. The king looked in amazement and admiration. The diamond had never been so beautiful.

This passage is in one of Pearl Buck's most recent novels: "He allowed the catastrophe to flow over him like a great wave. 'You cannot overcome the sea,' his father had told him. 'It is as endless as eternity, as unchangeable as fate. In comparison to the sea a man is less than a small fish. Don't fight the sea. Don't combat

76

B

the tides. Yield yourself and the waves flow. Let yourself follow them. Then you will be borne up. The sea itself will uphold you.' " *

When I read her autobiography, *My Several Worlds,* I realized that this wisdom was the distillation of many waves of sorrow and suffering on her own part. She expresses gratitude for the wonder and beauty of life; yet it was the kind of life that might have defeated and destroyed an average woman. The catalogue is dramatic: exile to a strange foreign land in her childhood; long stretches of poverty and loneliness; a domineering, zealous, fanatical missionary father; the heartbreaking death of her mother; an unhappy marriage; a defective child; the dangers of war and revolution; her eviction from China, her separation from the people she dearly loved. But from Pearl Buck came no whining, no wailing: with superb literary artistry she wove those tragic experiences into stories of beauty and inspiration. Not despite them, but because of them, she is today a Nobel Prize winner, and one of the noblest and wisest women of our time.

The principle of turning liabilities into assets is as old as civilization. The Eskimos, for example, keep warm in igloos made of snow and ice. The poets know that the uses of adversity are sweet: read any of the poems of Heinrich Heine, who died in Paris, exiled, to see how he converted his tears into diamonds. And in everyday life the principle operates. Listen to Frank Leahy, the great Notre Dame football coach: "While it made me heartsick at the time, the fact that I injured a knee and could not play in my senior year at Notre Dame actually turned out to be a break. That enabled me to watch the techniques of the great Knute Rockne. At the end of the season, when Rockne went to the Mayo Brothers' Clinic, he brought me along for another operation on my knee. We spent two weeks talking nothing but football. It

* From *All Men Are Brothers* by Pearl S. Buck; published by Grove Press, Inc.

77

was while bedridden in the same room that Rockne arranged for me to be an assistant coach at Georgetown."

The Chinese character for crisis consists of two symbols, one meaning "danger," the other "opportunity." We all pass through periods of danger, depression, suffering; we do not realize that these can be opportunities as well as obstacles. The late Joseph Fort Newton wrote: "We cannot tell what may happen to us in the strange medley of life. But we can decide when it happens—how we take it, what we do with it—and that is what really counts in the end. How to take the raw stuff of life and make it a thing of worth and beauty—that is the best of living."

A colleague of mine who was recently stricken with blindness in one eye (I rejoice to learn that a recent corneal transplantation has restored the sight), and who faced the grave and immediate danger of sympathetic blindness in the other, wrought from the tragedy this beautiful prayer: "Oh, God, we do not ask for perfect health, but for the power to transmute illness and affliction into service on Thy altar; we do not ask for perfect happiness, but rather for the power to shape suffering into service and tears into triumph of the spirit; we do not ask for a perfect world, but for the power to change and refashion it more closely after Thy will; we do not ask for the peace that dulls and stultifies the energies, but for the peace that passes all understanding and arms us with serene strength and vigor to establish Thy kingdom. Amen."

The eighth step is: Give it everything you've got. This is, of course, the constant plea of all athletic coaches. They know that even the most brilliant of their stars can let down the rest of the team if he gives less than his utmost. The halfhearted, indifferent, don't-care approach is a common cause of failure in many games, and most of all in the game of life itself.

Parents do a halfhearted job of child rearing, and then wonder what ails the family. Children give, grudgingly, only the leftovers of their lives to family relationships and to schools, and then complain that they are not getting much out of either. Husbands and wives cease to give of themselves shortly after the marriage ceremony, and cannot understand the failure of their marriage. Too many men—executives and workers, professional men and businessmen—bring to their daily work divided minds, unenthusiastic hearts, and bored souls.

The cliché says that you get out of life what you put into it. I go further: you cannot make a success of life unless you put your *all* into living it. Your life is the biggest game you will play, the most serious business in which you will engage; it is *you*. How can you expect fullness and satisfaction if you hold part of yourself back? Do you *really* care about your health, about the number of your years on earth, or do you mutter vaguely about exercising "later on, when there's time"? Do you really care about using that miraculously intricate—even if rusty—brain of yours? Does the state of your spirit mean anything to you? Can you respond to generosity, reverence, nobility? Or have you—*the chances are that you have*—drifted into a life of eating, drinking, halfhearted work, and cheap amusement?

In his book, *When a Man Comes to Himself,* Woodrow Wilson wrote, "We must learn to live by our enthusiasm." Note that he did not mean enthusiasms: bingo, sports cars, upswept hair, or adenoidal crooners. I think he was aware of the derivation of "enthusiasm"; it is from the two Greek words, *en theos,* meaning "in God"; that is, a spirit touched by divine ardor or frenzy. As the ancient Greek sibyl, touched by the gods, threw herself into her work with singleness of purpose, so must modern man give himself to the task of becoming himself.

You cannot work at success part of the time. Success is a continuing condition, born not of a number of good deeds, nor of a period of virtue, but of a life lived constantly at the service of one's real self. The forms it takes are many; *often it goes unrecognized, except in the heart of the man who lives it.* But one quality is always present where life is successful: enthusiasm. The spark. The divine passion for life in all its honest manifestations. The ability to give oneself wholly to one's life.

"I tell my people," says Charles F. Kettering, "that I don't want any fellow who has a job working for me; what I want is a fellow whom a job has. I want the job to get the fellow—not the fellow to get the job. And I want the job to get a hold of this young man so hard that no matter where he is, the job has got him for keeps. I want that job to have him in its clutches when he goes to bed at night and in the morning. I want that job to be sitting at the foot of the bed telling him, 'It's time to get up and go to work.' And when a job gets a fellow that way, he's sure to amount to something."

And when life gets a fellow that way, he cannot avoid the truest success, the truest happiness.

The ninth step is: Check up on yourself regularly. You check your car, your bank balance, your teeth; why not check your attitude toward life, your progress toward success? Take an inventory of yourself once a year; if you were a storekeeper, you would of your stock. Spiritual liabilities? Assets? Pay careful attention to the liabilities: the qualities you lack, the mistakes you've made, the opportunities you've missed, the people you've alienated, the friendships you've lost. And re-evaluate your assets; you may be overestimating a few of them, or you may even have too many for your own good. How are you using them? Are they simply ornaments? Are you proving something to the neighbors, or actually enlarging and enriching your soul?

Of course your inventory will not be accurate. Even a stock inventory is often inaccurate, because of the human element; and a personal inventory is all human. When Bobby Burns prayed God for the gift of seeing ourselves as others see us, he knew he was seeking the impossible. An office boy once called his boss —anonymously—from a telephone booth. "Do you have an opening for an office boy? No? Well, how is the one you have? A hard worker? Does he do a good job? Can you depend on him? Are you sure you're not planning to replace him? No? Well, thank you very much." Asked the purpose of the call, he explained: "I was just checking up on myself."

It's better, though, to have someone else check up on you.

80

That someone else should be able to see you impartially and objectively. Not, in other words, a father, mother, wife, child. Not a luncheon or golfing or drinking companion. Find someone whose integrity and intelligence you respect, whose criticism you will accept, whose counsel you will follow. See that person at least once a year. Behave much as if you were in a confession box or on a psychoanalyst's couch.

Don't just tell him your troubles. Don't use him as a wailing wall or sounding board. Submit to him your thoughts, feelings, hopes, dreams, fears, frustrations, expectations, accomplishments. Let him see the entire balance sheet. Regard him as your spiritual accountant.

And when he gives his report, don't just file it away and forget about it—why waste his time and your own? Study it carefully and critically; then act upon it. Don't doubt or delay; don't think it through so often that you fall into the trap of rationalizing away all your deficiencies. And remember that this is not a traditional balance sheet, where all is well if the assets match the liabilities. You are trying to convert yourself into pure asset; you are trying to bring your whole being into the pursuit of success and happiness.

For most of us criticism is difficult to endure; but faithful are the wounds of a friend. A real friend is not the man who glosses over our faults and mistakes, or who consoles us with sympathy, or who coddles us with flattery. Nor is he the man who recites a punchy pep talk, slaps us on the back, and grins jovially, "Now don't worry, kid, you're doing swell. Go right ahead the way you are." Very few of us *want* to continue the way we are; for most of us it would mean stagnation.

A wise friend tells the truth; he tells it with sympathy and understanding, but he will not lie. His purpose is beneficent and not malicious. He will be as pleased to help you as you are to have him help.

The tenth step is: Be patient. Be very patient. You can never know the exact moment at which success will come. You may for days and months and years see yourself driven inexorably down into the valley of failure, and then one morning you wake up and find yourself sitting on the very mountaintop of success. It is entirely probable that the truly successful man is too happy and too occupied to be consciously concerned about the question of whether he is a success. He is too busy persevering in those attitudes and projects which are making him successful.

On a recent European trip I spent an afternoon in Holland with a remarkable man. He is one of the few Dutch Jews who narrowly escaped death at the hands of the Nazis. For the last two years of the Nazi occupation of Holland, he successfully hid himself in the cabin of a ship moored in a harbor in the Zuyder Zee. I asked him how he had managed to evade capture, especially since the ship was always right under the nose of the Nazis suspiciously sniffing about for any sign of a Jew. His face filled with the wisdom of the ages. His quick answer was, "Patience, patience." To stay below decks day after day, going out for a breath of fresh air only on a dark night. The capacity to chain your restless feet and curious eyes to waiting, waiting, waiting. No, the answer is not courage, nor hope, nor faith—important as these may be—but just the power of patience. To wait out the day of success.

Columbus, for example, knew many discouraging and despair-filled moments. They laughed at his conception of the earth as round. They mocked his plans and hopes as those of a madman. They rejected his requests at Genoa and Venice and Portugal. They delayed his departure in England and Spain. But he never gave up hope for his dream or faith in himself. And on the 12th of October, 1492, he heard from one of his ships the long-awaited cry, "Land! Land!" He lifted up his eyes and saw success. Yes, a greater success than he realized. He had discovered a new world.

Philip Mickman is an eighteen-year-old English lad who swam the English Channel a few years ago. He first tried the swim, and failed, when he was seventeen. He tried again the following summer and failed. When he finally succeeded, he was in the ice-cold water for twenty-four hours. The channel is only nineteen miles wide, but he had to swim an estimated forty miles to buck rain and wind and ebb tide. His father, at his side in a pilot boat, begged him to quit. But not Philip; he persevered to victory.

The late Ezio Pinza wrote, "I thank my lucky star that I had a father who was willing to see me through the tribulations of trying to make myself a success as a carpenter, baker, and professional bicycle racer. He didn't seem worried when my friends pronounced me a failure, and he always stood by me with advice and help until I thought I had found the right road. One reason is, I am sure, that he had faith in an old Italian proverb, '*la vita comincia domani*,' life begins tomorrow. He knew that given a chance, life has a habit of taking care of a great deal of time itself. My life, like every life, has had many ups and downs, but one thing which has helped me to keep going is remembering this one fact, which is so true, so simple, and so powerful: However bitter this day has been, God will always give you a chance to start over and try again—for life begins tomorrow."

And often that tomorrow which brings success and happiness does not announce itself beforehand. You wake up, you look about you, you wonder momentarily at the strange peacefulness of the day; and you realize suddenly that whatever it was you had gone through life wanting, it is yours today. You are at peace with yourself, your fellow man, your God.

The ten causes of failure, and the ten corrective steps, have now been set before you. A physician can only prescribe; it is up to the patient to take his medicine. And remember that small and irregular doses will do no good. I have said it before: Success is an attitude toward life, based on a knowledge of the self. To win that knowledge, to build that attitude, the prescription must become part of your life; the medicine must be absorbed constantly, from day to day. There are no miracle drugs for the soul; there is only the miracle of man fulfilled.

HEAVEN'S
LIEUTENANTS

Chapter Five

*The voice of parents is the voice of
gods, for to their children they are
heaven's lieutenants.*

—SHAKESPEARE

"Why did I fail? Why did I fail?" cried Mrs. Portia Howe, blinking tearfully at a letter from her son. The heartbroken mother had just completed an emergency flight to Tokyo; and all that awaited her was a dirty sheet of foolscap sent on from a North Korean camp. "I have made up my mind," her son had written. "I am not going. Don't try to see me. You'd be wasting your time, and don't believe I've been forced, doped, brainwashed. I have chosen to follow the Communist way of life. I am not coming home."

Mrs. Howe held a small Bible in her trembling hands. In a low, firm voice she said, "I am not accepting this as final, and I am basing my faith on this Book, in which it says—Proverbs 22:6 —'Train the child in the way he should go and when he is old he will not depart from it.' I tried to train him in the way he should go. I believe God's promises and I am not giving up at this point. I would like to make this point clear: I've searched through my recollections. Where did I fail? Where did I fail?"

There is no record that Mrs. Howe's question was answered. It was not because her cry went unheard or unheeded: it found its way into every newspaper, and became a topic of conversation in city streets, village stores, and hundreds of thousands of homes. It was an echo of one of man's most primitive wails, first heard on that tragic day when Adam and Eve beheld their son Abel lifeless on the bloody ground, slain by his brother Cain.

I wish I had been in Tokyo at that sorrowful moment. I could have given Mrs. Howe an answer, perhaps not the correct answer, but one like that which I have given scores of fathers and mothers who have come to me with that same cry on their lips. "I know it's my fault," they weep. "I have loved my child; sacrificed for him; given him a good home, a fine education; tried to guide him, to keep him from evil companions and bad influences. And yet you see what has happened. What did I do that was wrong? What should I have done? Where did I fail?"

Mrs. Howe, I would have said, you haven't failed. You may have made mistakes in rearing your son; but all parents make mistakes. Parenthood demands decisions. Human decisions are always subject to error. The world alters quickly these days; needs and fulfillments differ from year to year. Each of us is unique; life fashions each child in a different image. The failure was no more yours than mine, or that of any other American. It was our country's failure—all 170,000,000 of us—to infuse him with love for, and faith in, our democracy; to save him for his native land.

And in the last analysis, it was his failure. Of all the thousands of sons released from Red China's prison camps, only twenty-two refused to return. He was one of them; yet you are just as passionately patriotic, as devoted to your country's ideals, as the mothers of the thousands who came back. Ask yourself, "Where did my son fail?" Perhaps for him this was the illusion of success; perhaps he felt it was what his soul required; perhaps he thought he was being true to himself. Why? Who can tell? Did it begin in the womb? Was there an association, a frustration, that changed the course of his childhood? An influence or inspiration that ignited a sudden youthful idealism? A temptation or torture that

85

preyed on the weakness of the flesh? Open your Bible again, to the Book of Job, and read this: 'But wisdom where shall it be found? And where is the place of understanding? Man knoweth not the price thereof. Neither is it found in the land of the living. Behold the fear of the Lord that is wisdom; and to depart from evil is understanding.' Go home, Mrs. Howe; ease your troubled heart. Be patient. And God's wisdom will reveal itself.

Parents have always been too quick to blame themselves for the follies and failures of their children. Many parents still behave as though they were potters, and their children lumps of clay. Like the potter, parents envision the ultimate form, mold and trim the clay, and apply pressures where necessary.

But a child is more than inert clay; and no human being can play God to another. A child has a mind, a heart, a will of its own; and life is an infinitely more complicated machine than a potter's wheel. Rare, too, is the parent with true insight, with the artist's touch in human relations. The average parent is undecided and hesitant: how much of himself shall he force upon his child? Where does guidance end and pressure begin?

When the parent seeks advice, he finds that the various schools of "child psychology" have starkly conflicting views on the subject. One subscribes to the traditional theories of bribe and threat, reward and punishment; another follows more libertarian principles of freedom and equality; and between the two are several variations and gradations of each theory. Under the conservative, traditional discipline, a child, breathing in notions of democracy on a national scale, may become bitter, belligerent, and rebellious toward his parents. Under the libertarian influence a child may mistake liberty for license, and equality for anarchy; he may become unruly, insolent, and tyrannical.

So parents, frustrated and confused, shift from one extreme to the other, vacillating between oversuppression and overindulgence. They command brutally, or they yield spinelessly. And the result is often the same: the child becomes, sooner or later, the master of the parent. The harsher the parental rule, the stronger the child's ultimate rebellion; the laxer the parental hand, the sooner the child usurps control. Is it any wonder that the modern parent feels like a failure?

It is of small comfort but of some interest to learn that the same frustrations embittered parents in ancient times. About 6,000 years ago an Egyptian parent observed, "Our earth is degenerate in these later days. There are signs that the world is coming to an end. Everybody wants to write a book. The end of the world is near." And a little over 2,000 years ago Socrates remarked, "The children now love luxury; they have no manners; contempt for authority; they show disrespect for elders and love to chatter instead of exercise. . . . They contradict their parents; misbehave before company; gobble up dainties at the table; cross their legs and tyrannize over their teachers."

Except for literary prolixity, which seems mercifully to have been spared the Greeks, three widely disparate cultures—Egyptian, ancient Greek, and modern American—have suffered from the same difficulties. ("Everybody wants to write a book. The end of the world is near." The words fascinate me. If the one followed the other, I would close my treatise here, advising my readers to take to the hills!)

The problem is universal, in time and in space. When parents, in a burst of self-pity, tell me of the jealousy and brutality displayed by one of their children to another, I recall Cain and Abel; I envision Adam and Eve asking themselves miserably, "Why did we fail?" When, in self-reproach, parents tell me of their inability to conceal a preference for one child over another, I see Isaac favoring Esau over Jacob; I see Rebecca choosing Jacob over Esau; and I see both bewildered in their old age because their sons are lost to them—one in exile and the other a forest bandit. When, in self-blame, parents tell me of futile attempts to save their sons from great hurt and even tragic death, I see Jacob losing Joseph; Jochebed, Moses; Mary, Jesus; all unaware of the

87

spiritual glory that will spring from their sons' suffering and sorrow, plaguing themselves with the eternal lament, "Where did I fail? Where did I fail?"

None of these parents really failed. Scant as the record is, it indicates that parents have always given their children all the love and care of which they were capable. But parents are not all-wise, or all-powerful; being finite creatures, they are entitled to a quota of mistakes.

I think it is important to remember that most parents who come to confess failure *do not really believe their own protestations.* The deeper cause of their dissatisfaction is a conviction that the children have failed—failed to be what the parents hoped they would be. And yet the children did not really fail; they simply refused to accept their parents' attitudes. They became what they had to be—even Cain. The parent, with a vague inkling of this, does not like to believe that the fault is the child's (after all, the child was made in his image and the basic fault may be his own), and with good parental self-abnegation protests that the fault is his own.

My first admonition to all worried parents is, *get rid of your crippling guilts!* Time and again I have asked, "Have you loved your son? Have you suffered and sacrificed for him?" The invariable and unhesitating answer is, "Yes, yes." Now, of course, you can pick out errors made ten years ago; you can regret misjudgments and omissions. But "you" now are not "you" ten years ago. You did your best at the time: and no human being should ever be asked to assume later guilt for earlier actions which were innocent—even praiseworthy—when performed.

Often the parent protests, "But I should have known better. I should have seen that my child was not like others. I should have put him in nursery school. I shouldn't have pushed him so hard in his studies. I should have moved to a better neighborhood; given him more of my own companionship; taken him to a child psychiatrist. I should have known that he was abnormally shy. I should have sensed his fears and anxieties; I should have done something about them before it was too late."

Or the parent will sigh: "I loved him too much and gave him too much. He was never disciplined. His word was law. I wanted to give him everything—all the things I'd missed myself. And now look at him: a selfish wastrel."

Let no one claim that there is a pat formula for rearing children. Solomon, with all his wisdom, confessed in the Book of Proverbs: "There be three things which are too wonderful for me; yea, four, which I know not: the way of an eagle in the air; the way of a serpent upon a rock; the way of a ship in the midst of the sea; and the way of a man with a young woman." He might well have added a fifth: the way of a parent with a child. Robert Louis Stevenson, near death, writing his last works on the island of Samoa, reflected, "You would think when the child was born there would be an end to trouble, and yet it is only the beginning of fresh anxieties, and when you have seen it through its teething and education and at last its marriage, alas, it is only to have new fears, new quivering sensibilities with every day, and the health of your children's children grows a touching concern as that of your own."

Many conspicuous failures as parents are those who are confident that they have succeeded because they and their friends look upon their children as successes. Often this is the failure of the child's life masquerading as the success of the parents' program. Over the years, I have known hundreds of children, watched them grow to maturity, enter businesses and professions, fashion marriages and build families. Most of them appear to be leading successful lives. Their parents are proud and happy, having "done so well by the children." Yet I know that these children are most often failures; and I know that the primary responsibility for the failure lies with the parents. The sons have followed in their fathers' footsteps, consolidating the family interest, upholding the family tradition; they have pursued paths carefully cleared for them, paths into which they were firmly pressured from their early years. The daughters are well married, financially and socially, if not romantically; their lives are respectable and tranquil, but their homes are modeled on the old homestead. They have been successfully molded in the image of their fathers and mothers; but they are failures. They have lived only to fulfill their parents' desires, and their own dreams have been wasted. They have realized the best in their parents, and not in themselves. And many of these younger people sense it. They are uneasy in the knowledge that they should have been the builders of a better world, that they should have scorned money and power and ease. They should have been guided and driven by a "divine discontent." They should have sacrificed and suffered for the ideals of their youth. They have, in the deepest sense, sold their birthright for a mess of pottage.

There is only one failure for parents: failure to save their children from failure. Occasionally children succeed best when they are helped least: they just grow, and they seem to find their true place in the world. But more often parents *can* help; they can plan intelligently, acknowledge the child's individuality. There is still no guarantee of success, of course; there are always roads not clearly marked, detours that could never have been anticipated.

Much is made of planned parenthood before the children come; it is even wiser after their arrival. Basic to the planning are a series of precepts, products of experience and observation. Like all rules and standards, these are occasionally hard to live by; it takes intelligence and determination. But they work. They yield results.

The first is: *Don't look upon your children as possessions.* Once conceived, they become distinct individuals, with bodies, minds, and souls of their own. There can be no question of "ownership," of possession. They are lent to you in sacred trust. Parents often lack the wisdom expressed in this Talmudic tale:

Rabbi Meir and his wife Beruria had two beautiful little children. While the Rabbi was at prayer in the synagogue, the two children were stricken by a fatal disease and died. Upon the Rabbi's return, his wife greeted him at the door and asked, most gravely, "My husband, suppose someone had left in our care two precious jewels which we might enjoy even as we guarded them. And suppose one day, two or three years later, with no warning, he came and demanded their return. Would we, despite our deep attachment, be duty bound to give them back?"

"Of course, my wife," the Rabbi answered. "At best, it was only a loan."

Without a word, Beruria led him into the bedroom where his sons lay wrapped in the arms of death. Quickly comprehending, the Rabbi bowed his head and cried, "The Lord hath given, the Lord hath taken away. Blessed be the name of the Lord."

There are parents who see their children as ornaments. Walking between my home and my Temple, I frequently meet young mothers wheeling baby-buggies; they gaze lovingly down at their bundles of joy. Average women, wearing ordinary clothes; but neither the raiment of a queen nor all the jewels of the Indies could enhance their appearance in public as does that newborn baby. As I smile in admiration, I cannot help wondering whether they will continue to see those infants simply as ornaments throughout their lives.

And fathers and mothers come to me to complain about their children. They explain that their sons and daughters are not really bad, but often what they say and do—and more frequently what they *don't* say and do, particularly in company—causes embarrassment. The parents don't feel that these are really their own children; they must be changelings; they are not at all like father and mother. They have strange interests, and choose odd companions. It is difficult to explain them to one's friends.

Obviously these parents are primarily concerned that their children be ornaments to them, adornments to their way of life, flattering evidence of parental heritage, intelligence and care. Yet the sons and daughters are upright, of good character. If

91

allowed to behave as individuals and exercise their own talents, they will succeed. But because the children's beliefs and behavior are *individual*—we might almost say, *in proportion* as they are individual—they fail to follow the socially acceptable modes of their parents. And the parents, in guilt and embarrassment, assume that they have somehow failed their children.

This assumption is, of course, partly due to the habit of protecting the child. A great portion of the parent's early function consists simply of saying "No" in order to keep the child from harm. As the physical dangers decrease, the social dangers replace them, and the parent finds himself automatically being corrective and defensive about the child. The path of absolute social acceptability is surely the safest for the older child, and the parent struggles to keep him on it. But "safest" is not the same as "best." Any process of growth—physical, mental, or moral—involves risk. Overprotection, overcorrection on the part of the parent may eliminate risk; they will also inhibit normal growth.

Perhaps the basic mistake here is treating the child as a toy. Parents very often play with their children just as their children play with trains: turn them on, enjoy them, become bored, turn them off. The attitude persists sometimes through the child's teens: he's handy to have around when a parent wants to while away some free time, or play the professor. When the game becomes dull, the child can always be sent out to join his gang, or sent up to bed. And this is called "being pals" with the child. But one-sided friendship is not friendship at all. Taking is not the same as giving; entering a child's room is not the same as entering his heart.

There are other parents who treat their children as tools. Not too long ago child labor on the farm and in the factory was accepted as a normal part of the pattern of American life. Children were valuable possessions to the poor farmer or the slum dweller. Their labor added needed income; the more children in the family, the greater the potential supply. It is true that some families were saved from starvation by child labor; it is equally true that some parents built the foundation of their own security on the sweat of their own children.

Today any such direct use of the child is both illegal and immoral. Yet there are parents who will enroll their children in certain schools, pressure them into associations, push them into vocations, for the enhancement of the parent's position, and not for the higher interest of the child. They use their children to add to their social, instead of financial, income. The principle is the same: this is simply a more subtle slavery. The essence of slavery is that it makes a possession, and not an individual, of the human being. Your children are not possessions: they are the future of the world.

The second precept is: *Don't consider your children as nuisances.* The attitude is more common than we think. Many children are unwanted even before they are born, and the sentimental happy ending—where the father chucks the newborn babe under the chin and says, "Well, he's not so bad after all"—is more a sugary fiction than an accurate reflection of reality. Other children are wanted, all right, but about a year after their arrival the parents begin to see what a tremendous responsibility they have shouldered—and disillusionment sets in. The light of their life has dimmed somewhat. The bundle of joy is heavier than they had expected. No more all-night parties, no more quick weekend trips, no more hobo-esque vacations. The good night's sleep is now interrupted several times; the day of rest is broken by bottle-warming, diaper-changing, and collecting the shards and chips of the best family china. And three cannot live as cheaply as two; even the money is spread thinner.

The day comes, then, when parents cease to see their child as a blessing. He is, they feel, subtracting from and not adding to their happiness. And once this feeling has taken root, it becomes stronger with the passage of time. As the child grows he needs more: more of his parents, more money, more love, more sacrifice. He pesters us with questions and demands. He maneuvers us into arguments with neighbors and teachers. He disobeys rules, breaks more china. He is firmly established as a nuisance, and his parents' once desperate desire for him has turned to simple despair.

Many parents feel this way. They may confess it to themselves; they rarely do to others. They fail to realize that the heart's deepest, most secret feelings must inevitably come to the surface, and betray themselves in attitudes and actions. I have had perplexed parents ask me why they and their children had ceased to be close; why a wall had sprung up between them; why conversation languished and confidences were no longer exchanged. The fault lay almost always with the parents; their own unconfessed resentments had subtly altered their approach to the children. The children had sensed it, but could do nothing about it. Love had yielded to anxiety.

Parents must learn early to pay the price of parenthood cheerfully. Emerson's "law of compensation" is emotionally unbreakable; for whatsoever you receive, you must give. If you wish to take, you must learn to "take it." And not like the "quarry slave chained to the dungeon"; not in annoyance and irritation, resentment and rebellion; but with grace and gratitude, aware that children are little miracles, and that when we are old, the world will be theirs.

One thing more: remember that to the child *you* are the nuisance!

The third precept is: *Don't make him in your own image*. Heredity has already done that, in large measure: the cut of his features, the color of his hair and eyes, the later form of his body. His early associations will add details to his portrait. And unless you find that portrait unbearable, trust nature and life to finish it properly. If it is unbearable—if you feel that the child is just *bad* —then bring in a master artist, and take his advice. More often than not you will find that faults of your own have initiated the damage; and your attempts to repair it may have aggravated it.

Natural protectiveness and a natural identity with our own children may lead to mistakes. When a father gives his own first

94

name to a son, and makes him a Junior; sends him to his own alma mater for schooling; directs him toward his own business or profession, he does so to help the boy. Rarely is he motivated by vain pride or a desire to perpetuate family tradition. He believes that there are aids and precautions available to his son, of which the most must be made. He is making a common error: the error of believing that what is good for *his image* of his son, is actually good for the son as an individual.

I know men who have never fully recovered from the psychological wounds inflicted by the word "Junior." In their early days it was a constant reminder of their inferior position in the home, and a constant source of embarrassment in the presence of their own friends. In their teens, it stood athwart the path to a distinct and individual personality: they were their father's sons, and that was, after all, a limitation: they were stamped with his characteristics, judged by his successes and failures. Even later, with their fathers dead and gone, these men were pursued by memories. Their achievements were belittled ("No wonder. He's old ————'s son") and their failures exaggerated ("Don't see how any son of old ———— could have done so badly"). These men may have reached old age without having felt for one day of their lives that they were unique and individual human beings.

Often the child rebels against this identification, and the rebellion may create a bitterness that time will not ease. The rebellion occurs generally in high school or college, when the pressures of public opinion are at their strongest: marks and athletic ability are the standards by which the developing personality is judged, and the judgment is a highly public affair. If Pop was a star athlete, the boy often feels that he must make the team or bust; if Pop was a Phi Beta Kappa, the son is under academic pressure from his first day in college. The fact that the first of these boys may be interested chiefly in research chemistry, and the second in physical education, is largely ignored, until one day the revolution comes. The unwilling athlete walks away from a scrimmage and never comes back; he leaves Princeton entirely, and writes his father from a Western state, where he is working his way through a small college and studying what he likes. And the "hereditary genius" makes the football team but flunks calculus—which he might well have passed without parental pressure. It would be pleasant if the inevitable result of these rebellions was, for the first lad, fame as a nuclear physicist, and for the second, fame with the Chicago Bears; but the chances are that neither will have an easy time of it. Both will suffer always from the waste of energy and individuality in their courageous battle against unnecessary parental decisions.

The surest way to drive your child to failure is to force him into your own footsteps. What gives you personal satisfaction will probably mean your child's ruination. You may think you have established a solid foundation for him—"given him every advantage"—but you have not considered him, the real him, at all. You may have forced him into a lifetime of depression and defeat. When you offer a child guidance, let it be for his good, and not for your glory.

The fourth precept is: *Don't give your child all the advantages you never had.* Of course, one of the most universal parental urges is to do exactly that. More pocket money, "nicer" companions, greater leisure, fuller schooling, are all apparently advantageous. And there is nothing wrong with the desire to see our children bigger and better and happier than we were—unless it is simply a disguised desire to bring credit on ourselves.

Parents would be wise to give children more of what they themselves *had,* and to worry less about what they themselves didn't have. "I can't understand it," the perplexed parent sighs. "My child has so much more than I had at his age. My family was so poor that the next meal was always a problem; my clothes were hand-me-downs; there was no such thing as a birthday party, and there were very few toys in the home. I never got beyond elementary school; I had to help support the family. Going to a movie was like a trip to the moon. So I took care of my own son, when he came along. He's never known what it is to want

96

for food and clothes. His playroom is full of toys, and his days are full of fun. We live in a fine neighborhood; he goes to the best private schools. He's had everything. And yet he seems to be one of the most dissatisfied and difficult youngsters in his group. He behaves as if he'd had nothing."

Well, think it over. You've given him everything you never had; but have you given him what you *did* have? I can imagine your home, your early life. Your father and mother lacked material things for you, so they gave you much of their time and companionship. They were not as rich and as busy as you are now. On the Sabbath they took you to worship with them; through discipline and example, they taught you good manners and a strong moral sense. They not only taught, but practiced openly, love of man and God. Have you given all that to your own child?

Every generation has material advantages the preceding generation lacked; this seems to be almost a law of history. But this is a quantitative advantage, and has little to do with our quality as human beings. More and bigger is the watchword; not nobler and better. And the farther we are from the acute dangers of material destitution, the more we should give to moral and emotional growth. It seems a shocking commentary on man's capacities that it always takes a major catastrophe—war or depression—to bring out the best in him; that during a time of ease and plenty, he forgets those very virtues—love, justice, fraternity, sacrifice—which make manifest the divine spark in the human being.

Many a parent owes his own success to the things he never had. His character was formed under adversity, when there was no time for complaining and no room for greed. But he forgets that his character, more than anything, is what he must hand down to his child. Without that, gifts and baubles are mere distractions; without that, the child will never learn to cherish the thoughts and talents within himself.

The fifth precept is: *Don't make your child the center of attention.* He is a member of the family, and not a "godlet." There is as much danger in allowing him too large a position in the family

97

as in neglecting him. He must have your love, yes, but he must understand that the world is not his alone.

In my study I have heard amazing assertions by spoiled children of five, six, or seven; even more amazing were the acquiescent replies of their parents. "Shut up," one child shouted at his father, "I don't like you."

The proud parent answered, "You don't know what you're saying," and sat there smiling indulgently.

Another child flashed, "You're a mean man. I'm not going to do it and you can't make me."

Meekly the mother sighed, "She has a lot of spirit."

"I'm not going to Sunday school."

"Religion is no good."

"I'm not going to Temple either."

And between the parents passed meaningful glances, as if they were assuring each other, "Pretty smart, for a seven-year-old!"

The day comes for any great star when he is asked to take second billing. It is a bitter day; but the explanation is there: he has passed his peak. As a rule he is old enough, and wise enough, to understand. Children, however, are not. From a position of absolute command, where all his needs are instantly satisfied, the normal child evolves to a less and less glorified position; his role becomes lesser, his billing smaller. And a conflict arises, because most of the small child's talents have been developed as a means to satisfaction of his needs; often before he has sufficient interest in the world at large, he ceases to be the center of attention, and is left to find channels through which to expend his juvenile energy. His first reaction is an immediate demand for more attention; he is accustomed to using his energies in that way.

And the doting parent finds it difficult to deny his clamors. The doting parent finds it painful to inform the child, by word or deed, that the world is full of a number of things, many of which demand a parent's attention. Even the sun gives way to the night, the moon, and the other stars. For the child, even partial eclipse is painful.

The Biblical story of Joseph and his brothers can be of help; it should be read aloud to children, and this passage in particular:

And he dreamed yet another dream, and told it to his brethren and said, "Behold I have dreamed yet another dream, and behold the sun, moon, and eleven stars bowed down to me." And he told it to his father and to his brethren, and his father rebuked him and said unto him: "What is this dream that thou hast dreamed? Shall I and thy mother and thy brethren indeed come to bow down to thee, to the earth?"

And the brethren envied him.

The brothers also hated him, threw him into a pit, and sold him into slavery.

The sixth precept is: *Have the courage to see your children suffer.* When a distinguished psychoanalyst suggests, "Parents who try to smooth all the bumps from their youngsters' paths and strive to keep childhood a rosy dream, actually hinder their children's growing up," progressive fathers and mothers nod agreement. But as a rule, they accept the theory without bothering to adopt the corollary practices. The average parent seeks instinctively to save his child from error and to spare him pain; but I have always suspected that he was saving and sparing himself as much as his child.

The father who, while spanking his son, says, "This hurts me more than it hurts you," is a familiar character; he means what he says. The son is also correct in answering, "But not in the same place." Yet he is mistaken if he thinks that the spanking is not emotionally painful to his father. Mothers who, for disciplinary purposes, send their children supperless to bed, or deny them movie, television, and party privileges, are often quite heroic in the sacrifice they make of their own natural desires and feelings. It is not easy to be a witness to, much less a cause of, your little one's hurts and sorrows.

It is not easy to withhold a more liberal allowance; to refuse permission for dates and late parties (particularly when their friends enjoy those privileges); or even to watch them struggling with arithmetic, grammar, and spelling when you might so easily do the homework for them. But then, it is simply not easy to rear children; these are only specific examples of the general self-denial and heartache true parenthood demands.

It was once common to refer to minor physical aches and pains among adolescents as "growing pains." There are emotional, mental, and spiritual growing pains as well, and a parent's natural tendency is to prevent them whenever possible. They should not be prevented. Nor should they be shrugged off. They are extremely consequential to the child's growth. A good sensitive feeling for aches and pains is a fine preparation for the problem of living.

An insensitivity to them—which can result from overprotection by the parent—will ensure an even greater hurt, for both child and parents, when the child is older. Jacob, I have often thought, must have known that Joseph's tales would arouse resentment in the hearts of his brothers, and some day bring him great harm at their hands. Yet he sent him out into the fields with them daily, probably realizing that some day he would not return. And though he said that Joseph was destroyed by some wild beast, he knew in his heart that his favorite child had been hurt by his brothers. The Bible tells us that he kept the knowledge, and the pain, to himself; he had the courage to see his son suffer on the road to salvation.

So it must have been with Mary, as she watched her son, Jesus.

The seventh precept is: *Be completely honest with your child.* Parents seem to feel that the words "I did it for your own good" excuse everything—even deceit—in the eyes of the children. They add, apologetically, "When you're older, you'll understand these things. We love you, and we want you to be happy."

If the child grew up to believe that the end justifies the means, his parents would rightly be shocked; yet this is exactly what the parents say in justification of their deceit.

The child knows. Almost as soon as he can distinguish between light and darkness, he can distinguish between truth and falsehood. Offer a hungry baby its bottle and snatch it away teasingly (often done in "fun" by loving parents!) and the reaction is immediate, definite, and loud, a violent rebellion born of passionate frustration. The baby cannot understand the nature of a love that will break promises—a dishonest love. I have yet to hear one sound argument for lying to a child, misleading a child, or failing to keep a promise to a child. The child will learn soon enough that the world is full of distrust, deceit, and hypocrisy. Teach it to know that there are at least two beings whom it can trust at all times, in all matters: its father and mother. Teach it that there is one place in which integrity flourishes: its home.

Too often the first professors of dishonesty are a child's parents; the first school of deceit, its own home. I have wondered whether Rebecca ever realized what she was doing to Jacob when, in her great love, she helped him deceive his father, Isaac, and cheat his brother, Esau. The home of Laban, who deceived and cheated Jacob, could hardly have been a wholesome environment for the character of his two growing daughters, Leah and Rachel.

When a parent complains, "I can't understand how any child of mine could get into the habit of lying; it's as though the truth weren't in him," I am tempted to quote the old saw, "The apple doesn't fall far from the tree." Honesty is not only the best policy in dealing with children (as it is in dealing with anyone); it is also the strongest foundation on which to build a good parent-child relationship. Fathers and mothers who lead their children into a failure of honesty, have led them into the possibility of permanent failure in life. And the surest way to teach a child dishonesty is to be dishonest with him. In deceiving a child you have cheated him; you have also deceived and cheated yourself. You are a Frankenstein, rearing a monster who will some day rise up and destroy you with the very weapons you fashioned for him.

The wages of dishonesty is dishonesty. The wages of deceit is the death of the dream.

The eighth precept is: *Be careful of the example you set.* In a

101

poignant essay, "Dearest Father," the youthful Franz Kafka pleads, "Please, Father, understand me rightly—the man who was so tremendously the measure of things for me, yourself, did not keep the commandments you imposed on me. Hence, the world was for me divided into three parts: into one in which I, the slave, lived under laws that had been invented only for me; then into a second world which was infinitely remote from mine, in which you lived, concerned with government, with the issuing of orders and with annoyance about their not being obeyed; and finally into a third world where everybody else lived happily and free from orders, and from having to obey." *

"Do as I say, but not as I do." For many parents, as for many preachers, this is the easy way. They forget Emerson's comment: "What you do shouts so loud, I can't hear what you say."

Children find it difficult to understand why they should be unequal to others under any law. However kind and logical the explanation, they will not understand the necessity of their going to bed early while their parents stay up late; they will not understand that they may not drink and smoke when their parents derive pleasure from both; they will not see the value of Sunday School when their parents rarely enter a church.

If we have an image of goodness, of the life of worth, toward which we urge our children, an ounce of example is better than a pound of exhortation. Conduct means more than command in the life of a child.

It was about a generation ago, when I first read the late Christopher Morley's *Thunder on the Left*, that I became acutely aware of the sensitivity children brought to the scrutiny and appraisal of their parents. I began to hear more keenly, and with greater understanding, what children had to say about their parents and their homes. I know now that much of the revolt of

* From *Dearest Father* by Franz Kafka; published by Schocken Books Inc.; copyright 1954 by Schocken Books Inc.

youth is against the hypocrisy of parents; much of it springs from early disillusionment, from awareness that fathers and mothers do not behave as though they believed what they proclaim so piously. I know now that many young men distrust certain businesses and professions not because of anything distasteful or dishonorable in those vocations, but because they distrust their own fathers in them. I know now that many young married women furnish their homes and deal with their families in patterns radically different from those of their mothers, in reaction against unpleasant memories.

Bringing up children takes the best you have. It may, if you bring heart to it, make you better than you were. It is, in the strictest sense of the phrase, a labor of love. Its only reward is spiritual. And life holds few, if any, greater rewards. To feel that your children are grateful because you kept the commandments you imposed upon them; because the good in their lives was a reflection of the good in your own; because your beliefs and your behavior squared; because the family was a family, and not a hierarchy; because they know, through you, what is valuable in life—to feel all that is in itself a great measure of happiness, a great measure of success.

The ninth precept is: *Don't expect too much or too little.* They say that one day when Elizabeth II was a little girl, out riding with her grandmother, Queen Mary, the car stopped for a red light. A flower vender bowed, smiled, and presented Elizabeth with a corsage, saying, "Flowers for the little lady."

Pertly, Elizabeth spoke up, "But I am a Princess."

Queen Mary reproved her: "Everybody knows that, but we're trying to bring you up to be a little lady."

Close to the desire to give children what the parents never had, is the desire to make of children what the parents never were. "Success" where the parents "failed" can become an obsession. The children must, in a manner of speaking, redeem the parents. They must be brilliant in school because the parents are still embarrassed about their own poor grades. They must make money, attain position, marry brilliantly, because the parents never scored better than "fair" in these areas.

But suppose the children are not innately equipped to rise higher than their parents? Suppose they would be happier as plain citizens, leading useful but ordinary lives? And society rates certain professions and businesses higher than others; but have parents the right to do the same? There is—and I offer this for very serious consideration—a bond between competent people which transcends vocational categories. A good actor, in other words, will appreciate the work of a good lumberjack; a good ballplayer will appreciate the work of a good public servant; a good chef will appreciate the work of a good mechanic. Each feels that the other is a "pro"; that he has mastered his chosen field. *It is only among the failures, the envious, that a point is made of the differences between talents.* What then are we to say of the father, a successful steel executive, who writhes in embarrassment because his son wants to be a good naturalist? Of the socialite railroad magnate who is unhappy because his son wants to raise beef cattle? What right has any parent to establish a hierarchy of jobs, and to insist that his son be a poor specimen of upper-bracket executive rather than a happy and conscientious hardware retailer, or librarian?

But there are many parents who will simply not let their children be happy, who drive them on, who force them to try to be more than they are. These parents, whatever else they do for their children, make failures of them; and the failure reflects only the vanity, the greed, the egotism, of the parent.

At the other extreme is the parent who expects too little, who refuses to challenge, even tentatively, the latent capacities of his child. This happens often with children who are "given the best of everything," reared in a hothouse atmosphere of excessive protection. Their bodies have never been tired, their mental capacities extended, their hearts moved, their souls stirred. As a result, they have never had the opportunity to discover what there was within them.

It is generally the parents who are afraid of taxing children beyond their capacities who really ought to fear dooming them to fruitless lives. Demanding too much of him can make a child a nervous wreck; he will have been overused, but somewhere along the line he will have come to know and value his own capacities. Even in disaster, there will be something to salvage, and there will be a knowledge of correct salvage techniques. But when too little is demanded of a child, he grows up not knowing any of his capacities, and consequently afraid to try anything of more than elementary difficulty. And when the pinch comes, when the crisis is upon him, he will be helpless. One day he will realize that he has not done with his life what he might have done; by then it will be too late. The period of growth will be over, and only the time of decay will remain.

Parents give up too easily. In their fear of overdisciplining a child, they allow him to waste himself. How many of us have not heard children reproach their parents for failing to insist on music lessons, harder study, more mathematics? And parents can only take refuge behind the excuse that they were unwilling to bring pain to the resisting child; that they knew piano lessons would some day be of great satisfaction, but they were unwilling to risk the child's resentment.

The most tragic sorrow a parent can experience is the death of a child. But to watch a child's instincts and talents decay and wither for lack of work, lack of persistence, lack of courage, is also a great sorrow. To take a human being, with all his potential, and to kill his capacities either by overwork or by neglect, is a true sin.

The tenth precept is: *Don't be your children's servant.* Be a partner, a pal, a helper, a friend—but neither a master nor a servant. For the past three generations we have all worked so hard to cure parents of their master complex that we have given them a servant complex. Someday a new Samuel Butler will write a new *Way of All Flesh* which will arouse sympathy for a father subjected to the authoritarian cruelty of his son! One writer has already asked, in an article entitled "Why Be a Slave to Your Chil-

105

dren?" "But why shouldn't Mother's and Daddy's welfare and needs be at least on a par with Junior's? . . . Under the convenient guise of being good parents, more and more couples seem to be letting their lives and leisure, their social and cultural pursuits, their inspirations, their relationships with friends, all revolve around the rulers of the roost—their children." Not so long ago a group of eminent specialists speaking at the Child Study Association Institute in New York agreed: "Parents need fun as much as children do. It is as important for adults to meet their own needs for satisfaction in living, as it is for them to provide the love and attention their children require."

There are parents, I know, who have found their greatest satisfaction in being full-time slaves to their children. It is a sort of reverse sadism, a joy in martyrdom. There are women who are slaves to good housekeeping, and men who are slaves to money-making; the house, the family, the marriage itself may be neglected. So it is with parents who enslave themselves to their children; everything else in life may fall apart, and ultimately the family relationship will, too.

As a rule, a child comes to dislike—and occasionally despise— a parent who caters to his every wish and whim. That kind of parent is capable of serving the child in little matters, but not in great ones. There are times when a child's most important needs are denial and discipline and defeat. Before he takes his place in a man's world, he must be taught that life is not a bowl of cherries.

And there is another danger. The child who sees life in terms of masters and servants will grow up determined to be a master at all costs. He will not be comfortable in normal, affectionate, give-and-take circumstances; and he will certainly not want to be a servant. He will have no choice but to become a master. The average doting mother would think twice about catering to the little fellow, if she realized that overindulgence might make him a totalitarian personality.

But most parents who are willing to sacrifice their own happiness for that of their children do not have much to begin with, themselves. They are trying to compensate for their own real or imagined failures by successfully subordinating themselves to the children. This is no answer; this is simply adding a new failure to previous failures.

The answer is in the Bible, in that verse which describes the journey of Abraham and Isaac up the mountain of Moriah—"and they went both of them together."

The road to success and happiness cannot be walked alone. Parents must learn that; they must learn that the only answer for a family is to "go all of them together."

BABES

IN

THE

WOODS

Chapter Six

Children begin by loving their parents. After a time they judge them. Rarely if ever do they forgive them.
—OSCAR WILDE

"What a child says in the streets, it heard from its parents at home," says the Talmud.

On a Sunday morning in Chicago a little girl was seen circling the same block for hours. A puzzled policeman stopped her, finally, and asked, "What are you doing?"

"I'm running away from home," she explained.

"Where do you live?"

"In that house." She pointed to one in the middle of the block.

"Well, if you're running away why do you keep walking around the same block? Why don't you go far away?"

"Oh, no," was the firm answer. "I can't. My mother told me never to cross the street by myself."

The story symbolizes the relationship of parent to child, which is one of opposites: repression and liberation, instruction and neglect, freedom and discipline. These opposites reflect the world itself, and their function is to prepare the child for the fluctuations of pleasure and pain that will make up his life.

Another word for "life," in this sense, is "reality." I like to call reality "the fourth R," but I think of it as a discipline that precedes, by far, Readin', 'Ritin', and 'Rithmetic. Reality is a discipline that should begin with the very dawning of the child's consciousness.

There are, of course, certain natural realities, like light and darkness, sound and silence, which the child learns of through habit and repetition. But once we leave this primal level of simple perception, reality becomes very complicated. And it is no exaggeration to say that the parents' role as interpreters of reality begins on the first day of the child's life.

In general the process of interpreting is not complicated until the child himself is capable of thought and motion. But by the time a child is a year old his parents have often begun to concentrate on his future, rather than his present. They have begun to look forward, as all parents will who have to change diapers or warm bottles, to the day when he is self-sufficient. The result is too often a concentration on the child's future, to the serious neglect of his present.

We forget that at best the child has a difficult time of it. He is required always to deal with more than he is equipped to handle. He is called upon in every stage of his growth to be more than he is and do more than he can. Adults intensify his difficulties because they see in him not only the child but the future adult. The child is required not only to be successful as an infant, but to give promise, at the same time, of the praiseworthy adult to come.

Failure—sometime, somehow—is inevitable. In order not to fail in the present, the child must occasionally sacrifice some opportunity to advance rapidly; more important, he is often forced to frustrate his own natural desires for comfort or sensual gratification (e.g., mudpies) in order to fulfill his parents' desire that he be a young gentleman. Pressures like those are, to state the case baldly, bad for the child psychologically, but necessary for him socially. There is no growth, as we have noted, without effort and risk. But the effort must be controlled, the risk calculated. The parents' responsibility is great. Without delicate care, the child may, like the legendary chameleon on a swatch of plaid, drive himself to destruction in the compulsive need to be all things to all men.

That delicate care is not often taken. Parents will hazard any number of physical risks for the child, will undergo great mental anguish themselves, realizing that all this is necessary if the child is to learn to walk, eat, run, climb trees. But the task of teaching morality, love, plain dealing with one's fellow man, is left to nature, or the school, or "time"; parents will delay and debate, explain and excuse, anything rather than bring the stern realities of individual existence into the child's early life. Failures of the body —scraped knees, abrasions, bad bumps—are tolerated as necessities. But failures of the soul are unthinkable: "Don't you believe it's too early to send him to school and to subject him to discipline? Won't he find it strange and frightening? Wouldn't he be better off playing with his toys at home?"

But those fears and failures are inevitable; and they are as much a part of growth as scrapes and cuts. Of course a child will find school strange and frightening; a young man will often find his first job strange and frightening, and would be better off had he not been spared the earlier, easier adventures into new worlds. But generally the child is watched too cautiously; one little cry at separation from his mother, one protest against newness, and he is whisked back into familiar, and safe, surroundings.

Part of the problem is that children feel before they understand. And part of the solution lies therein: when they are too young for understanding, only feeling—love, encouragement, acceptance—can help bring them through the bitterness of early development. When they are too young to learn about the origins and patterns of fear and faith, they can be made to feel secure emotionally. And by far the most important factor in that security is the acceptance of failure.

A child must learn very early to realize that failing is part of living. To lead him to believe otherwise is to deny reality, to bring him up in an atmosphere of false—and destructive—superiority. Eternal triumph exists only in the world of fantasy. And children love fantasy; they are susceptible to the legend, the fairy tale. They will readily accept the parental feeling that they must always succeed, always be little men and women; and when reality makes them conscious of failure, the emotional scars may be long-lasting.

To love your child for his perfection is nothing. To love him for his failures is to love him well. It is that love which will form the later man—*the man whom failure cannot defeat.*

The acceptance of failure is simply a part of the acceptance of reality. Reality is often unpleasant, but to deny it, to base our lives on retreats and illusions, is to court disaster. There are times, for example, when bereaved young husbands or wives ask me seriously whether or not their small children should be permitted to attend the funeral rites for their lost parent. In general they plead, "Don't you think they ought to be spared the pain? Won't it just upset them, and wound them emotionally? Will it do any good to drag them through all that sorrow?"

My answer is that it will do much more harm if they are denied the truth; to allow them to attend the service will cause them pain, of course, but the death of a parent is a reality, however harsh, and they cannot afford to live a delusion. Let them learn early that death is a part of life, grief is joy's partner, separation is the ultimate price of every union. Slick phrases and half-truths may choke off, but will never answer, the troubled questions in a child's heart.

If your children must experience death, let them see it as it

111

really is, and not disguised in the garments of fantasy. Whether it is a pet dog or a dear one, let them understand "that no life lives forever; that even the weariest river winds somewhere safe to sea." They must know, sooner or later, the pain of denial and despair; they will be better off if they learn that shadows are cast only when there is sunlight; that love is cruel only to be kind; that the Lord taketh away only that which He giveth.

There is more than enough fantasy in the child's life. What he cannot explain, he will cloak in illusion. Fantasy is an integral and wholesome part of childhood; it should even be encouraged, as it contributes to the child's mental flexibility and powers of imagination; but it should not be allowed to smother reality. Parents are called upon, throughout the child's early years, to step into never-never land; to share the child's myth-making and fancy. There are problems: how can adults help their children to retain the wonder and beauty of childish fancy? How can they separate the harmful illusion from the necessary fairy tale? How can they explain the chemistry of fear without exposing the child to a private terror?

Buried deep within most of us are childhood memories of witches, enchanted woods, changelings, pirates. Millions of Christians still recall the wide-eyed wonder with which they opened packages on Christmas morning; shattering a child's belief in Santa Claus is not easy. Somehow we must keep alive the glory of this imaginative world, at the same time making clear its unreality.

A child who takes his fancies literally is of course not equipped to face the facts. He may become an addict, so enthralled by the constant triumph of light over darkness, good over evil, and living happily ever afterward, that he will refuse to accept the complex vagaries of human existence. He will not be prepared to make the transition when the stern voice of reality and responsibility is heard.

In our Sunday school (especially in the nursery and kindergarten classes) children are told many stories out of the folklore

112

and legends of centuries past. But their teachers are instructed to distinguish clearly between the simple tale and the underlying truth; between illustrative fiction and informative fact. Stated simply, our rule is: Don't say or do anything that must be unsaid or undone later. And we find that on a foundation of fact, fun as well as faith can be fashioned in a child's mind.

John Locke (among others) described the mind of a newborn baby as a *tabula rasa,* a clean slate. We have questioned this concept, and many of us have rejected it. We have come to believe that the introduction to a life is written in the genes and chromosomes of the unborn child. The general outline of the story is there indicated; and each story is unique.

There are a few children whose introduction is so poorly written that not the most consummate artist could make the story a success. Through no fault of their own—because of heredity—these children will never be as normal, natural, healthy, happy, attractive, or alert, as others. Their parents must accept them as they are. Most parents do, and with fine compassion and great love make the best of things.

But these children are few. Most normal children who fail because of early inadequacies are innocent; the failure is their parents'. We have discussed parenthood, and pointed out that it is an art, developed through careful preparation and hard work. The simple process of giving birth does not make a woman a good mother. Pride in the fact of physical creation often blinds parents to the more difficult job ahead: the molding of the mind, heart, and soul. There must be love; there must be understanding. And there must be example. Perhaps none of these is possible without compassion, without the emotional ability to feel as the child feels, to suffer and rejoice with him.

One of the most perceptive passages on parenthood I have ever read is in William Saroyan's *The Human Comedy.* Mrs. Macauly is speaking to her small son: "Oh, I've had good luck, and I'm thankful. My children are human beings besides being children.

They might have been children only, and then my luck would not have been so good. Last night you cried because you are human. It was pity that made you cry. Pity, not for this person or that person who is suffering, but for all things—for the very nature of things. Unless a man has pity he is inhuman and not yet truly a man, for out of pity comes the balm that heals." *

The force of pity—for the child, and for the very nature of life —is never more valuable in a parent than during his child's early years. To keep the child from reality is to disqualify him for life; to thrust him rudely into the world may cripple him emotionally. Ideally, he will take his bumps and frustrations—and he will conquer them, at this stage, in proportion as his parents share them. The classic analogy here is learning to swim. To stay away from the water is futile. To throw the baby in will, contrary to a popular belief, more likely drown him than teach him anything. What is essential is that the parent get into the water with him. Only by sharing the difficulties, by patience and intelligent instruction—by getting wet, to come back to the metaphor—can the parent make the child feel that life is neither a menace nor an illusion.

What is important is not the instruction, or even the intelligence, or even the patience. It is the compassion: the sharing of your life with another.

Let us now consider other influences upon the young child. During his first years it is not only the parents who affect his growth. There are, for example, brothers and sisters, whose very presence exerts pressures that alter the course of development. They may arouse a spirit of unwholesome competition, or of destructive resentment; they may bully or belittle or, conversely, overprotect and overpraise. Looking again at Margaret Mead's

* From *The Human Comedy* by William Saroyan; published by Harcourt, Brace and Company, Inc.

Coming of Age in Samoa we find that even in relatively primitive societies the education of children is accompanied by much sisterly and brotherly tongue-lashing and cuffing. The dialogue of adolescent Samoans with their juniors is freely sprinkled with slaps, with "Quiet!" or "Sit still!" or "Shut your mouth!"

Relatives, friends, neighbors all play vital roles in the rearing of a child. They may ignore him, leave him out of conversation, neglect his birthdays. Or go to the other extreme: shower him with attention and presents, exaggerate his qualities and abilities. The wise parent must be a buffer. No one else, after all, can know the child well enough to draw the line between damaging discipline and outright spoiling. And this is a crucial area. The child's reactions to the "outside world" as seen from the home will determine his later reactions to the world at large. If he is neither to be frightened into sullen acquiescence nor made proud before a fall, his parents must stand beside him.

As a buffer, the parent is in a delicate position. Because growth is essentially a matter of conflict, there exists a normal conflict between parents and children. And when the parent guides, directs, takes sides, the child is prone to transfer his natural frustrations and resentments from their real objects—relatives, friends, teachers—to the parent. This exaggerates the conflict; and if there is not true love on the parent's part, a state of war, usually cold, sometimes hot, may spring up between him and his child. There are many families in which this is true. Most of them achieve an uneasy truce which lasts through adolescence, when the child becomes more rational and more aware of his parents' motives.

Psychiatry has a good deal to say about this. Sigmund Freud threw light on it, but many of his followers, and many of his popularizers, have neglected to point out that he was striving to make us see that an unshakable and unashamed love was a large part of the solution to these difficulties. His theories of mother-son and father-daughter fixations (the "Oedipal situation") have come down to us strangely distorted; many feel that love between parents and children is somehow wrong, and the result is a

115

greatly heightened tension in family relations. This is, as we have shown, a gross misinterpretation of Freud's doctrines. The whole goal of his life's work was to eliminate the irrational, the misunderstood, the stupid, often involuntary hostilities that keep human beings from love and compassion.

As a result of misinterpretation and oversimplification, a little knowledge—of psychiatry—has become a dangerous thing. Children's (and particularly adolescents') suspicions have been strengthened, their resentments deepened. Popularized and unscientific versions of psychoanalysis have encouraged them to feel that their frustrations and failures are the fruits of their relationships to their parents. Some time ago I was startled when a bright ten-year-old, who had become a behavior problem at home and in school, pleaded with me to help him understand himself. "Why do you do these things?" I asked him. "What is there in disobedience that pleases you so?"

With what I thought was a smirk, he answered, "Well, I guess it's to get attention. I don't know what's wrong with me. I try to make friends but nobody likes me." Obviously, he had heard a smattering of psychiatric talk somewhere; he was using it now as an excuse and a defense.

He challenged me to show him the way to success. How could he transform his father from a constant critic to a compassionate companion? How could he get his teachers to stop picking on him? How could he make his schoolmates more friendly? How could he get into his neighborhood gang? He didn't know. Couldn't I tell him?

My first impulse was to follow the example of the ancient sage Shammai, who, when a heathen asked that he teach him Judaism while he stood on one foot, angrily drove him away with a broom. What restrained me was the worn and troubled expression on his mother's face. I knew that it was later than she thought; that her boy needed much help, more than she herself could give. The boy had to be retrained, retaught—retooled, as it were—emotionally. He was right about one thing: he had to learn to understand himself. His social problem was learning to live with others; he would never solve it until he had learned to live with himself.

In 1931, on a study tour of Russia, I found, in a Moscow Park of Rest and Culture, children of kindergarten age playing games with a distinctly warlike flavor. Carrying long sticks on their shoulders, they were marching and shouting and laughing—universal signs of great fun. I asked about them, and was told that they were being directed in "purposeful play"—to teach them the rudiments of close-order drill and riflery. On a collective farm, I ran across some five- and six-year-olds playing at a shrewdly devised game of wheat harvesting. In 1933, on visits to Nazi Germany and Fascist Italy, I saw the same purposeful devices used to train kindergarten children.

The question of play is intimately connected to a problem of timing, which can be best expressed briefly: "How fast shall I let—or make—my child develop?" A too rapid or too slow rate of development may have disastrous consequences for the later adult. One extreme is the child whose parents love him as a baby, and keep him babylike: refuse to cut his hair, give him toys that he should have outgrown, force him to play with younger children. Aside from the emotional scars caused by these restrictions, the boy may find that when the time comes for him to grapple with problems appropriate to his age, he is ill-equipped, and even frightened. The other extreme is more common: it is the child who is pushed faster and faster by his parents, given too complicated toys, forced into the company of older boys, pressured into a position he should not be asked to fill. Here our example of the young play-soldiers is instructive. The real danger in this kind of artificial growth is not that the boys become proficient in drill or shooting, but that later, when their minds have matured, they will retain toward arms and discipline their earliest childhood reactions; they will see the world as a child sees it, in terms of a chain of command, absolute obedience, with "our side" absolutely good, and "their side" absolutely evil. They will, in other words,

117

grow up robbed of much of their individuality, capacity for choice and judgment, and flexibility of mind.

(Victor Hugo tells of a band of gypsies who put certain infants into large glass containers and kept them bottled up so that they became monstrosities. They were freaks, much in demand by circuses. They were mentally and—perhaps—emotionally adults; physically they were children. The process is reversed in our time; too many of us are physically adult but mentally and emotionally children—the result of a premature bottling-up of our possibilities.)

The tendency in our own time has been to allow young children more and more freedom, which is equivalent to allowing them more and more play. In the general loosening of social mores since the nineteenth century, pleasure—except for certain specified illicit pleasures, which we are assured are not pleasures at all—has slowly ceased to be a source of vague guilt. Play is a part of pleasure, and the enthusiasm for play and pleasure, in America particularly, has become a cult. The "playboy" is an abundant crop. "Oh, let the child have a good time," is a plea that settles many domestic discussions, but does not solve the basic problem: what is a good time? Good not only in itself, but as a part of the child's growth?

Americans have a knack of starting to solve their problems even before the problems are stated. With the emphasis on "play" and "freedom" has come an emphasis on educational toys. Manufacturers and parents have realized that toys can be much more than a passing influence in a child's life. Toys and games open channels of thought and release streams of emotion. They can help shape the child's future. More and more parents are selecting toys with the same care they give to food and clothing. They are taking the trouble to learn—from nurseries, psychologists, and careful observation—that toys and games, like food and books, must be timed properly. Each must have meaning and value, or it is wasted; and the meaning and value must be applicable, must help the child in his search for reality, or they in turn are wasted.

I remember the early thirties, when my son was a small child, that the dream of universal disarmament was a shining hope for all of us. Like other young parents, my wife and I eliminated guns and tanks and lead soldiers from our son's toy-box, and discouraged games that might arouse warlike sentiments. We followed the same course with the stories we told him and the books we read to him. When he was five years old an uncle presented him with a tank. He thanked him, but didn't touch it. Later, looking at it with puzzled distaste, he asked us, "What do I do with it?" We removed the guns and made a tractor of it. He played with it, and kept it for a long time. His childhood was, I think, as happy as that of anyone I have known; and it was a very fruitful one.

Play with a purpose—a purpose for *children*—cannot come too early. It can help a child to appreciate his home, to develop independence, to conquer fears; it can make success a quiet habit, and can teach him to accept occasional failure.

Through the back door, into the kitchen of a typical American home, comes thirteen-year-old Johnny, fresh from his first brawl. His shirt is torn, one eye is turning purple, his nose is bloody. Cleaning his face and treating his wounds, his mother asks, "Darling, did you cry much?" With a flush of triumph and a note of surprise in his voice, he answers, "I didn't cry at all. You weren't there to cry to."

Johnny has entered the most difficult period of life: adolescence. He is becoming a teen-ager. Books, pamphlets, magazine articles, and committee reports attacking the problems of boys and girls like Johnny appear in ever increasing numbers. Discussions of juvenile delinquency are printed in every Sunday supplement. Johnny is at an age when the shadowy, imperfectly differentiated qualities that make him an individual will begin to take more solid form; when, in other words, his character will crystallize.

Adolescence has been defined from many points of view. The physiologist refers to the physical changes that take place: Johnny's voice will change, his shoulders broaden, his beard grow,

119

his sexual instincts mature. The educator refers to his mental capacities: Johnny is ready for symbolic learning (algebra) and for conceptual thinking (history, the sciences). The judge—if he ever sees Johnny, which we hope he will not—thinks of him as too old for parental probation and too young for prison: Johnny is at the reform school age. His English teacher feels that he is ready to memorize long passages; the baseball coach thinks he may learn now to "take two and hit to right." His father sees the day coming when the family car will have to be shared; his mother begins to worry about "dating," and, quite naturally, to be slightly jealous of all the girls on the block. Johnny's younger sister sees him as a man; Johnny's cousin, in college, sees him as a boy.

Johnny belongs to two worlds, and this may be the most helpful definition of adolescence. He has been encouraged to look upon himself as an adult—to accept family responsibilities, like mowing the lawn; but he is constantly reminded that he is still a child. Before the teen years this is not a problem, because Johnny's impulses to maturity—or to the status of an adult—are poorly defined and weak. But in adolescence Johnny changes, and for the first time he begins to take seriously the notion that he is capable of adult responses and accomplishments.

And, to some extent, he is. But he is hardly reliable. He lacks education, he lacks experience of life. He will do a good job on the lawn unless a call goes out for a shortstop, in which case he may disappear for three or four hours. He will save money diligently, displaying a mature sense of its value, and then buy an air rifle and yield to the temptation of street-lights. We have a hard time defining his rights and responsibilities, his privileges and punishments. Natural parental pride makes us allow teenagers to attempt more than they are capable of doing; and natural parental caution makes us occasionally deprive them of pleasures to which they feel they have a natural right.

Small wonder that adolescents are confused! Physically, of course, it is a confusing time anyway; and we add to the distress by being unsure of our own attitudes. The result is often a span

120

of bitter years for the adolescent; and the bitterness often affects the rest of his life.

Basically the blame for much adolescent difficulty must fall upon the parents. There is a kind of alternating current that passes from adolescent to parent and back; it consists of attraction (protection and pride on the parent's part; desire for help and approval on the adolescent's) and repulsion (weary thanks on the parent's part that Johnny is becoming independent and is less of a chore; scornful rejection of help and advice by self-sufficient Johnny). Unfortunately, the attraction makes itself most obvious when Johnny has done something independent and praiseworthy —so that the parent seems to be reducing him, in his moment of triumph, to a child; and the repulsion generally occurs when Johnny most needs help, and the parent gets just plain tired of an adolescent who can't seem to do anything right by himself.

This is a paradox. It is not new. The problem is not "solvable." It is one of the continuing and fundamental problems of mankind. Johnny is, after all, moving out of a group to which he has belonged all his life. This will cause him mingled pride and anxiety. And his parents are slowly losing a son for whom they have made many sacrifices over a long period, and in whom all their fond hopes lie; they too will feel pride and anxiety. But their anxiety is Johnny's pride; and their pride is his anxiety. There, in its briefest form, is the problem of adolescence.

There is no easy way out. There are precepts we can follow when dealing with certain specific problems—we shall examine three of them in a moment; but the general subject of adolescence is too broad to be covered by rules.

One general helpful suggestion can be made; it will affect all the relationships between parent and adolescent. Cultivate a sense of equality, and restrain both pride and anxiety.

Each half of that suggestion implies the other. Among acknowledged equals there is rarely occasion for excessive pride or excessive anxiety. When the inequality is stressed, see what may happen: Johnny will react to his parents' obvious pride by feeling that he must always bring home the bacon; he will sense an obligation to please them by competing and winning in all areas of life. The winner of the school spelling bee will feel that he must go on to the football team. He will, through love for his parents and a newly awakened pride in himself, extend himself too far, and enter areas where he is handicapped. He will, in short, expose himself unnecessarily to failure and disappointment. He will begin to see life as a series of trophies to be brought home. You can't win 'em all; and when he fails, his bitterness will turn first against himself, and then against his parents.

Or this may happen: Johnny will be aware of his parents' anxiety, and will scorn it; feeling grown-up, he will ignore good advice and refuse help. He will go his own way, and he will be ill-equipped to make the serious choices before him. Or, feeling a need for security but not wanting to admit that his parents' anxieties are justified, he will join a gang, and adopt its values for his own.

A firm sense of equality between parent and adolescent will diminish feelings of pride and anxiety on both sides. Again, compassion is necessary; equality between individuals means that each feels an identity with the other, that the pleasures and sorrows of each are shared by the other; and this is true compassion. It should be easy for parents to feel that; somehow it is not. It takes generosity and self-confidence; it takes courage. The reward is a deepening of maturity for both.

In ancient times the Talmud taught that it was a father's duty to teach a child three things specifically: swimming, a trade, and the Torah, which is God's law. Swimming, to save him from physical drowning; a trade, from mental and emotional drowning; and the Torah, from spiritual drowning.

Since then, division of labor has become a condition of life, and we find those functions taken over by many outside the home: the teacher, the journeyman, the psychiatrist, the printed word of book or magazine. Of all the direct influences on today's child, the teacher is probably the most important—a fact certainly not reflected in the small respect and smaller wages granted that noble profession within recent years.

Teachers teach facts, directly; indirectly they develop capacities. They are often as responsible as parents for the views and visions of children. But teaching is a profession undervalued in our country, and the result is that many teachers are inadequately trained and insufficiently interested. There are teachers who have been discouraged to the point of indolence and indifference. There are teachers who are forced to supplement their income by outside work, so that their pupils become of secondary interest to them. Some become tyrannical, almost sadistic; they drive children from the fount of knowledge by fouling it with their own bitterness. Others take the easy way, and pass on to their pupils the counterfeit coin of superficiality instead of the sound metal of instruction. Others decide simply that until society acknowledges its responsibility to the teaching profession, they themselves will shirk responsibility toward their pupils. One way or another, there are too many drains on the child's rightful heritage of solidity of mind and strength of character.

This story, for example, told me by a close friend, appalled me. He was passing an elementary school playground and saw some children throwing stones at passers-by, some of whom were injured. He marched to the office and asked why something wasn't being done about this. "Well," said the principal defensively, "I didn't tell them to do it." *I didn't tell them to do it!*

"Yes," said my friend, "but have you told them *not* to do it?" There was no answer.

But regardless of the quality of the school, it tends more and more to supersede the home as an authority for the child. The child is busy discovering the world, and the school is a large part of the world. The child begins to compare his parents with other parents; he begins to compare the restrictions at home with the freedoms at school. Psychologists have pointed out that a sure way to lose a friend is to make him dependent upon you; to put

123

him in your debt. And certainly the child depends more on the parent than vice versa; there is a natural child-parent hostility that makes the independence of life at school even more attractive.

But this independence has a dangerous aspect. When too much of the domestic function is abdicated to the outside world, terrible insecurities may arise in the child; faced with obstacles too great for his own understanding, and forced to rely on relative strangers for help, the child may lose the strength that true intimacy creates. His world will be peopled with enemies, or at best neutrals; there will be no one to whom he can turn in complete confidence. Ulysses Macauly, in *The Human Comedy*, went through a moment of that bleak emptiness; but fortunately for him his world contained enough love to see him through it:

He looked around. Day had ended and everybody had gone—the only thing left anywhere was something for which he had no word— Death. The small boy looked back suddenly at the mechanical man. It seemed then that the man was looking at him. There was swift and fierce terror in the boy. Suddenly he was running away. The first people he saw in the streets now seemed full of death, too, like Mr. Mechano. They seemed suddenly ugly, not beautiful as they had always seemed before, and Ulysses ran until he was almost exhausted. He looked around, feeling a deep silent steady horror in all things— the horror of Mr. Mechano—Death! He had never before known fear of any kind—let alone fear such as this. And it was the most difficult thing in the world for him to know what to do—the world was surely wonderful and it was surely full of good things to be seen again and again, but now the world was only a thing to escape.*

We have discussed fear; we know that it is an instinctive reaction to the unknown. All normal beings feel it. It is helpful; it

---

* From *The Human Comedy* by William Saroyan; published by Harcourt, Brace and Company, Inc.

warns man of danger. Fear can, in this sense, be a friend. But the experience of fear is not pleasant, and the constant companionship of small fears can warp a child's personality beyond salvage. To the child, don't forget, many fears are real which seem laughable to adults. Many acts of coldness or indifference which will pass unnoticed by adults can add to the sum of a child's anxieties. And it is these relatively incomprehensible childhood fears that require the most delicate attention from parents. As with failure, the first step is to convince the child that fear—somewhere, sometime—is inevitable; that we are all occasionally afraid. The second step is to teach him what fear means, to make him understand that fear can be a valuable ally. The third step is to teach him to act reasonably and conscientiously even when under the influence of fear. As these steps are taken, the fears will diminish.

And as the fears diminish, independence becomes a less formidable condition, and the child's gropings toward independence become more assured. The insecurities we have mentioned, the occasional coldness of the world, the shattering realization that he is only a small part of a large society, will cease to paralyze the child's emotions, or to provoke bitter reactions of withdrawal or aggression. Through understanding—which must derive from the parent's acknowledgment that he is an individual, and from the parent's compassion for him—the child will win through to a balanced view of life, to an awareness of his own importance, to an awareness of his own responsibilities. His break with his parents—it comes, sooner or later, in all families—will be a natural growth, and not a childish rejection. He will appreciate the difference between standing on his own feet and stepping on his father's toes; and he will be capable of accomplishment and pleasure without the irrational burden of guilt that spoils so many lives.

The concepts of guilt and conscience are difficult for adults to handle; how much harder they must be for children! Perhaps the ultimate truth of guilt is that each of us bears his own within him, and is harmed by it more than those he has sinned against;

en if true, that metaphysical statement is of little value in ing conscience with children. Our general attitude toward d dishonesty is expressed in the following story.

A little boy had fallen into the habit of lying his way out of difficulties. His father scolded and punished until he realized that the boy was not responding; he resolved then to go about the matter more subtly. He erected a white post in the front yard, and said to the boy, "Son, every time you lie, I'll drive a nail into that post. That's all I'll do." The boy shrugged, and went on lying. After a month the post was studded with nails; it began to look black. The boy saw it every day, and became troubled.

At the end of another month there was barely room for another nail. Worse, his friends in the neighborhood had begun to question him. He was embarrassed, and finally ashamed. He begged his father to remove the nails. "All right," his father agreed; "every time you tell the truth when it matters, I'll pull a nail." In another two months the nails were gone, but the boy remained discouraged.

"I know," his father said. "We've taken out the nails, but the marks will always be there. The post will never be all smooth white again."

The surface moral of the story is a simple one. If you drive the nail of a lie into your soul, the truth may remove the nail but the scar remains forever. Repentance can atone for a sin and receive absolute forgiveness, but it cannot achieve complete forgetfulness. There can be redemption, but there will always be remembrance.

The marks can never be entirely erased. But the effect of the marks upon the conscience, the sense of guilt, can be eradicated —especially early in the child's life. We have confused fear, guilt and failure, all three of which are inevitable, with shame. Shame is not simply embarrassment or uneasiness; shame is a powerful emotion, and is evoked only by powerful sins. We need not be ashamed of such normal and occasional manifestations of the human spirit as fear, failure and guilt. Sins may leave their marks which will become faint and almost invisible in time. But we can learn to be merciful to our souls. No sin need corrupt us permanently; we can not only atone for it but use it as a signpost to wise correction and strong character.

Churches, schools, parents, other agencies, can teach children to understand their fears and frustrations. Hidden away, repressed, left to fester, fears and frustrations can create a permanent climate of bitterness and failure; but brought to light, discussed honestly, seen as only a part of the vast and wonderful complexity of the human spirit they can be miraculously effective as aids to maturity.

We have already indicated a possible haven for frustrated adolescents who feel surrounded by failure at home: the gang. Frustration at home is not always responsible for the formation of gangs; there is more to it than that. But it is certainly an outlet for the emotions of "belonging" that may be repressed when there is a bad family situation.

There are two factors at work here: one is the desire for security, for the comfort of the group; and the other is the natural instinct of uncertain men to conform. The adolescent, belonging neither to the world of the child nor to the world of the man, tries to create his own intermediate world. In that world the values are half-juvenile (respect for power, love of violence, preoccupation with form and ritual) and half-adult (loyalty to one's friends, occasional courage, abiding strictly by the society's rules of conduct). Once that world is created, the adolescent can feel secure within it, and in proportion as he turns to it for a sense of security, he will conform to its established rules.

Not all adolescent gangs are delinquent, by the way. There are innocuous conformities which serve simply to identify the teen-ager, and certainly do not imply that he is a budding criminal. Haircuts, for example; a whole high school may one day show up with all the girls in pony-tails and all the boys in crew-cuts or scalp-locks. Clothes—whether blue jeans or more formal wear—tend to conform to a style set by the most popular students. Language changes; expressions come into use that no other generation will ever hear, unless one or two of them survive as jokes.

As the group grows more restricted, more to be a gang, the rules tighten, and the rebellion against accepted conventions becomes more obvious. Schoolwork, or even friendly conversation with teachers, is scorned. Fear of, or respect for, the other sex is considered childish and weak. The law is made to be flouted; this includes, of course, parental regulations. Generally the most admired members of a gang are those who have violated the greatest number of conventions in the home, school, and community.

It is important to notice that there is as much conformity within the gang as within the society from which it has seceded. In my years of working with children, I have found it almost impossible to achieve real communication with them when they are firmly entrenched in a neighborhood or school gang. The approval and security that a child needs, and usually gets from his parents, teachers, and communities, gang members get from the gang; they are flippant about society because they can afford to be; they have their own society. And the gang gives its members a comfortable anonymity; the "we" covers the "me," the sense of individual responsibility is diluted, and the member stands or falls, on any given issue, with the group. Numbers furnish strength; guilt is diffused through the group. The gang is an appreciative audience, and its approval is an accolade far more precious to the budding adult than any praise from elders—the elders are, after all, those who hold you back, stand between you and adulthood, and when taken all together, the elders are the community.

The cliché has it that there are no delinquent children, only delinquent parents. This may be true for children up to the age of about thirteen. After that, when the school, the police, the municipality, the national magazines and the cultural climates have taken over much of the parents' function, the statement should read, "There are no delinquent adolescents—only a delinquent community." The fact is recognized by the courts. Penalties

128

for criminal acts are less severe for teen-agers than for adults; which is, I think, society's way of acknowledging a certain general guilt, shared by all, in the sins of the adolescent. When the adolescent oversteps the bounds of decency and law, he violates the community's regulations; previously he had simply violated a rule of the household. And as the mother may feel that she has erred somehow when her child proves to be rebellious, so the community understands that the responsibility lies with all of us when adolescents go beyond the law.

Here is the interesting statement of an ex-convict, the theme of which runs counter to modern theory: "I am twenty-two years old, and this is the first period of my life since I was nine that I have not committed a crime or been in prison. It has been more than a year now that I have lived straight and I have a good job and a pretty fiancée to show for it. . . . I have held up more people and robbed more stores than I could even count. I often had a gun in my pocket or a bayonet tucked inside my sleeve. 'No good' is putting it mildly. But now I'm straight and I'm straight from here on out. And do you know what did it for me? Prison—that is what I want to get across. Despite all this talk about criminals being sick, and strict prisons are out of date, and conditions should be nice and pleasant—don't lose sight of the fact that some men will stop committing crimes if the penalty is bad enough. At least that's why it worked with me."

But most authorities—and most criminals, by the way—feel that punishment is not sufficient either as a deterrent or as a corrective. Certainly to the overconfident adolescent, absolutely sure that he himself will never be caught, or that the gang will protect him, punishment is only a vague notion, not even a consequence to be feared.

Adolescents have enormous energies, experimental natures, and, in a sense, the minds of outlaws (this, because they no longer belong to the world of children, but have not yet accepted the world of men). The community has not made allowances for the adolescent—and the community is criminally delinquent when

129

it does not provide wholesome outlets for the normal interests and urges of teen-agers. The truth of this has been recognized, but there has been little subsequent action. We may give a few dollars to the local youth organization; we may make a contribution to the Off-the-Street Club; we may vote "Yes" on a referendum to build a new playground. But all that is sporadic action of limited effect.

We must not only recognize but act on the needs of adolescents just as conscientiously and unselfishly as we recognize and act on the needs of infants. Most cities should maintain, for example, a vast network of playgrounds, ball parks, basketball courts, swimming pools, tennis courts, gymnasiums, each, perhaps, with its own snack bar and sports library. Most cities might have a chain of small, open, well-lighted libraries, rather than the one huge stone Public Library guarded by two lions and generally forbidding. Most cities require planned programs to stimulate the constructive use of leisure time—the dance and the theater, arts and music, crafts and games. Most necessary are guidance centers, for orientation in the intelligent choice of vocations.

We need, in short, to revise our own opinion of teen-agers. They are not helpless children; neither are they taxpayers; consequently, we ignore them. The fact is that it is more important to the community to take care of its adolescents than its children (whose parents can manage them). Most mature criminals, let us remember, are formed in adolescence; presumably a generation of happier adolescents would do more to reduce the crime rate than any number of noisy newspaper campaigns.

But the real tragedy is that teen-agers are people, people in trouble, passing through a difficult time. We owe them an even break. The making of good adolescents depends on the whole community; but the making of tomorrow's community depends on today's adolescents.

The most tragic, and often the most consequential, anxieties of children—particularly adolescents—are those that rise from the

130

ever-urgent sexual instincts. Primarily, we adults are at fault. We must reject absolutely our popular definition of sexual impulses. Too many of us feel that when a boy over fifteen whistles at a girl over fifteen, sex has reared its ugly head. This view is incorrect, and any discussion of sex on the basis of it would be futile at best and dangerous at worst.

The sexual impulses in the earliest years are inextricably intermingled with other sensory impulses. To the infant, gratification of a desire is simply gratification of a desire; he does not feel one desire as belonging to a different category from others.

As the child grows, he becomes aware of a difference in his desires; he appreciates the difference, for example, between hunger, demanding food, and thirst, demanding liquid. This we may call the "differentiation" of desires.

As he grows older he differentiates more and more, until finally (first, psychologists say, at around the age of five, and then from puberty onward) he is aware of the sexual drive as a drive distinct from all others.

What we must remember is that originally his drives were undifferentiated;

that originally there was no difference in quality, legality, or morality, between his sexual drives and his other drives;

that we ask the adolescent to accept the general opinion that sexual drives are somehow less legitimate than others;

that this opinion is absolutely incorrect, as all desires rise from the original undifferentiated desire for gratification;

and that we therefore impose upon the adolescent, who is not yet mentally or emotionally mature, and who is already grappling with the purely physical problem of emerging sexuality, a devastating secondary problem: that of adjusting his normal and vigorous sexual drives to a prejudiced and repressive public opinion which insists that those drives are not normal and must be restrained.

Arbitrarily, we fix the age of relative freedom (within the law) in these matters at eighteen or twenty-one. But exploration of the physical apparatus of sex begins in infancy; even before puberty boys find erotic satisfaction in dirty stories, lewd pictures, and occasional glimpses of women in states of partial undress. Girls, who are thought to be not so brazen, display a giggling interest in these naughty male activities. Children of all ages know and feel more about sex than most of us believe.

At puberty the drives become imperative; and it is therefore when our children reach puberty that most of us deliver the dire warnings that completely confuse the child. The drives hammer at them constantly, and so do we, warning them against their use as well as their misuse. Yet—and we would do well to remember this—some of the great love stories of our literature are about teen-agers. Juliet, legend has it, was fourteen. Fourteen!

There are relatively few marriages now involving adolescents. In the state of Illinois, for example, children are required by law to attend school until the age of seventeen, or graduation from high school, whichever comes first. The long schooling is demanded by a complex and industrial civilization; and until his schooling is over, a young man is hardly in a position to marry. I am sure that there are valid sociological and economic reasons for the minimum marriage ages established by law.

And there are, of course, the best and most imperative reasons for chastity before marriage; there are no logically valid exceptions to moral and religious law. Premarital chastity is socially desirable and morally healthy; no matter how "modern" and "scientific" the theories which deny this assertion, they cannot stand up as sound under the microscope of rigorous analysis.

But here we are not concerned so much with righteousness as we are with the paradox which remains unsolved: *the violence of sexual drives must be subdued the hardest for years during that period when, apparently, it is at its strongest.*

There is no way out. There is no such thing as "semichastity." The adolescent must face this overpowering problem; and if he is ever to be happy in life, he must learn to solve that problem.

Many, many teen-agers have come to me for guidance in this

132

area. "I'm shy with girls." "I'm ashamed, because I want to kiss them and touch them." "I watched my mother undress. I couldn't help it. I know it's wrong, but . . ." "I like to be with boys, but they want to kiss me and I know it isn't right." "I'm afraid I'm different from other boys. They seem to know how to get along with girls. I freeze up. Is there something wrong with me?"

And I tell them this: of course there's nothing wrong with them. If they *didn't* have those thoughts and feelings, *then* there might be something wrong with them. Their sex-hunger was given them at birth, with food-hunger and knowledge-hunger and adventure-hunger and success-hunger. To be ashamed and afraid is wrong; they must be glad and grateful. All of us—their parents too—were troubled in the same way as children. And many of their elders—though few will admit it—are still troubled today.

"Yes," they say, "but what do I do? How do I deal with it?"

Most of all, I advise them, stop feeling as though the impulse is the sin. Make up your mind to accept the impulse as something natural; learn to live with it.

When sexual impulses arise, do not ask yourself, Is it wicked? but Is it wise? Is it good for me? For my body, for my peace of mind, the conscience I carry with me before all men and God? For my self-respect? And what will it do to my future? Will I ever be able to grapple with serious problems, to deny temporary happiness for the sake of the future, if I cannot manage to do it now?

Cast aside guilt over the impulse. Man, alone among the animals, is capable of lofty thought, ideal creation, sublime nobility; the price he pays for that capacity is an awareness that he is also capable of the lowest infamies. But to be aware of sin is not the same as sinning. To recognize evil—and even to feel evil—is not the same as doing evil. Unnecessary guilt can have tragic consequences. It can confuse us, until right is truly indistinguishable from wrong. It can create in us the attitude, "Might as well be hanged for a sheep"; having felt the guilt, we also feel that we

133

have paid for the pleasure. But most dangerous, it can lead us to deny our own complex natures; it can drive us into neurotic patterns, and make our lives unlivable.

And when you are clear in your mind that the impulse is natural, you will be better able to fight it. Your energies, your thoughts, your ability to reason, will be stronger. You will have avoided the trap of self-deception, of feeling that you are hopelessly depraved and that therefore nothing matters. You will see yourself more clearly as you are: a magnificent creation, given life by God, with the strength and intelligence to do His will, to find happiness, to become what He desires all men to be: human beings, strong and free.

The community can help. The community has ducked the sexual question in adolescence for too long. Schools should have guidance centers—attendance must, of course, be voluntary, but parents should be pressured to use them—with instruction in the nature of adolescent drives and the solution of adolescent problems as the primary objective. Communities should co-ordinate many agencies, religious, medical and social, athletic and constabulary, to deal with the problems of the teen-ager at all levels.

The objection is often raised that sex education is a matter for the home. In a sense this is true—a child's original knowledge of the reproductive process must come from an understanding and intelligent member of his own family. But by far the greater part of the sexual problems for the adolescent consists not of gaps in his knowledge, but of his inability to deal with the moral and social aspects of sexuality. And his parents, a generation removed, not living in adolescent circles, nor as acutely aware of the manners and morals, the temptations and attitudes, of today's adolescents, may have a completely unrealistic picture of the teen-ager's problem. It is often easier for a stranger to get to the root of those problems; a child is sometimes more embarrassed before his own parents, and less likely to tell the "humiliating" truth. And

134

too many parents themselves are often misinformed; ignorance in these matters is not the prerogative of adolescents alone.

One of the most charming stage scenes I have ever witnessed is the one in *Life with Father* where Clarence Day, at the insistence of his wife, ceremoniously leads his son, about to leave for college, into the dining room, anxiously closes the door, and awkwardly launches a discussion on "the facts of life." After circling the subject, touching upon every area except sex, in the true Victorian manner, he finishes by telling the boy nothing of consequence. As I watched the scene I could not help reflecting that when the same interview takes place today, and the father says, "Son, I'd like to discuss the facts of life with you," the young man's answer may well be, "All right, Dad. What do you want to know?"

In any case the greatest harm comes not from the fact that we have evil impulses, not from the fact that the marriage age is fixed by law, not from the fact that teen-agers are natural outlaws, not from rock 'n' roll and not from paternal hesitation, but from the fact that on the common, workaday, community level of ordinary life, the subject has been taboo for too long. Parents will discuss practically anything else with their children, with teachers, with doctors, with ministers; but sex, the most natural and indeed essential of the human drives, is left to the national magazines. Can we require mature intelligence from our teen-agers, when we ourselves display such arrant and prejudiced stupidity?

This chapter has taken up many aspects of childhood and adolescence. Instruction and correction during these early periods is of extreme and obvious importance to the later adult. His life will be a search for success and happiness, and what he learns as a youngster will determine the paths he takes later.

Perhaps the sum of all the lessons imparted to the young is independence. No teaching can create, or even promise, happiness and success; what instruction does is to create qualities which will in turn create success. Being an individual is a requisite for success; and independence—within, of course, a basically interdependent society—is a requisite for individuality.

In one of his poems, Alfred, Lord Tennyson asserts, "Self-reverence, self-knowledge, and self-control; these three alone lead life to sovereign power." Through the ages religion, by the power of the sacred word, has inspired men to revere themselves as children of God. For centuries schools have imparted to children more and more knowledge about themselves as persons. But parents, teachers, and ministers have not yet succeeded in teaching any great number of children to develop real self-control—the quality of self-reliance, the true spirit of independence.

That this is an essential part of maturity should be obvious. The baby, normally, feels that the world was created for his pleasure, and all creatures in it to serve him. Too many homes do little to correct this attitude, and by the time the child enters school he tends to be a petty tyrant, seeking to control others, unable to control himself.

The compulsive need to control others is a clear symptom of lack of self-control. To be independent does not mean to be free from all outside restraint. The world does not belong to any one of us, and in general as the child's social horizons widen, much of his selfishness rubs off, which is another way of saying that he acquires a measure of self-control. The child who remains domineering remains a child. Later on, we find that the most dangerous potential for delinquency lies deep within the child who has never been taught self-control, or has refused to accept it. Lacking self-reliance, confidence, independence, he will be too ready to join the group that can supply him with substitutes for those qualities. And when accused of cowardice or failure, he will blame the "others"; he will say that he never chose to be a failure, but was forced into it by frustration. What he means really is that he never learned independence and personal responsibility.

Traditionally, the blame for the failure of children has been assigned either wholly to the one or wholly to the other. In the

Bible we read, "The fathers have eaten sour grapes and the children's teeth are set on edge." The blame for the behavior of children was thrust on the parent. In violent protest against this practice, the Prophet Jeremiah exploded, "In those days they shall say no more: The fathers have eaten sour grapes and the children's teeth are set on edge. But everyone shall die for his own iniquity; every man that eateth the sour grapes, his teeth shall be set on edge." This is the other extreme; the child is made wholly responsible for himself.

The truth lies, of course, somewhere in between. The shortcomings, stupidities, and sins of parents are many. Those of children are necessarily few and their capacity to deal with them limited. But parents love their children so much that they experience inexplicable disappointment when the children seem to deny their heritage for no reason at all. Perhaps it would be better to concentrate less on casting blame, and more on correcting troubles.

The principles enunciated in this chapter can help us all to achieve many aims. They can be applied differently to meet various difficult situations. They have been set down here to provide immediate help to parents, but their ultimate aim is to help children:

1. To accept the full reality of their world, without distortion or omission, but without destroying the beauty of fantasy and imagination.

2. To accept fears as part of life; to learn to recognize and overcome them.

3. To play not only pleasurably, but purposefully; and thereby to learn to work happily.

4. To grow at a good pace, living each period of childhood to its fullest, and moving on to the next period when the step comes naturally.

5. To live with conscience, and understand that mistakes can be rectified, guilts purged, sins expiated.

6. To remain individuals; not to commit themselves totally to any one group or person; to be free to break the circle of a gang when the call of individual conscience makes it necessary.

7. To be compassionate toward their parents (even as the song goes: "Be kind to your parents, though they don't deserve it") realizing that parents have problems of their own, and have a right to work for their own happiness.

8. To accept the sexuality of man's nature as something natural and normal; to learn to control it without guilts and humiliations.

9. To achieve genuine independence as individuals, which may be called a combination of self-control, self-reliance, and human compassion. To remember that "the child is father of the man."

MARRIED

LOVE:

HIS

Chapter Seven

A man's home is his wife.
—RABBINICAL SAYING

Heaven only knows how the comic muse would have survived without marriage.

Marriage is a wonderful institution; but who wants to live in an institution?

A bachelor is a man who doesn't make the same mistake once.

A widower who marries the second time didn't deserve to lose his first wife.

Report from a Los Angeles paper on a local romance: ". . . and the couple were married last Wednesday, thus ending a friendship which began in their schooldays."

What first strikes us about these tasteless witticisms is their cheap humor; and then we notice that they elicit their chuckles by being destructive. Sour grapes? Man's last gibe in the face of the inevitable? In every joke, they say, there is a kernel of truth; they also say that no one bothers to kick a dead dog. The answer

139

is probably concealed in these two clichés, and may run as follows:

(a) Responsibility is one of the marks of maturity.

(b) Most men are not truly mature.

(c) Most men shirk responsibility—particularly permanent and serious responsibility.

(d) Marriage is a covenant setting forth obligations; it is therefore a responsibility.

(e) For centuries, in the face of attacks from every quarter, marriage in one form or another has survived. It seems to be here to stay.

(f) Man, as usual, accepts his responsibilities with a maximum of griping, some of which, by the law of averages, will be funny.

(g) The result: 365 bad jokes a year.

The analysis may seem more farcical than scientific, but it's basically true.

Any careful statistical study will reveal that marriage itself is never a failure. Its demise has been announced by several cynical philosophers and radical governments, but it has thrived, while its would-be assassins have been swept into the dustbin of history. In the early days of stormy revolutions, like the French and the Russian, marriage is mistakenly identified with the "old order," rather than, properly, with humanity; and the zealous revolutionaries strike a blow for freedom by abolishing it. What then happens is amply reflected in this Associated Press dispatch from Moscow, which was reported about a year ago, one generation after the fall of the Czarist regime: "Throughout the Soviet Union a campaign is under way to stamp out immorality among Communist party members in particular and Soviet citizens in general. Especially condemned are cads and bounders, bigamists and alimony dodgers who desert their wives and children and betray un-

140

suspecting maidens." And the Soviets once busied themselves nationalizing women and outlawing marriage as a decadent capitalistic bourgeois invention!

For most of us this startling Soviet revelation was unnecessary. I have long cherished, as the most beautiful affirmation I know of the possible glory of marriage, a love story from the Talmud. Under ancient Rabbinical law a husband was expected to divorce his wife if, after a reasonable time, the marriage had produced no offspring. A couple, deeply in love, one day faced the necessity of separation under this law. Weeping, the husband begged his wife to take from their home as a keepsake that which she considered her most precious treasure. When the night of parting came, she plied him with strong drink and he fell into a deep sleep. In the morning when he woke he found himself in strange quarters, and his wife standing at his bedside.

"Where am I?" he asked. "And why are you still with me?"

"This, my husband, is my new home. You said that I might take my most precious treasure. I have done so. It is you."

The story has a happy ending, because in tribute to such love the law was waived, the couple were reunited, and they lived happily ever after.

One of the lessons I often read to a bride and groom standing before me during the ceremony is a reminder that the ring with which they plight their troth carries no magic power within itself. In fairy tales, by placing a ring on a finger and twisting it properly, two people can be swiftly transported on the wings of love to a distant land of perfect bliss. But we do not live in fairyland. For us the magic is not in the ring but in those who use it: the magic of their mutual love.

Marriage is a human institution, and there is nothing wrong with any marriage that human beings, exercising their powers of intelligence, tolerance, patience, forbearance, can't cure. It is not marriage that changes; it is the people in it, who have sworn to love each other throughout eternity, to honor the highest moral

141

standards, to obey the holiest sanctions under God. It is they who made the marriage, they who made it fail, they who could make it succeed.

A distinguished professor of sociology and recognized authority on marriage has pointed out that today people marry for one or a combination of a number of reasons. He has listed love, economic security, parents' wishes, escape from loneliness or from a bad situation in the parental home, money, companionship, sexual attraction, protection, notoriety, social position and prestige, gratitude, pity, spite, adventure. Some couples, he added, are drawn together by mutual interests which make their relationship richer. Some weddings are based on psychological need; they are a modern kind of shotgun wedding. Some people will tell you that they married to fulfill their personalities. But the truth, he concluded, is that people marry because marriage is the socially accepted pattern through which they most satisfactorily achieve certain desired ends.

Ben Hecht, in his *A Child of the Century*, restricts his speculations on this score to men. The catalogue is uncomfortably cynical, until we remember that Mr. Hecht married for love, and was quite happy. "Many inscrutable and wanton forces bring men and women together. I itemize some of them: There is a great tribe of men who do not marry women at all, but marry fetishes, who promise to love, honor, and obey a coiffure, an odor, an over-meaty breast. There are fortune hunters and misfortune hunters, romantics playing blind-man's-buff, and lonely hearts looking for someone with whom to play cards. There are jilted men who marry somebody else rather than commit suicide. There are men who marry in order to convince themselves that they are men. There are men too shy to undress in front of strangers, and men weary of undressing before strangers. There are men and women who marry because they have nothing else to do with themselves. There are politically-minded young men who marry party constituents (this is particularly true of Communists). There are men who marry because they want to be like their mothers, and still others who want to be like everybody else. There are men who offer marriage as a bribe to women they could not otherwise seduce; and men who marry women as the only way of pulling them out of other men's beds. There are men who marry kitchen stoves and vacuum cleaners, and men who get trapped into wedlock by a female determination stronger than their own love of freedom." *

I have not had Mr. Hecht's picaresque experiences and associations, but after three decades of officiating at marriages—over three thousand of them, many for young people whom I had known and taught for many years—I am convinced that a vast majority of couples marry believing that they are in love. Their hearts, and not their minds, take the last leap of decision. At that moment they behold the person; eventually they may see place and power. There is even an old quip for this contingency: If you love a girl you shouldn't hold her money against her.

In Hebrew the word for marriage is Kiddushin. Literally it means sanctification, deriving from the same root as one of the most significant words in Jewish thought and tradition—Holy. In ancient times, when most other peoples looked upon marriage as just a biological relationship, sanctioned by the law of man, the Jewish people gave it the new dimension of sanctity. They raised it to holiness, and called it blessed by the love of God. They made the Jewish union a sacred one, and the Jewish home a shrine, where husband and wife, in a spirit of devotion and dedication, loved God and their fellow men as well as each other.

One of the most beautiful stories of marriage in all literature is that of Rebecca and Isaac in the Old Testament. Abraham, Isaac's father, now old and desiring to see his son married to a woman of his own people possessed of specific qualifications, sent a servant to find the bride. Seeking the bride, and mindful of Abraham's

* From *A Child of the Century* by Ben Hecht; published by Simon and Schuster, Inc.

injunctions, the servant, standing at a watering-place, prayed: "Oh Lord, the God of my master Abraham, if now Thou do prosper my way which I go; behold I stand by the fountain of water, and let it come to pass that the maiden that cometh before me to draw, to whom I shall say, Give me, I pray thee, a little water from thy pitcher to drink, and she shall say to me: Both drink thou and I will also draw for thy camels; let the same be the woman whom the Lord hath appointed for my master's son." And Rebecca did come to the fountain, and the servant's prayer was answered. But look at the basis of Abraham's choice: not beauty, not family, not riches. Only her character!

It was an arranged marriage, and not a romantic affair. The Bible tells us simply: "And Isaac brought her into his mother Sarah's tent and took Rebecca and she became his wife and he loved her." The commentators are often curious: "Why does it say first 'she became his wife' and then 'and he loved her'? Could he not have loved her before marriage?" The answer is yes; but he made certain that he continued to love her after the marriage. His marriage was *Kiddushin,* sacred, a relation founded on the enduring quality of holiness, filled with unceasing devotion and everlasting dedication. Isaac made sure that his marriage would succeed.

Many of the most unsuccessful marriages are those which seem to have all the "big things" that make for happiness; and some of the most successful, those which have few, even of the little material things regarded as essential to the home. I have attended golden wedding ceremonies of couples whose marriages had been dead or dying for fifty years; I have seen failing unions given new strength by tragedy; and I have seen two people steadfast in their love and faith through a lifetime of disappointment and disaster.

For the last decade in America, statistics have generally recorded the ratio of divorce to marriage as about one to four. On the basis of my experience in marriage counseling and my observation of many couples, I would estimate that among the three fourths who remain together, the ratio of successful unions —really successful—to unsuccessful is the same, about one to four.

Opinions differ as to what makes marriage a success. The ready answer is "happiness." But what is happiness? How does it manifest itself in marriage? Happiness at best is a variable and elusive quantity—or rather, quality. There is no single act which we may call the finding of happiness; it exists in the striving after fulfillment. Yet many of us strive all our lives without experiencing what we would call happiness. Others live in a state of happiness and never bother to use the word, or to speculate on the quality. They are just happy.

Outward appearances may be deceptive. In Denmark recently there was a rush to the divorce courts; an ignorant observer might have been justified in assuming that marriage had gone to pot in Scandinavia, and that mass neurosis had set in. The explanation was simpler. Under a new old-age pension law, all men, married or single, but only single women, were eligible for pensions upon reaching the age of 60. Married women had to wait until they were 65. Many couples, married for years, secure and confident in their love, arranged to be divided in law when the woman reached 60, but remained united in love and life!

Often what unites men and women in marriage has a direct bearing on what divides them later. Without sacrificial effort and mutual sympathy, a wrong beginning rarely leads to a happy ending. If an American heiress marries a European baron, she may later divorce him for a duke, or he her, for a settlement. Meanwhile a struggling coal miner and his wife may be so united in their constant struggle against difficulty and adversity that nothing will ever separate them. In general the reasons that lead to marriage are far less important than the qualities and values later brought to its service, but often the reasons remain the qualities that each partner brings to the relationship.

In *Cass Timberlane*, Sinclair Lewis wrote, "Will the world ever be truly civilized? We always assume so, but will it? If the world ever learns that it knows nothing yet about what keeps men and women loving each other, then will it have a chance for some brief happiness before the eternal frozen night sets in. You cannot heal the problems of any one marriage until you heal the problem of an entire civilization, founded upon suspicion and superstition, and you cannot heal the problems of the civilization thus confounded, until it realizes its own barbaric nature, and that what it thought was brave was merely cruel; what it thought was holy was only meanness, and what it thought success, was merely the paper helmet of a clown more nimble than his fellows, scrambling for a peanut in the dust of an ignoble circus." *

It will be a long time before we heal the problems of our American civilization, still founded upon much suspicion and superstition. But that should not deter us from striving to find out what keeps men and women loving each other, and what keeps them together in marriage. When Mr. Lewis says that we know nothing, he is wrong. Many are the reasons for failure in marriage, and many are the remedies which—if faithfully applied—can save couples from disaster and secure their success.

Why do men fail in marriage? The first, and most general, reason is that they have clung to an outmoded conception—almost a superstition—of women. Their image of woman is ancient, or at least mid-Victorian. They no longer see her as a chattel, a slave, but they do, consciously or unconsciously, regard her as inferior. She is, they feel, unable to match men in certain fields of activity and accomplishment, and incompetent in specific areas of knowledge and understanding. To them woman's place is still in the home; her goal, perfection as a helpmate.

When men marry, they think of the wife described in the Book of Proverbs:

* From *Cass Timberlane* by Sinclair Lewis; copyright 1945 by the author. Published by Random House, Inc.

A woman of valor who can find? For her price is far above rubies. The heart of her husband doth safely trust in her, and he hath no lack of gain. She doeth him good and not evil all the days of her life. . . . She riseth also while it is yet night and giveth food to her household. . . . Her lamp goeth not out by night. She layeth her hands to the distaff. . . . She is not afraid of the snow for her household, for all her household are clothed with scarlet. . . . Her husband is known in the gates when he sitteth among the elders of the land. . . . She looketh well to the ways of her household and eateth not the bread of idleness. Her children rise up and call her blessed; her husband also, and he praiseth her. Many daughters have done valiantly, but thou excellest them all. Grace is deceitful and beauty is vain, but a woman that feareth the Lord, she shall be praised. Give her of the fruit of her hands and let her works praise her in the gates!

Or they envision the women John Ruskin depicted in his *Sesame and Lilies* at the end of the nineteenth century:

Now their separate characters are briefly these: The man's power is active, progressive, defensive. He is eminently the doer, the creator, the defender. His intellect is for speculation and invention; his energy for war and conquest. . . But the woman's power is for rule, not for battle . . . and her intellect is not for invention or creation but for sweet ordering, arrangement and decision. She sees the qualities of things—their claims and their places. Her great function is Praise. She enters into no contest. . . . The man in his rough work in the open world must encounter all peril and trial. . . . But he guards the woman from all this; within the house as ruled by her unless she herself has sought it, need enter no danger, no temptation, no cause of error or offense. This is the true nature of home; it is the place of peace.

Many men fail in marriage because they can never rid themselves of this feeling of superiority—some, of course, are unaware that they have it—or keep themselves from acting upon it. They speak of the "little woman." They exclude her from certain discussions because "she wouldn't understand." Business

147

problems and political issues are deemed too complex for the lesser minds to comprehend. The management of the home, on the other hand, is simply child's play—not fit for an adult male. The old notion that woman's only concerns are *Kinder, Küche, Kirche* (children, kitchen, and church, which are assumed to require more feeling than thought) still persists today.

This sense of superiority encourages men to practice the double standard in marriage. An ancient Oriental philosophy invades the American home: the King can do no wrong. But let the Queen make a false move, and off with her head. This philosophy runs through the man's thoughts, feelings and actions. It manifests itself in small ways—thoughtlessness, and large—tyranny.

This is particularly true in the realm of sexual fidelity, where the term "double standard" is usually applied. There are still many American husbands who regard a private harem as the special prerogative of the male. (The fact that it must be private indicates their cowardice.) Let a wife try, just once, and the philandering husband reacts like a Renaissance prince; he is shocked and furious; his eyes roll wildly; he reaches for the dagger. His own harem is not as conveniently located or as large in numbers or as public as the traditional seraglio. But in one respect it is infinitely more evil: the master of the traditional harem had never promised eternal fidelity to one wife and he had publicly assumed responsibility for all its members.

It is not only in the realm of sex that wives complain of the double standard. They want to know why a husband will spend large sums of money on entertainment and liquor for himself, and then quarrel over her bills for clothes and hairdos. If the first are for his pleasure, the others are for hers. And they want to know why their husbands must be briefed on the wives' interests and activities, when the men are unwilling to admit that the women may share an interest in business, financial affairs, and the general problems of men. They want to know why their husbands must have regular nights out with the boys and occasional trips away from home for a rest, while the wives are expected to enjoy the same routine, the same round of chores—*Kinder, Küche, Kirche*—year after year with no relief.

And why are all the mother-in-law jokes directed at *his?* What about the mother-in-law *she* has to endure, who is convinced that she is not good enough for her son? Why should her husband ignore and even humiliate her in public, and then regard it as lese majesty if she offers an objection or criticism before friends? Why should the household be blanketed in an abnormal quiet, the atmosphere charged with solicitous care, when he returns from a day's work, while she is expected to be ready for a wild night on the town whenever his lordship decrees?

The double standard is obviously pernicious, yet men persist in refusing to concede its existence. I am only amused, no longer amazed, when a philandering husband complains to me about his wife's flirtatious ways, about a real or imagined come-hither look in her eyes. (He is usually so frightened by his own inability to control his emotions that he imputes to her actions and guilts that are properly his.) I am no longer shocked when married men openly boast of affairs with other women, shortly after having praised the character and fidelity of their wives. I know that they are unconsciously reflecting the general, still prevailing, pattern of male dominance. I also know that wives are usually aware of their husband's liaisons, and that many are resentfully resigned to a meaningless marriage consisting largely of a public display of unity and tranquillity.

Jealousy is a natural result of this kind of life. This original green-eyed monster may have been the serpent of the Garden of Eden. Even the happiest marriage is not immune to its poisonous venom. Occasionally a trivial incident can arouse it; a handkerchief flaunted by an Iago can lead to a murdered Desdemona and a self-destroyed Othello.

Sex is, of course, the area in which jealousy arises most quickly. I have discussed their general dissatisfactions with many husbands, and I have found that usually they think of their relation-

149

ship to their wives in the traditional, or mid-Victorian, terms. They demand—again, consciously or unconsciously—exclusive possession of their wives; not only of their favors in love, but of the light in their eyes, their smiles, the touch of their hands, often their conversation. The unreasonable possessiveness of the domineering husband can make tragedy out of the wife's most innocent friendships with other men; a smile, an animated conversation, an innocent touch, can rouse the dumb beast in a possessive husband to unreasoning fury.

Not only the occurrence of those incidents, but even a reminder that they occurred once in the past, can stir up husbandly jealousy. Perhaps this is not true jealousy, but it is painful. A bundle of letters found after years of happy marriage will create no real insecurity or loss; but a man will feel a sting just the same. There will be no vulgar doubt on his part, but any such reminder of the premarital past will seem tasteless and indelicate. It will discomfort him to realize that he was not always her liege lord.

Social scientists have pointed out one of the significant personal and social changes of the twentieth century; those who feel inferior, or are so regarded, are no longer willing to accept their fate. This change has affected the modern family. A renowned psychologist asserts: "There is a new equilibrium between men and women. It is drawing rapidly toward equality. Equality between the sexes has never been seriously accepted. We have not yet reached it, but have more of it than mankind ever had before. Women no longer accept the position of the second sex. Men who still feel obliged to live up to the masculine pattern of the past find it increasingly difficult to prove their superiority and become apprehensive and neurotic. In this way husband and wife become suspicious and antagonistic to each other, despite their best intentions, despite their love and affection, and their sincere desire for peace and harmony. The fear of losing out in the competition, of being dominated and defeated, abused and humiliated, creeps into their relationship."

150

Ashley Montagu, in *The Natural Superiority of Women,* goes even further; he makes a good case for women as the stronger sex. We can certainly agree that she is not inferior to man, only different. She is no longer wholly on the distaff side within the home. She often has power and prestige in the marketplace. She is frequently more active and progressive than man in civic and church affairs. Her intellect soars high in speculation and achieves much in invention. Her energies are used in war; she shares conquest and defeat. Her labors for peace are no longer confined to the home; she belongs to the world.

Modern man must realize that woman is truly his equal. The modern husband must take his wife not as a helpmate, but as a whole mate—an equal partner. The ancient sages taught, "If thy wife is small, bend down to her and whisper in her ear." Many husbands do and say things which make their wives feel small; they then shout further belittling remarks in her ear. Many husbands bully their wives into permanent submission. A husband must learn to look up and out with a woman—never down upon her. As Anne Morrow Lindbergh puts it, "Love does not consist in gazing at each other (too often with condescension and contempt) but in looking outward together in the same direction." If the male is to establish superiority, let it be through growing accomplishment and revealing wisdom, not by tradition—and irascibility. Let him lead with love, hold his wife's hand in partnership, and help her walk with dignity by his side.

A happy marriage demands a single standard for both mates. The wise husband will strive to take his wedding vows seriously: to love his wife exclusively, in body and in spirit; to cherish her needs and wishes as of equal importance with his own; to honor her confidence in him, and her position in the eyes of others. He will seek to do unto her as he would expect her to do unto him. The sages went even further; they taught, "Love thy wife as thyself; honor her more than thyself."

Lack of fidelity is not the husband's only sexual failure. It is the most serious, of course; most wives feel it deeply as a viola-

151

tion of basic decency and a blow to their pride, though they may tolerate it. Inwardly they never accept, though outwardly they condone, often for the sake of children or economic security or appearances.

There are other failures in the sex relationship, some of them so serious that wives are tempted to hope that their husbands *will* find distant pastures greener. There is, for example, the over-passionate husband, who acts as though sex were the be-all and end-all of marriage. His honeymoon becomes an orgy, his home a brothel, his wife a slave to his physical desires. I find occasionally that a couple whom I have married will immediately separate after the honeymoon and head for the divorce court. The usual reason is the husband's failure to show consideration, and to establish compatibility during those first few vital days. He seems not to realize that his wife is not simply a creature fashioned to fulfill his desires. She is his partner, a flesh-and-blood companion, with urges that may differ from his own.

Even after many years of marriage, some husbands never seem to understand the peculiar make-up (mental and emotional as well as physical) of many women. If the wife begs off from love-making, the man will take it as a personal affront, a sign of resentment or repugnance, a proof of frigidity, or of interest in another man. He suspects her of being unwilling, when she is simply emotionally unable, at that moment, to respond with the kind of enthusiasm essential to joy.

There is also the under-passionate husband who cannot realize that sex is just as important, though not always as urgent, in a woman's life as in a man's. This particular ignorance often accompanies the general mid-Victorian attitude toward women: woman was not only inferior, but, if she were a "good" woman, almost sexless. Because of prudish notions, idiotic theories about health, or genuine physical incapacity, many husbands reveal themselves as slow to arouse or respond, and infrequent in performance.

These husbands must learn that a wife is not a wanton simply because she possesses a stronger sex drive than they had expected. They must try to understand it and adjust to it; even to rejoice in it, though it may mean a rude awakening from their dream of male superiority. In some marriages it is necessary that the husband emphasize the sexual element more than his natural inclination may require, even as in many marriages it is essential that he stress sex less.

Recently a couple came to see me for counseling. For months the husband had been withdrawn; he had retreated into a hard shell, and was moody and uncommunicative. He refused to engage in any sustained conversation with his wife; he rejected her tentative advances, her evidences of affection. He had thrown up a solid barrier between them. And she had exhausted every means of breaking through to him. She came to me, helpless. He wouldn't tell her what was wrong, and she was afraid that he wouldn't tell me.

I persuaded him to come to my study. When I had gained his confidence the story came out. He was convinced that his wife found other men more attractive than him. He was sure that she was faithful; but lately she had been flinging herself at their male friends in a flirtatious manner which he had never seen before.

His wife confessed that what he had said was partly true— but she maintained that the basic responsibility was his. Their marriage had had a very bad beginning. She had been completely ignorant and untutored; he had been importunately insistent. She had been given no time to understand and to adjust. She had suffered emotionally and physically. And now for years she had suffered from mental resistance to the sexual act; added to it was the fear of pregnancy.

We examined their fears, and for the first time each of them spoke to the other in utter frankness. When they left me I knew that they were back on the road to success.

Sex is a small word that means many things. It does not always mean the sexual act. Often a certain light in the eyes, a lilt to the voice, a tender word and a gentle caress, a considerate gesture, a small courtesy, are sexually more effective and exciting than direct courtship, or the sexual act itself. It is more important for the husband to be sexually artistic than sexually powerful. The Greeks had a word for it; the Latins have a way with it; and American husbands would do well to speak the word and learn the way.

They tell the story of the young man who heard that his fiancée's father had just gone into bankruptcy, and remarked bitterly, "He's just trying to do all he can to prevent our marriage."

Money can be a strong incentive to marriage; it can be equally destructive to marriage. Too much money is more dangerous to a marriage than too little. Instead of contributing to the quality of married love, money often blinds a couple to the real values in life.

King Midas converted whatever he touched to gold; a husband obsessed by money converts his marriage bed to a marketplace. Having money to place on the altar of love, he neglects to couple it with a part of himself—with affections and attentions. Emotionally sterile, substituting money for human values, he becomes an easy prey for women on the make, willing for a price to become back-street wives. It simplifies the process of divorce, which can become impersonal and stripped of human values if only there is enough money to establish the proper residence and hire the best of lawyers.

And too much money frequently drives a couple out of the home, into free-spending crowds of social dilettantes. The marriage bonds and family ties are weakened. Children become an annoyance, books and conversation are neglected, there is none of the compassion generated by the multitude of small problems that more modest families must solve together. And when the obsession is principally the husband's, the wife may become a gold-widow, like a golf-widow or a card-widow. Wives of wealthy husbands often find that the gilded goddess is a more demanding mistress than any fleshly woman.

Often it isn't the possession of much money, but rather the spending of too little, that makes a man a failure as a husband. In *The Last Resorts*, Cleveland Amory reports that a Mrs. Kent, who still summers at Bar Harbor and winters at Palm Beach, recalls one symbolic moment in the 1920s when her husband called her on the carpet. "Mabel," said Kent sternly, "you aren't spending enough money." Few husbands make this complaint; most cry out against extravagance on the part of their wives, and a few miserly souls complain if she spends money at all.

Marriage is the best investment a man can make. The sooner and the more generously he puts money into it, the larger and more frequent will be his dividends. Let him follow Mr. Kent's example—a word of caution here: this won't work with all wives! —and he will find his lady scolding him (affectionately) for extravagance. The money a husband preserves through stinginess is the most costly of his possessions; he has purchased it at the price of marital happiness. People are amazing: we have come so far from the days when a man counted himself happy if he had his health, a square meal, a good woman, and a place to lay his head, that we find men giving up all that happiness for the sake of money—the purpose of which is supposedly to supply him with what he has renounced!

At the other end of the scale are husbands who fail because they cannot make proper provision for their households. Often it is not their failure alone; their wives, who are stubbornly unable to adjust to a lower financial scale, share the blame. The husband's heart fills slowly with a sense of failure and inadequacy; the end of that road is suicide.

Yet some of the happiest marriages are found in the poorest of homes. Poverty may make life more difficult, but it need not destroy it. Many unions are strengthened when husbands and wives must struggle and suffer together to maintain themselves and their marriages. Paradoxically, the less some people have, the closer they are drawn together, and the nearer they come to fulfilling the copybook maxim that two can live as cheaply as one. This is far from praise of poverty. Poverty is more often degrading and limiting than inspiring. The truth is that adversity often brings out the best in us; and when we have the strength to withstand adversity, we generally have the strength to withstand the corroding temptations of later prosperity.

Still, the most degrading and devastating of all marital rows are those that involve money. More often it is the stinginess of the husband, rather than the extravagance of the wife, which is to blame. Even—or should I say particularly—when the wife supplies the major part of the income, the quarrels can be vicious.

It is difficult to determine to whom the greater sympathy should go. A man who slaves to earn and keep his money can feel legitimate resentment when it is used up on what he considers luxuries. He can make do with old clothes; but his wife must have new ones. He enjoys the old furniture; his wife must constantly buy new pieces. He is satisfied with the old car; his wife wants the latest model. He is balanced enough not to worry about keeping up with the Joneses; she would consider it a tragedy to be left behind. He tips modestly, and occasionally neglects it entirely; she is terribly embarrassed. What is common sense to him, is stinginess to her.

No two individual families have the same attitude toward money, or the same financial problems. There is no solution to the riddle of money. The best advice is: if the choice is between more money and human happiness let the money go. Money can be replaced; humanity cannot.

Thoughtfulness—chiefly on the husband's part—can do much to preserve even a dubious marriage. To many wives, marriage is their whole existence, and keeping the family together their main business. But the average husband gives much of his thought, time, and energy to making a living, and he often forgets to attend to the business of keeping his marriage alive. The problems of his life outside the home loom large, and he tends to look upon domestic difficulties as of small account or consequence.

But marriage is a most important activity; being a husband is a very worth-while occupation. You can't make a success of marriage any more than of a business, without giving it constant attention. And it is often wisest to concentrate on the niceties (which you are most likely to forget) rather than on the large responsibilities (which you will be unable to forget).

Too many husbands give to their marriages only the outer edges of their thought and occasional fleeting moments of their time. They feel that once the wedding ceremony is completed and the honeymoon over, life will take care of itself. A nod here, a smile there, a gift or two, a promise of better times to come, and the marriage is bound to succeed.

Of course it doesn't work out that way. To be a successful husband a man must make a substantial investment of himself—of his time, his emotions, his activities—even if it means making less money, winning less fame. When a woman marries she wants a home and happiness. But more than all else, a husband—a husband who will be part and parcel of that home and happiness. A husband who will always be her lover in deed as well as word—ever kind and considerate, thoughtful and true till death do them part.

She wants a husband, too, who will be thoughtful enough to realize that his wife may enjoy activities outside the home; who will understand that her interest in the world at large equals his own, but that she is deprived of his opportunities for daily outside experiences. Women need female friends as men require male comrades, and they want time to be with them. Women participate in community activities, and occasionally rise to local prominence. Yet many men are jealous of their wives' time and energies and seem to expect that women must find complete fulfillment in domestic chores. This is obviously unrealistic. Women have spe-

157

THE ROAD TO SUCCESSFUL LIVING

cial interests and talents; it is natural that they will try to express them. They want to feel that they are not just wives and mothers; they want to feel that they are individuals.

Instead of being jealous of his wife's activities (sometimes he fears that they are a threat to his own leadership in the home or community), the wise husband will understand and encourage his wife's participation in them. He will find that in the fulfillment and flowering of her own special talents she will become better equipped to preside over the household. He will discover that she has a better understanding of his own non-domestic problems and needs. He will, in short, have a happier wife and a better life. It takes appreciation, understanding, and sympathy; but without these, of course, he scarcely deserves a happy wife and a good life.

In marriage, as in literature, there is nothing so deadly as *ennui*, which is a very tired French word meaning "boredom." The late William Allen White wrote in his diary, "Solomon was bored to a crisp. Madame Bovary was bored to a crisp and so she went out and had three successful adulteries. And I am satisfied that Madame Bovary was not a very bad woman. She was simply bored to extinction. . . . The next time I hear of a man or a woman going wrong, either socially or politically or commercially, I am going to look and see if that man or woman isn't bored to a nice brown crisp, and see if he wasn't seeking excitement rather than anything else." *

In an article called "How Not to Love a Woman," Judy Garland writes, "The mechanization of love we dread more than anything. It means death to us. I know a husband who sent two dozen roses a day to his wife. Every day, every day in the year. In the end the routine arrival of the flowers, such a lovely gesture in the beginning, became a bore to her. Her 'Thank you, darling'

---

* From *The Autobiography of William Allen White*; copyright 1946. Used by permission of the publisher, The Macmillan Company.

became phrases to choke on; her pleased smiles curdled on her lips. 'What did I do?' he asked bewilderedly when she sued for separation. Well, he hadn't done anything terrible. And yet he had." *

When wives come to me to discuss their dissatisfactions in marriage, and to talk about divorce, before offering any opinion I insist upon talking to their husbands. As a rule, after a long and detailed recital of their earnest efforts to supply their wives with everything a woman's heart desires, they end up with that same puzzled query: "What did I do?"

It is hard to tell them that their wives are just plain bored. They have everything; yet they feel that they have nothing. Nothing but a dull daily grind; the same thoughts, actions, and possibilities from day to day. Nothing exciting to wake up to, and nothing fascinating to go to bed with. The same topics of conversation, the same forms of amusement, the same friends in the same places. They may remember the old wedding joke: A minister started the ceremony by saying that there are three things in life which we all must do: we are born; we are married; and then there is nothing left to do but die.

The illusion that material plenty is a firm foundation for marriage finds its way into the minds of many husbands. A wife may have everything—money, prestige, a home, beautiful clothes, trips abroad, presents—yet if her husband is dull as a person, generates no sparks of excitement, repeats the daily and yearly routine with dogged perseverance so that there is no variety in their program, no expectation of change, no sense of adventure, no room for the unexpected, no opening up of new horizons, she will settle down to endure the marriage, but she will never enjoy it.

I once copied these words, which every husband would be wise to heed:

* Reprinted from *Coronet,* February 1955.

When you have married your wife, you would think you were got upon a hilltop and might begin to go downward by an easy slope. But you have only ended courting to begin marriage. Falling in love and winning love are often difficult tasks to overbearing and rebellious spirits; but to keep in love is also a business of some importance to which both man and wife must bring kindness and good will. The true love story commences at the altar, when there lies before the married pair a most beautiful contest of wisdom and generosity and lifelong struggle toward an unattainable ideal.

Years of counseling have convinced me that if a husband makes himself interesting and exciting to his wife, she will cling to him despite his obvious deficiencies and immoralities. But he can be as pure and pious and perfect as the most rigid standards of integrity and decency demand—if he is a bore, she will long to leave him. She may appreciate him with her mind and praise him with her voice, but her heart will be burdened.

Some months ago, Dr. T. F. Schlaegel, Jr., of the Indiana School of Medicine, speaking before the Academy of Psychosomatic Medicine, told of a case history in which a husband's kiss was credited with keeping his wife from blindness. The woman had suffered an attack of acute congestive glaucoma, a common cause of blindness. In these attacks the flow of aqueous liquid from the eyeball is blocked, and pressure builds up within the eye until sight is lost. But the woman reacted emotionally to her husband's kiss; the reaction reduced the dangerous pressure in the eyeball; the attack was beaten back. Here was a woman who was not bored; a woman who loved life so much that her whole organism fought for it!

When a husband is thoughtless about the little things—gentlemanly courtesies like opening doors, letting his wife precede him—the wife is often blind to his larger accomplishments. There may come a time when she not only fails to appreciate them, but even fails to consider them worth while. Even major successes become as dust and ashes, and lose all meaning.

160

Not every man can give his wife wealth and glory, and thus gain her gratitude and adoration. But every husband can be thoughtful and tender, considerate, sweet, sympathetic, and thus gain his wife's respect. Someone has said, "Our idea of a model husband is one who thinks his wife's headache is as important as his own arthritis." The wise man's wife is queen not for a day, but for a lifetime. By valuing his wife's respect, a man can create happiness.

A woman will more readily endure her husband's lack of respect for her than hers for him. Women have come to me with horrifying tales of mistreatment at the hands of their husbands—tongue-lashings, vile names and foul curses, vilifying remarks about their intelligence, integrity, and fidelity, blows on the head and body—and yet they pleaded that I help them find a way to preserve their marriages. They always remind me of a scene in Ferenc Molnar's *Liliom* when Julie speaks to her child about her departed husband—it is a very perceptive line—"Sometimes one can beat you—and beat you—and beat you—and it doesn't hurt at all."

Other wives have told me of words and deeds of great gentleness, kindness, thoughtfulness—the highest consideration for them, the greatest generosity toward them—but they wanted a divorce. Why? Because they had lost all respect for their husbands. They had discovered that the men they had married were weaklings, weak in mind—stupid—or weak in spirit—craven—or both. Their men had no character, would not hesitate to lie or cheat or steal in order to attain an objective, had no self-respect, no scruples or morals, no sense of honor or decency. These men could supply no strength of leadership, no purpose in life.

In that same article, "How Not to Love a Woman," Judy Garland pleads, "Don't yield your leadership. Don't hand us the reins. That's the main thing. We would consider this an abdication on your part, and quicker than anything else it will fog the clear vision of mutuality which made us love you in the first place. It would confuse us, it would alarm us, it would make us pull back.

Oh, we will try to make you give up your position as Number One in the house—we will seem to be fighting you to the last ditch for final authority on everything for a while. But in the obscure recesses of our hearts, we want you to win. You have to win, for we aren't really made for leadership. It's a pose. If you can't teach us that, I think it would be better for you to leave. I really do. It means we really can't be women at all." *

In his novelette *The Colonel's Lady* Somerset Maugham tells the story of a complacent Englishman who one day finds his wife famous for a book she has written, and himself the laughingstock of friends who have read the book. When he examines the volume, he finds that it tells the tragic tale of the author's loss of a great love. He confronts his wife angrily, demanding to know the name of her secret lover. After many threats and much pressure, she confesses (I paraphrase): "You were that lover. You—when we first married—when you were a wonderful, noble, idealistic young man, filled with lofty principles and noble visions—the man with whom I fell in love. But that young man died long ago. All I have left now is you as you have become—a successful man as the world measures it, but a man without any integrity or decency—a man for whom I have lost all respect—a man whom I can no longer really love."

Most husbands are concerned with their desire to respect their wives, and not concerned enough with holding their wives' respect for themselves. Without respect, love cannot live. A woman who cannot look up to a man will soon look down upon him. And when respect is once lost, it is rarely restored. It is replaced by pity, which is the gravedigger of love.

Let him lose all else, this husband, let him lose fortune, fame, and favor; but let him keep his wife's respect for him as a man. Let him lead; his wife expects it. But let him establish leadership by proving himself worthy of it, not by insisting upon it because

* Reprinted from *Coronet,* February 1955.

he is the male partner. To be worthy of society is good; to be worthy of your peers is better; to be worthy of a good woman is quite the best.

"My wife's an angel!" a happy husband exclaimed enthusiastically.

"I'm terribly sorry," a realistic friend answered dryly. "When did she pass on?"

To call your wife an angel is good tactics; to expect her to be one is bad judgment. There is an old joke—this seems to be our chapter for old jokes—which holds that all women are angels, for three reasons: they're always up in the air about something; they're always harping on something; and they're always needing clothes. It's quite cynical; but like all cynicism and all sentimentality, there is a germ of reality in it.

"In the first," Robert Louis Stevenson once wrote, "he expects an angel for a wife. In the last, he knows that she is like himself —erring, thoughtless, and untrue, but like himself also filled with a struggling radiancy of better things—and adorned with ineffective qualities. You may safely go to school with hope; but ere you marry you should have learned the mingled lesson of the world: that dolls are stuffed with sawdust and yet are excellent playthings. That hope and love address themselves to perfection never realized and yet firmly held become the salt and staff of life."

Angels are perfect; no human being is perfect; a wife is a human being (there are some moments in every marriage when the husband believes this); therefore no wife is an angel. It is only the rare woman who is as perfect in beauty as Helen of Troy, whom legend calls the woman whose face launched a thousand ships. It is only the rare wife who is as devoted and faithful in love as was Penelope in her patient vigil for Ulysses.

The wife of reality—not of romance—is possessed of the human frailties to which we are all heir. She is not perfect in wisdom or beauty or kindness or love. She is most often good to look at, pleasant to be with, conscientious in intelligence and industry, comforting in sweetness. At times she is vain and overbearing, unreasonable and demanding. Frequently she is petty and inconsiderate, overambitious and arrogant. But for all that, she is usually much finer than her husband, if only because she is closer to the life of domesticity and love which is ruled by human values, while her husband is closer to the life of the public market, which is ruled by profit and loss.

A husband does well to think of his wife as an angel, but he must know in his heart that to require her to be one will destroy both her and the marriage. The wise husband takes his mate's imperfections—*but not her good qualities*—for granted. He will view them with understanding and sympathy, and will leave off criticism and deprecation. If he is truly wise he will understand that she is putting up with his faults; and if both are wise they will seek subtle ways to help each other overcome those faults.

The husband must remember that he fell in love with an earthly creature; that it was her earthly qualities that first attracted him. If she had been an angel, perfect in all virtues, he might never have asked her out a second time and she probably would not have gone out with him the first time. He loved her for what she was; let him continue so to love her. If he deceived himself, is she to pay for the deception? Let him share with her the struggle for perfection, and let him rejoice that they can make that struggle together.

There is one more quality, perhaps the most important, which husbands must share with wives if marriage is to be successful. This is the most basic emotion in any of the world's religions, and the most noble in any of the world's civilizations: forgiveness. William Faulkner, writing about man and woman, said this: "Love, but more than love too; not depending on just love to hold two people together, make them better than either one would have been alone, but tragedy and suffering, having suffered and caused grief, having something to have, to live with—even when because you knew both of you could never forget it. And then I began to believe something even more than that; that there was something better, stronger than tragedy to hold two people together—forgiveness."

Faith, hope, and charity: and the greatest of these is charity. Remember that forgiveness is not simply a negative acceptance, a willingness to forget. It is an active quality, one of the deepest of man's emotions. It is a denial of all that is base, and an affirmation of all that is human.

Forgiveness is the spirit without which all other brave qualities are useless. Forgiveness is what we shall ask on Judgment Day; it is what we must all extend now.

To recapitulate, here are a few precepts of value to the husband in any marriage:

1. Get over your mid-Victorian concept of women. They are not inferior; you are not superior. Accept your wife as an equal partner in a great adventure.

2. Reject the double standard. Ask no more of your wife than you are prepared to give her.

3. Try to understand your wife's attitude toward sex, whether it is more or less enthusiastic than your own. Remember that she is not a chattel. She is a human being, with her own needs and desires. Help her to fulfill them.

4. Remember that money can break a marriage as easily as make it. Don't use it as a measuring rod. Don't hold it back when human values are at stake. Let it be your mutual possession; don't be possessed by it.

5. Try not to be jealous. It means that you don't trust your wife; and more often it means that you are seeing the light of your own reflected guilts. If you can't restrain your jealousy, get it over with as quickly as possible, and try not to say anything you'll regret later.

6. Don't be a bore. One way to make yourself exciting to your wife is to concentrate on her and forget about your own excel-

165

lences. Cultivate new values; keep an open mind; try to keep growing.

7. Be thoughtful. The little things to you are not always little in your wife's eyes. Make consideration a habit, and see what a difference *it* makes.

8. Consider your wife's respect for you as more vital to the marriage than yours for her. Don't be a showoff in anything, expecially in money or prizes or honors. Your wife must respect you as a man, not as a bank account or trophy.

9. Don't expect perfection in your wife until you have attained it yourself; you're safe, because you will never attain it. You are both human, which is a wonderful thing to be; don't spoil it by asking too much.

10. Forgive. That's all. Just forgive. It's hard, sometimes; sometimes you want forgiveness yourself and it isn't granted. True forgiveness is probably the noblest human quality; if you never do anything else, but you learn to forgive, you're a better man than most of us.

Forgive.

MARRIED

LOVE:

HERS

Chapter Eight

> *Matrimony: the high sea for which*
> *no compass has yet been invented.*
> —HEINRICH HEINE

A book written sometime before 1620 and entitled *A Good Heart*
contains a chapter on marriage which today seems quaint, to say
the least. The chapter is in the form of a fable, the story of a
Queen who gave her only daughter in marriage to a King. The
King ruled over a far domain, and the Queen knew she might
never see her daughter again. Now, if ever, was the time to pass
on whatever advice she had for her daughter; fittingly, the advice
consisted of instructions for the bride. There were ten rules; they
guaranteed success; and they went like this:

"The first, my dear, is to beware of his anger, lest you enrage
him. When he is cross, don't be jolly; when he is jolly, don't be
cross; and when he is angry, smile at him and answer him with
soft words; thus you will still his anger.

"The second, dear daughter, concerns his eating and drinking.
Consider his tastes; and urge him to partake strongly. Let his

meals be ready at their hour; hunger does no one good. When he has been drunk, refrain from telling him what he did or said in his drunkenness; when he commands you to drink with him, do so, but remember that when he has once seen you drunk he will hate you.

"Third, dear daughter, when he sleeps guard his sleep that he be not wakened; rest is magic to the disposition.

"Fourth, dear daughter, be careful with his money, and give nothing away without his knowledge.

"Fifth, dear daughter, pry not into his secrets, and if you learn aught of them, keep them from all others, and also the things he may boast to you in private, tell them to no one.

"Sixth, dear daughter, whom he likes, do you like; whom he dislikes, do you dislike. Do not favor his enemies, and do not frown upon his friends.

"Seventh, dear daughter, do not contrary him. Obey him. Let his words find favor with you. This is easy when he is right, and difficult when he is wrong, but it must be done.

"Eighth, dear daughter, ask him naught that is beyond him in skill or labor, lest his pride turn against you.

"Ninth, dear daughter, heed his requests, knowing that when you do he will love you, and will be your slave to serve you with joy.

"Tenth, dear daughter, take care not to arouse his jealousy, by word, sign or deed.

"Please him in all things; treat him as a King, and he will call you Queen. Take this advice with you as provision, and let it nourish you all your life."

The reader is probably outraged. This is not marriage, he will say; it is slavery, concubinage. Rules outlined over three centuries ago must strike the modern mind as barbaric. We may smile ironically, or laugh derisively—and perhaps a husband here and there may grimace bitterly, sorry to be reminded that such a Golden Age once existed.

Yet each of those rules contains a germ of truth; each of them reveals an understanding of one or another of the problems central to the marriage relationship. *In essence,* if not in form or practice, they hold as true for our times as do the Ten Commandments Moses brought down from the heights of Sinai 3,000 years ago. We must avoid the tendency to interpret these rules as a perpetuation of the traditional view of women as inferior; but let us examine them for their truth, and take from them what help we can.

John Ruskin, in his *Sesame and Lilies,* only a little over half a century ago, described the "true wife" in basically the same way: "She must be enduringly, incorruptibly good; instinctively, infallibly wise—wise not for self-development but for self-renunciation; wise, not that she may set herself above her husband, but that she may never fall from his side; wise, not with the narrowness of insolent and loveless pride, but with the passionate gentleness of an infinitely variable because infinitely applicable modesty of service—the true changefulness of woman." Essentially, that is a husband's conception of a true wife today. And that is fundamentally the kind of wife a wise woman will want to be today.

We do not express the rules and suggestions in such arrogantly blunt form today. Over three centuries life has become more complex and love has become more liberated and sophisticated. Vast changes have occurred within marriage itself. The nature of the family has been altered. Men and women meet in a freer manner and live and love under higher tensions. But women still pursue men (being careful to make it appear that the reverse is true), and wisely so (object: matrimony). Wives still value their husbands; a bad marriage is still a tragedy.

Women have always had—and still have—a greater stake in matrimony than men. Wives have made—and still make—more sacrifices for the sake of the family and home. Lord Byron wrote, "Man's love is of man's life a thing apart; 'tis woman's whole ex-

169

istence." He might easily have substituted "marriage" for "love." Whatever the prevailing theories of equality, men remain the adventurers, the providers—men are busy outside the home, and their marriage is only a part of their lives. To most women, marriage is all their lives, and anything else is incidental.

Most wives who fail today are unable or unwilling to accept this fundamental truth. In many of my wedding ceremonies the bride asks the privilege of placing a ring upon her husband's finger; the ring—unbroken and unending—seems deeply symbolic to me, and I have often wanted to hope aloud that she would do all in her power to keep the circle of marriage unbroken and unending.

Wise wives know that marriage means not only the possession of a husband, but also the welfare of the children, economic security, social status, protective companionship, and hope for future happiness. They also know that the success of the marriage generally depends much more on the behavior of the wife than on that of the husband.

Most wives who make a success of marriage do so because they begin with the realization that it is their most precious relationship, and plan an ordered, calculated program for its preservation—making a large allowance for necessary sacrifice and even suffering. In *The Neurotic Personality of Our Time*, Karen Horney has pointed out, "While men grew up into the conviction that they had to achieve something in life if they wanted to get somewhere, women realized that through love and love alone could they attain happiness, security, and prestige. This difference in cultural positions has had a momentous influence in the psychic development of man and woman. One of its consequences is that in neuroses women more frequently than men will use love as a strategy." *

* From *The Neurotic Personality of Our Time* by Karen Horney; published by W. W. Norton & Company, Inc.

Although she was not explicit, Dr. Horney must have meant *married* love. Certainly in our social order the strongest love cannot bring a woman lasting happiness, real security, or prestige if it is outside the bonds of wedlock. Woman has made great advances in our century, in political rights, educational advantages, economic opportunities, social privileges, but her lasting happiness as a woman still depends on marriage.

It is not so much the getting as the holding of a husband that is woman's greatest challenge. Marriage itself is only a beginning, the consummation of all the desires and affections that rise between a man and a woman as they come to know each other. It is when the emotional exploration is over that the spiritual exploration must begin, and this occurs sometimes long after the wedding ceremony. This is not conquest or the fulfillment of desires; this is the establishment of compassionate and mature love, based more on giving than on taking. And there are many men and women who never acquire the capacity for this kind of love; who never outgrow their immature longings for immediate pleasure or exotic sensation.

A few years ago, speaking before the American Association of Colleges, Dr. Lynn T. White, Jr., President of Mills College for Women, expressed his conviction that women were losing their hold on men. "One of the things to blame for this," he said, "is the concept of romantic love. Untold numbers of women have been deluded by the romantic craze into entering inherently unstable marriages. The movies, the radio, and the entirety of modern fiction today present marriage as the consummation of a courtship—based on sex attraction and nothing else—rather than as a process by which a man and a woman live together for a lifetime.

"Another reason women's hold is growing weaker," he added, "is that women live longer than men. Women are . . . tough and men die in higher proportion than women and now in America we have a surplus of women. What of the future, when perhaps several million American women will be unable to have husbands and families, even if they want them? The road back is the development of self-confident womanly women."

Many brides believe that the marriage license, the ceremony, the wedding ring, the exchange of vows are enough to transform a romantic attachment into a permanent relationship. Their great love, they feel, will conquer all. Well, love will conquer; but not their kind. Not a love which ignores and does not prepare for the problems and purposes peculiar to marriage. Not a love too romanticized to face reality: the threats and tragedies that lie in wait for every couple. Not a love, in short, based on medieval romances rather than modern realities.

I wish I could make every bride understand that once she has her man, her work has only begun, not ended; it is play which has ended. Her beauty, the small attentions and strategems with which she has won him will not be enough alone to hold him. Living together reveals on both sides unsuspected faults and deficiencies; and if marriage is based on the temporary illusion of perfection, it will crumble when that illusion is shattered. Both bride and groom must add new strengths and virtues to the union —and often they are the strengths and virtues of self-denial; they must extend their love to wider areas, not restrict it to each other's persons; they must lift their love to higher levels of communion.

The key to success as a wife is to be confident, foresighted, and womanly; taking romanticism as her luxury and realism as her necessity; bringing intelligence as well as sentiment to the relationship; working at marriage as her vocation; and regarding the role of wife as a skilled profession that requires learning through experience and applying new skills to new problems.

The love that is woven into marriage is stronger than the love that started it. This later love is born of mutual respect; it is born of troubles shared; it is born of the frustration as well as the realization of common plans; it is born as much of losing as of winning. It becomes, ultimately, the love described in the Song of Songs: "For love is as strong as death—the flashes thereof are flashes of fire. Many waters cannot quench it; neither can the floods drown it."

Marriages, in other words, don't stay young forever, and neither do the parties to them. Even in the early years there are new problems every day. The wise wife will bring new understanding to each day; she will try always to be a few steps ahead of trouble. She will realize that love and happiness are intertwined, and she will want her husband to have much of both. She will smile appreciatively at the story of the man applying for life insurance, who filled in the name of the beneficiary, his wife, and under the word "relationship" wrote, "Nice."

But so many brides simply cannot understand all this, because of stupidity or stubbornness or smugness or arrogance. Carried away by the first flush of love, they relax, and assume that happiness is theirs forever. And when it's too late, when they have wasted their early years in romantic dreams, they waste their later years in weeping over lost joys. Remember Lola, in *Come Back, Little Sheba?* She told her husband of her dream: "I saw Little Sheba—she was lying in the middle of the field—dead. I cried and cried. . . . That sweet little puppy—her curly white fur all smeared and no one to stop and take care of her. . . . I don't think Little Sheba's ever coming back, Doc. I'm not going to call her any more."

"Little Sheba should have stayed young forever," Doc mutters. "Some things should never grow old. That's what it amounts to, I guess."

So much for the first failure in marriage: the failure through sentimentality.

Two men are talking. The first says, "These shoes are so tight they're killing me."

"If they're so tight, why don't you take them off?"

"Listen," comes the answer, "when I get home tonight, supper won't be ready; if it is, it won't be fit to eat. I not only have to look at my mother-in-law, I have to listen to her. My daughter married a man I can't stand, and they have four of the meanest kids that ever walked. My dead-beat brother-in-law will be sitting in the only easy chair in the house, and the only pleasure I have when I get home is taking off these tight shoes!"

If a man's moods are normal and whims reasonable, he deserves to have them respected. When he wants quiet at home in the evening, the chances are he needs an antidote to the bustle about him all day, and it's not a lack of interest in the household. If his temper is short, his manner impatient, he is probably taking out on his wife and family some anger he couldn't express to an employer or employee or customer. This is hardly praiseworthy— see a fine James Joyce short story, "Counterparts"—but it is surely understandable. And where can he go for peace and sympathy, but to his own home, created by his own sacrifices?

There *are* times when children should be seen and not heard; when in-laws ought not to be visiting, or relatives intruding; when garrulous friends should take their gossip elsewhere. There are also times when the children ought to be swarming all over him like puppies, when relatives and friends ought to be adding to the cheer of an evening at home. If a wise wife grants the one thesis, she must grant the other. There are times when a soft answer turneth away wrath, when silence is more soothing than speech; and there are times when nothing is as animating and heartening as a good noisy conversation. Must a husband have all of one and none of the other? Home, says the cynic, is where you hang yourself. It is up to the wise wife to prove him wrong.

And now we come to the housewife, which is a less and less respectable word in this country as time goes on. The image usually conjured up is that of a sweet old lady with white hair and octagonal spectacles, bearing a vaporous apple pie and an imbecilic smile. We laugh at this image occasionally, as though the true sign of female emancipation was a pile of cigar ashes on the living-room rug, or a husband having a gloomy supper in a cafeteria. But we forget that it does not take an old-fashioned wife to create the old-fashioned comforts of home. If a free man's home is his castle, then an emancipated woman's home may be her kingdom. She can still take pride in running it well, making it not only a place where "they have to take you in," as Robert Frost says, but also where there are comforts and pleasures—where, in short, the husband will find more happiness than in other places.

A man has little time for the expression of love when he comes home simmering from a day's activity and finds his living room looking like a nursery school, his bedroom like a Montparnasse garret, and his kitchen like an abattoir. He is not likely to feel proud of his lunchtime economies when supper proves to be a can of sardines, a soggy tomato, and a cup of the morning's coffee. The notion of having left an inferno to return to Paradise will flee when he finds his wife's hair in curlers. His desire for cleanliness and bright spirits will be dampened by the sight of a hanging garden of stockings where the shower curtain should be. And when he finds opened jars of finger paint reposing on the seat of his easy chair, his cup of bitterness will be full; he can hardly be blamed for lurching out into the night, never to darken his wife's hand towels again.

No one demands that a wife be a chambermaid; but there ought to be at least a room for hubby in his own house. No one demands that she be a graduate of the Cordon Bleu; but a man who has spent eight hours in honest labor has the right to ask for one good meal. No one demands that she be an interior decorator, but dirty curtains on the windows, or wet diapers in a corner of the room, can certainly take the edge off a husband's bliss. She need not enter a class in hotel management; but she ought to be able to plan her day, organize her activities, as well as her husband does his. No home ever rises above the level of the woman who lives in it; and the most affectionate husband may be discouraged by a poorly managed home.

There is, of course, the other extreme. One of the fine classics of the American theater is *Craig's Wife*, which tells the story

175

of a woman who tries to fashion her whole life within the walls of her own home. Every room is planned with precision; the furniture has to be in its proper place at the proper angle at all times. Her husband must not lean on the piano—it scratches easily—or use the living-room couch too often—the fabric wears. No speck of dust can be tolerated on any shelf or window.

Hearing her, watching her, the audience realizes that her home has become the supreme and only love of her life. Her housekeeper, Mrs. Harold, scornfully remarks, "I've worked for three of them; you'd think their houses were God Almighty." Her aunt, Miss Austen, so fed up that after living with her for many years she decides to leave, finally says, "You want your house, Harriet, and that's all you want. And that's all you'll have at the finish, unless you change your ways. People who live to themselves, Harriet, generally are left to themselves." And the aunt proves right. When the curtain falls, everyone, including the husband, has gone out of her life forever. She is alone.

Excessive housekeeping can drive a husband to distraction and a marriage to destruction. A little dirt and a little disorder are far better than uncomfortable sterility. When in doubt, follow this rule: let the house be upset rather than those who live in it!

Even cookery can be carried to a destructive extreme. American cuisine has a bad reputation generally, and many housewives go all out to prove that they are exceptions. (The late Henry Mencken—I cannot find the passage, and will paraphrase—who had distinctive and emphatic opinions on practically everything, once wrote that the villainousness of American cuisine was so offensive to the cultured uvula that if one of its masterpieces were set before a French hack driver, he would promptly brain his wife with his linoleum hat.) But tarragon and Brie and exotic mushroomery should not become a fetish. However Dionysian the cuisine, a woman who devotes so much care to it that she neglects her appearance, the cultivation of her mind, her consideration for others, normal conversations with her husband, is in danger of losing him.

176

A woman may become a demonic housewife because she is unable to face the more demanding and complicated responsibilities of marriage. It is easier to cook and clean than to read widely, converse intelligently, and share compassionately in the deep and urgent problems of life and love. It requires less concentration, less giving of oneself, to knit and sew—women knit and sew while playing bridge, watching television, listening to (but not necessarily hearing) lectures—than to cultivate the mind and spirit, or to participate in community affairs. And many a wife will sometimes duck those greater responsibilities by busying herself with housekeeping.

She also limits herself. What possibilities are there for a future of broadening intellect and expanding vision, if she is buried in housework? How will her husband ever be able to say to her these words of Carl Sandburg: "I love you for what you are, but I love you yet more for what you are going to be. I love you not so much for your realities as for your ideals. Not always will you be what you are now. You are going forward to something great. I am on the way with you and therefore I love you." Her becoming is over and ended. Her future is in the past. Her ideals are now repetitious ruts.

When God made woman a mate to man, He commanded, "Therefore shall a man leave his father and his mother. He shall cleave unto his wife and they shall be one flesh." Not all men are able to obey that injunction to independence; but women by far are the greater offenders.

Women frequently cling with such tenacity and intensity to their parents, their mothers particularly, and occasionally brothers, sisters, and other relatives, that they can never become real wives. And when motherhood comes it is often the end of wifehood. (It is interesting to note that the happy union of Adam and Eve was not complicated by children until they had left the Garden of Eden.) With his usually cynical, but always quotable, expressiveness, Ben Hecht asserts, "I have observed that children are as likely to wreck marriages as to cement them. A thing in common is not the same as a man and a woman having each other. A child is always a lover's rival and usually another child's undoing —which is the same thing. For lovers are in part children, with the demands of childhood lingering in their embraces. . . . In marriage a woman fulfills herself by child-bearing; a man does not; nor does a marriage fulfill itself by producing children, nor even cement itself."

These remarks are as open to exception as any generalities; they do, however, call attention to one of the commonest dangers— often unperceived—to marriage. A husband and a wife, when they have a child, too often fail to learn how to hold each other along with that child. If a wife really feels that she fulfills herself by bearing a child, she will fail her marriage. A child is only a partial fulfillment—as is a home, or a special interest, or a career. A wife must remember that only her husband can bring her complete and eternal fulfillment.

Why cease to be a mate as soon as you have become a mother? Yet women do. There is the fanatical mother even as there is the fanatical housewife. She takes far too seriously the old sugary sentiment, "God could not be everywhere, so He made mothers." She is so completely mother that she ceases to be wife. It was Cornelia, the wife of Sempronius Gracchus, who, when a Roman matron pointed to her own precious gems, presented her sons and said, "These are my jewels." I have often wondered how good old Sempronius felt about that statement.

There are even childless wives who lavish maternal affection on their own mothers and fathers, or sisters and brothers, or nephews and nieces. They transfer to them too large a proportion of the affection and attention that is normally due to their husbands. And most wives are proud of this; they flatter themselves on being "good daughters," and cannot realize that what they give to others, they take from their husbands. I have even seen remarkably happy and stable marriages ultimately broken because of the wife's excessive devotion to a relative.

A wise wife, whatever her fondness for relatives, however many children she has, will always give her husband the major portion of her thought and time. He is not her first love in time; but he is in importance, and he always will be. And it is worth remembering that the most valuable service she can perform for her children is to present them with a constant example of devotion and happiness in marriage. (Probably the broken home is a cause of delinquency not only because there is no time for, or interest in, the children, but also because the children have no example or atmosphere of genuine human affection. A good marriage, then, ought to be an effective preventive.)

There is no substitute for a wife's close relationship to her husband. Other relationships and friendships may supplement it, but should never supplant it. In devoting herself to others whom she loves, the wife must not hurt him whom she promised to love with all her heart for all her life.

So much for a second group of failures in marriage: failures through misdirected effort.

Companionship, through a few of its synonyms, has become a very popular concept in the last few years. What it consists of is still not clear. The general opinion is that two people who are physically together, of the same level of intelligence and emotional maturity, and who enjoy doing the same things, can live their lives in transports of togetherness.

But couples can be completely together even when they are far apart in space and time, in thought and temperament. During the last war there were wives and husbands separated by thousands of miles and two or three years, who yet had a sense of companionship. There have always been marriages where one spouse was much older than the other, more intelligent, more sensitive, better educated, where there was nevertheless full companionship between the two.

Compassion comes back into the picture here—indeed, it has been implied in every paragraph of this book. A good companion is one who senses the needs, desires, and difficulties of another. In marriage our opportunity to learn these needs, desires, and difficulties is much increased, which enables us to develop compassion, sensitivity to the other partner, as a high art. All the words used to describe the companionable wife or husband bear this out: "good sport," "pal," "she understands me."

In *Immortal Wife*, Irving Stone has Jessie respond to John Frémont's proposal with these words: "I could not marry a man who would not let me work by his side as an equal partner. Call me Anne Royall, if you will; my mother has done that a hundred times. But I am not a feminist. You will never hear me cry for equal rights for women. I believe that the greatest job a woman can do in this world is to be a good wife. But I believe to be a good wife a woman must stand shoulder to shoulder and brain to brain alongside her husband. . . . I will never embarrass you, John Frémont. I want no credit or limelight or public acclaim. I will never stalk the street with a bundle of causes in my hand so that friends will duck down side alleys when they see me coming. But I want to help you. I want to make my own small contribution to your work. I want to extend your reach by just a little bit. That little bit of which I am capable." *

There is a vital difference between the good companion and the submissive wife. The latter makes a good wife, but not a Jessie Frémont. Her chief concern is her husband's welfare. She ministers to his physical needs, eases his anxieties, soothes his irritations. She is with him when he wills it, and out of his way at other times. His word is law, his deeds are praiseworthy. Like Ruth of old, this wife asks only, "Entreat me not to leave thee and to return from following after thee; for whither thou goest I will go and where thou lodgest I will lodge; where thou diest I will die, and there will I be buried."

There can be no complaint about this wife; but the good com-

---

* From *Immortal Wife* by Irving Stone; copyright 1944 by Irving Stone. Reprinted by permission of Doubleday and Company, Inc.

panion is made of sterner stuff. She helps make stronger the will and substance within her husband. She makes sacrificial efforts to understand him, to appreciate his qualities honestly. She helps in his struggles, and is not content merely to heal his wounds; she shares his suffering, and does not simply offer solace when it comes. She does not rest until she has poured a part of her own spiritual strength into his being, so that because of her he is just a bit finer, reaches a bit higher, becomes a bit nobler than he was before she came his way.

Here is Jessie Frémont again: "I know that most men prefer the amusing and charming wife who will bear their children and manage their houses and be there when they come home from a day's or a year's work. It is a full-time task to bear children and raise them and watch after the health of the family and keep the home beautiful and peaceful so that they can grow up to be fine human beings. It is enough for any woman. . . . It is not enough for me. . . . Since I am a woman I must work through my husband and so I must find a husband who will let me achieve this ambition, who will allow me to become as indispensable in his work as in his life."

We would have little sympathy for an athlete, a judge, a soldier who trained rigorously for the heights of his profession—the major leagues, a general's star, a Supreme Court appointment—and who, upon reaching those heights, threw everything away by allowing his mind to dull, his body to grow flabby, his instincts to atrophy. Yet we accept the same course of conduct on the part of a woman who remains attractive and companionable only until she has snared her husband—at which point she begins to let herself fall apart. An attorney explained a recent divorce situation: "All was well in this family for years until Mrs. K. started eating too much. When they were married she weighed 125 pounds, and was very attractive. Then she stopped watching the calories. Now she weighs 190. Mr. K. is willing to try a reconciliation, but only if she regains her old svelte figure."

181

"How far down does he want her to slim?"

Mr. K. spoke up. "Oh, to about 125 or 130."

I have seen brides diet themselves down to 110 pounds for the wedding day, and then balloon to 150 a year later, without benefit of pregnancy. And I have sensed their husbands' disgust even as the women giggled, "Oh, well, he doesn't mind. He loves me."

He does mind. To assume that physical appearance is of less importance after marriage than before, is to insult the husband gratuitously. Men fall in love with individuals—with minds, hearts, and souls, as well as bodies—but those individuals are women, and their husbands love their femininity. A wife must keep herself as trim and clean and lovely as possible. How many wives even consider their husbands' taste when buying clothes? Yet they should. The dressing gown at breakfast is as important as the nightgown at bedtime, and at forty even more than at twenty. It has been said: "A German looks down on a woman; an American looks up to a woman; a Frenchman looks at a woman." A wife ought to be very sure to bring out at least this one Gallic trait in her husband. Sacha Guitry once said, "An ideal wife is one who remains faithful to you but tries to be just as charming as if she weren't."

I have read and noted this perceptive passage: "The woman must be talented as a woman, and it will not much matter although she is talented in nothing else. She must know her *métier de femme* and have a fine touch for the affections. And it is more important that a person should be a good gossip (the word is here used in its old meaning) and talk pleasantly and smartly of common friends and the thousand and one things of the day and hour than that she should speak with the tongues of men and angels —for a while together by the fire happens more frequently in marriage than the presence of a distinguished foreigner to dinner. . . . You could read Kant by yourself if you wanted, but you must share a joke with someone else. You can forgive people who do not follow you through a philosophical disquisition; but to find your wife laughing when you had tears in your eyes, or staring when you were in a fit of laughter, would go some way toward a dissolution of the marriage."

Keeping the feminine touch is of prime importance. Often a woman finds that she must assume leadership in the household; that her husband, whom she loves, is unable to provide enough money, or is unable to command the children's respect. She faces the job of taking command in areas that are traditionally the man's. She must, in other words, assume certain masculine obligations. The danger is that the masculinity will affect her manner, her voice, her attitude.

Even when she is most bowed under responsibilities—when she must endure, and command—let it be her heart that guides her in the relationship with her loved ones. Let hers be the gentle mood, the sweet thought, the kind word. Let people not say of her, "She has the brains in that marriage. She wears the pants in that family." Overdomination of a family by the wife is as serious a tragedy as oversubmission on her part.

In one of Balzac's novels a young married woman says, "Before marriage I was a person; now I am a possession." No intelligent modern wife will want either herself or her husband to be a possession of the other. She will not consent to being entirely subservient to her husband's demands, though she will try to satisfy them. She will not be subdued by him or submerged in him. She will know that whatever she does for him or the home, her most valuable attribute is her individuality. She must not lose her life in his.

Every woman is unique. She must demand respect for her individuality. Her own talents are as valuable in their context as those of any living being; and to be forced to deny them, or waste them, in marriage is nothing short of tragic. One way to keep respect, to fight the domination of the husband, family, or world, is to assert femininity; to remember in all you do the nobility of your sex.

So much for these failures, which are the failures of femininity.

Occasionally—more and more in our time—a woman develops talents for work outside the home: for a career. These talents naturally clash with her domestic responsibilities, and a good deal of the periodical literature of the last two decades has dealt with this conflict.

In its most serious form, the conflict disables the woman for domesticity not because she gives time to an outside interest, but because she fails to do so—because in repressing a desire that yearns for fulfillment, she drives herself to a point where she is psychologically unfit for true wifehood, regardless of her years of rich experience and conscientious work. She resents denying herself the outside interest; and has nowhere to express the resentment but in the home.

This happens generally because the conflict between career woman and career wife is blown up disproportionately. There is no necessary contradiction between the two. All wives have some interest that is not purely domestic, some thought or talent which develops as their own, some program that they carry through to completion and stamp with the mark of their individuality.

Many of the most successful wives I know are also successful in a profession, a business, church or charity or civic task. And their husbands never complain about these outside activities; on the contrary, they praise them constantly. One among my friends is a concert pianist; another a college professor; another a crack saleswoman; another a private secretary. A number of them are dynamic leaders in community welfare organizations and agencies. Their hearts are rooted in the home; but they share their gifts with the world. Their husbands come first; but there is something valuable left over for others.

Of course there is a problem of mechanics. If there are many small children, outside work is almost impossible. With slightly older children, nursery schools or governesses must be used, and not all of us, even with both parents working, can afford these. But the mechanical problem is not the area of difficulty; mechanically, it is either possible or impossible to do outside work. The trouble lies in the psychological problem; women are convinced that by working outside they are becoming inferior parents and wives. That is not true.

For most women, outside interests are more important than we think. Childless women particularly must share in the activities of the world around them. The home, as we have said, is the free woman's kingdom; but there is no need for her to confine herself to its borders—travel, as so many have said, is broadening. Woman's roots may still be in the home; but woman's place is just about everywhere.

Women feel this unconsciously; and they may, in trying to keep their sense of home and marriage inviolate, lose their souls in the process. A woman who feels an unreasonable fear of and resistance to going out into the world may be actually afraid of something else: that she might like it too well, and come to despise her domestic responsibilities. For the woman of wisdom, this fear does not exist. She understands that her value to the home —to her husband—depends somewhat on her value as an individual. If going out into the world will make her a better individual —it usually does—she will be more of a woman, and therefore more of a wife. Her husband expects the career as a wife; he respects the career as a woman.

I heard a man say the other day that medical statistics indicate that women suffer from ulcers as much as men, but from the same ulcers—their husbands'. Not long ago Benjamin D. Paul, a professor of anthropology at Harvard, told delegates to a meeting of forty-nine health organizations that a good deal of the responsibility for the masculine ulcer could be attributed to the anxiety-generating social push of their wives. Dr. Erwin Stransky, a prominent Viennese professor, blamed women for some of the neurotic breakdowns among business executives. Women, he said, drove men harder and harder toward big money, to satisfy their feminine desires for luxury. One of the latest descriptions of the American success myth is that of the husband who achieves a stomach ulcer or cardiac condition at an early age in order to support a well-dressed widow and a handsome headstone.

There is no doubt that an overambitious, overdemanding wife can be responsible for the destruction of a husband and a marriage. I have seen wives literally drive their husbands to death (in some cases suicide) by their fanatical insistence on a standard of living higher than their husbands could afford. Measuring their needs by what their neighbors possessed, rather than by what the husband could earn, these wives are eternally restless and unsatisfied. (They are also, incidentally, very unappreciative of what they *do* have.) Occasionally these women do spur their husbands to superhuman efforts, and find, when they arrive at the top, that their husbands are no longer with them—even if the men have managed to survive the struggle.

Women often cling to the old notion that the primary test of a husband is his ability to provide. In this they are encouraged by parents, whose first question is traditionally, "What are his prospects?" Parents will even make great sacrifices in order to supplement their married children's income, thus habituating the children to a standard of living they could never reach under their own power. The psychological effect on young wives is very harmful. Inevitably, many of them become demanding and ambitious. They want a three-bedroom apartment when their own income would allow for one. Or they want a home in the country, ostensibly to give their children fresh air and good schools, but actually so they can be near their childhood friends whose husbands are doing well enough to live out there. They want a two-car garage, and they want it fully occupied. They want vacations in stylish resorts. They want, in short, what their richer or luckier friends have. The appearances are all that count; there is no appreciation of the true realities of marriage.

(The Talmud tells a symbolic story. There was a man in his prime, his hair sprinkled with gray, who became bald because he had two ambitious wives. One was young, the other old. One night the old wife pulled out all his black hair, so that he would look her age; the next night the young pulled out all his gray hair for the same reason.)

The demanding wife ends up as a nagging wife. And here is one possible fate for a nagging wife, taken from a Reuters dispatch datelined Paris:

Pierre Cotten, 47, who pushed his wife out of a window to her death because he was tired of her nagging and panning him, had his five-year sentence suspended because it was a first offense. Cotten was said to have had an excellent moral record. He told the court he seized his wife by the legs as she leaned out a window, and shouting, "If you want some fresh air go and get some," threw her out. He did not go to see what had happened to her because he was afraid she might be dead.

Nagging takes various forms, and silence can do it as well as speech. Significantly long periods of silence are often more effective than repeated pointed remarks. Nagging can be subtle as well as sharp. Withholding from a husband what he considers his rights in marriage is a form of nagging; in *Lysistrata* the Trojan women refused to cohabit with their husbands unless the men forswore war forever.

Most frequently, however, nagging consists of talk. In its extreme form, the talk is constant and tireless. Women are partial to talk as a weapon because it is not only the most effective and disturbing they have, but also the easiest to use. Not all women possess great sexual charm, fine intelligence, financial independence. But very few women lack a tongue and a temper.

There is a whole folklore about the female tongue. Thomas A. Edison, introduced at length by a toastmaster who dwelt on the invention of the talking machine, replied modestly, "I thank the gentleman for his kind remarks, but I must insist upon a correction. God invented the talking machine. I only invented the first one that can be shut off." An eight-year-old, asked to compose an essay on Quakers, wrote, "Quakers are very meek people who never fight or answer back. My father is a Quaker, but my mother is not."

Nagging women will often achieve their immediate goals—the temptation to yield for the sake of peace is irresistible to most men —but they fail to realize that in doing so they may have laid the groundwork for a resounding failure in marriage. To change the metaphor, nagging is a boomerang.

A marriage expert has written, "A large proportion of our divorces would never have been, had there been habitual nice things instead of bitter and unhappy things said during marriage." This reminds us of the man who came running out of his house in high glee. A friend asked him, "What's it all about?"

"My wife almost called me 'Honey'!"

"Almost?"

The man shrugged. "She called me Old Beeswax."

Some time ago psychologist Nathan Kohn, Jr., a personnel consultant, delivered an address entitled, "The Care and Feeding of Husbands." He was speaking to the wives of men gathered in Washington for a convention of the National Industrial Advertisers Association. Among other things, he said, "Your husband and all of us who try to think have tremendously increased pressure. When he comes home, he wants to discharge tension. He wants to get something out of his system. But there is the wife. She is thinking, 'Oh, good; he can watch out for the kids so I can get things on the table.' Try to put yourself in his place; try to understand." He continues with specific advice, and concludes, "You have to be willing to not talk too much so he can tell you his troubles."

The wise wife must remember that if she herself puts the marriage relationship on a material basis—if she concentrates on what her husband can give her—he will soon fall into her way of thinking, and lose all affection for her. Marriage will then become a business, at best a system of barter. But the wise wife will know that it is more essential not to fall from her husband's side than to rise above him, or even to help him rise above others.

She will become ambitious for him, but for his own spiritual good, and not for herself. She will help him demand the best within himself, not for his or her vanity, but because she knows that both should be struggling to find the best in themselves. She will help him, in short, to fulfill his human potentialities.

In John Klempner's book, *A Letter to Five Wives*, which became the excellent motion picture, *A Letter to Three Wives*, Addie Joss, a seductive, man-hunting, unattached female, wrote her social friends as follows: "Afraid I can't be with you, dears—I'm on a little mission which may interest you greatly because it's going to take me from you for good. Do I hear you shouting, 'Good'? All right. Shout while you can. And then it will be my turn. I'd hate to leave you empty-handed, so I thought I'd take along a little souvenir, something I hope you can spare—one of your husbands. Do you mind? . . .

"Which one? You do want to know, don't you, dears? Well now, it might be any one. Any one! Any one of five—five devoted husbands running off with Joss. Unfortunately, I could take only one. Some day I may make the rounds, but which one this time? Go ahead! Stare at each other. Try to look unconcerned. Pretend that it couldn't possibly be yours, and know in your heart it could. So worry, my dears, and suffer." *

Each of the five wives who receive this letter does worry and does suffer. Each reassures herself time and again that it couldn't be her husband; yet each, thinking back on her marriage, knows full well that it could be. Each, facing herself as a wife, becomes conscious of many things done, many things left undone, that might, cumulatively, have brought her marriage to this tragic climax. Each spends a long and unhappy day, waiting for the night to reveal one broken home. The story ends happily for all five; the tempted husband has changed his mind. But the wives

* From *A Letter to Five Wives* by John Klempner; published by Charles Scribner's Sons.

have learned a lesson: that you can't love a husband for a time and then ignore him; that keeping a man is a full-time job; that a woman can have faith in a man only if she has kept faith with him herself.

The suspicious wife is a permanent torment to a man. The psychology of suspicion is one thing; psychologists agree generally that the oversuspicious woman is probably accusing her husband of faults and sins for which she herself has a secret hankering. But the mechanics of suspicion—the form it takes in the home—are unbearable. In its extreme form it consists of a constant hostile inquisition. The husband buys cigarettes; the matchbook advertises a well-known hotel; his wife sees it, and demands to know what he has been doing at that hotel. The husband tips his hat to a friend in the street; the wife, who is no longer aware of the small politenesses her husband lavishes on her, sees a sinister affair in the making.

Every oversuspicious wife ought to keep in mind this story. A husband who had a very suspicious wife let her catch him one day holding a slip of paper and tiptoeing upstairs. She followed, and saw him put the paper under a shirt in his bureau drawer. She flounced into the room, and demanded, "What's that?"

"Oh, nothing," he said, and shrugged.

As soon as he left the house she ran to the drawer, found the slip of paper, and read, "You can have that fur coat if you can resist nosing around in my bureau drawer." The poor girl was in a terrible dilemma; we have no report on the outcome.

Curiosity is a normal and valuable trait. It can be a creative and constructive source of human advancement. But in close human relationships, great curiosity that grows into acute suspicion can be deadly. This is particularly true, of course, in marriage; and it occurs most often in wives.

Consider the low opinion of wives voiced in this letter, which appeared in a "your problem" newspaper column: "As I was leaving a public building, I was pushed quite rudely by a crowd of students entering the elevator. During that moment I lost my balance, fell against a gentleman, and knew that some of my lipstick came off on his suit jacket. Before I could get his attention, he left the elevator. I had intended offering to clean it off, or at least call his attention to it. So please print this, just in case he might be married and his wife might not understand."

There must have been a few guilty husbands in town who were grateful to the writer. But I trust that there were more oversuspicious wives who were given slight pause by the letter, and who may even have examined their consciences, and recalled incidents that were most likely entirely innocent, over which they raised a fuss. Most husbands who work late are doing just that; they are not out drinking or doing the town with another woman. Most husbands who make frequent business trips do not have a sweetheart in every town. Most husbands who enjoy the company of pretty and vivacious women are not dissatisfied with their own wives.

A clergyman has told the sad story of a young woman who came to him for comfort and advice, convinced of her husband's infidelity. For a number of weeks he had told her he would be working late every evening. At first she had thought nothing of it. Then she had begun to wonder; he was arriving later and later at night. She called his office several times and got no answer. She drove around to the building; it was darkened. She became certain.

The minister persuaded her to call her husband in. Faced with her charges, he was shocked. Then he said, "My wife has accused me of infidelity. Isn't infidelity a lack of faith? If it is, my wife is more guilty than I. I've been doing extra work at night for extra money, and the extra money is for a birthday gift better than anything I've ever been able to give her before. I work in a back room far from my own office. I haven't been guilty of infidelity. My wife has. After all our happy years together, she had no faith in me."

A marriage can live on, however tenuously, without love; but without faith it is no marriage at all. A wise wife will hold on to

191

her faith in her husband regardless of any doubts, any "circumstantial evidence." She will believe the best until she *knows* the worst. And then, she should have faith in the possibility of his repentance; his self-redemption may be the salvation of their marriage.

She will keep her sense of proportion. Whenever she fears that she is losing her husband, she will consider very carefully the idea that she may be losing some quality in herself which her husband once admired and no longer finds. She will not let small differences and petty quarrels affect her judgment on large problems. She will be eager to forgive and happy to forget, if she can; she will not harp on yesterday's unhappiness, but will think more of tomorrow's possibilities. She will remember that "Love suffereth long and is kind; love envieth not; love vaunteth not itself, is not puffed up; doth not behave itself unseemly, seeketh not its own, is not provoked, taketh not account of evil—beareth all things. believeth all things, hopeth all things, endureth all things."

And so much for the failure of faith.

To sum up, a wise wife will:

1. Not simply wait for her marriage to be happy. Watch carefully and work diligently to make it so. Be sure that the end of the honeymoon is not the beginning of the end of marriage.

2. Not be too proud to be a good housewife. Know that with whatever big operations her husband is concerned outside the home, he will appreciate all the small but important things that make his house a home.

3. Beware of becoming the fanatical housewife, whose home takes precedence over the people in it.

4. Not cease to be a wife as soon as she becomes a mother. Realize that the example of a beautiful marriage is one of the most important that she can set for her children.

5. Be sure that she is at her husband's side. Be his permanent partner. Comfort him and inspire him.

6. Be feminine. Even if she must assume more than her share

of responsibility, be womanly. Whatever else he admired, her husband married the "woman" in her.

7. Not forget that a woman is an individual in her own right. Not be a servant, not be a slave. Keep her individuality.

8. Try to find satisfaction in little things, when a demand for more and better things will endanger the marriage. Not sacrifice her husband's health or happiness to her own desires; and remember that many of her own desires are vanity and nothing more.

9. *Not nag.* Not prod her husband constantly, even if she feels that it is for his own good. Not try to talk him into submission. Realize that this may gain the immediate object, but at the cost of the marriage itself.

10. Not be a snooper. Not pry, not accept suspicion as certainty. Accept, if necessary, the knowledge of her husband's waywardness with love and charity—with faith—and with the greatest of all virtues, forgiveness.

THE

PERPLEXITIES

OF

YOUTH

Chapter Nine

If youth only knew! If age were only able!
—FRENCH PROVERB

Dogmatic quotations are often as misleading as they are inspiring. The following is an example: "Youth is not a time of life; it is a state of mind. It is not a matter of rosy cheeks, red lips, and supple knees; it is a matter of the will, a quality of the imagination, a sign of the emotions; it is the freshness of the deep springs of life. . . . Youth means the pride of courage over timidity. Of adventure over the love of ease. . . . Nobody grows old merely by number of years. We grow old by deserting our ideals. . . . You are as young as your faith, as old as your doubt; as young as your self-confidence, as old as your fear; as young as your hope, as old as your despair."

But youth *is* a time of life. It *is* a matter of rosy cheeks and red lips and supple knees. Everybody *does* grow old by number of years. No matter what your state of mind—however energized you are with positive thinking, however strong the spirit of courage and adventure summoned "out of the deep springs of life," however great your faith, self-confidence, and hope—when you have crossed the border into the middle years, when your muscles are weaker and your reflexes slower, when your lungs can no longer take the long pull, or your heart the high climb, you are no longer young.

Thinking and feeling and even acting young are not the same as being young. Some of the most ludicrous, the most tragic, sights I have beheld were of older men and women trying desperately to behave like young people. I have known them to dye their hair, pluck their brows, undergo plastic surgery. They wear the wrong clothes and talk about inappropriate things. They indulge in silly flirtations and romances. They drive themselves physically, in backbreaking sports or heartbreaking work schedules. They push into associations which do not become them. All this, to convince themselves, and perhaps a few others, that they are still young.

It is sad, but youth is not a state of mind and spirit; it is a particular state of being and having. In youth our energies and abilities are at their strongest; we replenish strength and tissue faster than we use them. In youth we have drive, we are impelled by our passions and purposes. Almost everything appears attainable; certainly very little is impossible. Youth is the flood tide, the time of great expectations and unquenchable enthusiasms, when hope is highest and faith strongest. Youth looks to the future, and not to the past.

"Youth is wonderful"—either Voltaire or Shaw said it first— "but what a pity that it must be wasted on the young!" Older people sigh, "If only they had our wisdom, our knowledge and experience! How much better their choices, how much wiser their decisions; how much smoother and simpler the course of their lives." Which misses the point entirely: youth is precisely that time of life when thoughts and emotions run fast, when the visions are grand. Youth's temper is hot and quick.

There are rare exceptions among us who are able to carry the vigor and daring of youth into later life, who retain its passionate

THE ROAD TO SUCCESSFUL LIVING

devotion to dreams and ideals, and who will suffer and sacrifice for them. But as a rule only the young possess that spirit. We may deplore their lack of judgment; the fact that they carry that spirit into inconsequential or even harmful areas; but we cannot help admiring, and missing, the spirit itself. The young do not have the experience of failure and frustration to guide them; they are not cautious or calculating; and this is perhaps the true difference, spiritually, between the young and old, even those older folk who try hardest to stay young.

The strength of the youthful spirit has done much more for the world than older observers usually admit. Take the great religious movements, for example. Moses was a young prince when, in protest against the inhumanity of slavery in Pharaoh's kingdom, he slew a brutal overseer, fled into exile, and returned to bring freedom to a people in bondage. Jesus was a young prophet when he took his first step on the road to Calvary. Buddha was a young noble who left the pleasures of his father's house to search for a solution to the problems of the human spirit. Mohammed was a young camel driver when he first stirred his people to the worship of Allah.

Out of the youthful spirit have come the great scientific discoveries. Galileo, at 17, was curious about a hanging lamp in the cathedral at Pisa; his startling later conclusions were the fruit of early speculation and early labor. Newton was in his early twenties when he saw the apple fall; legend says that his statement of the law of gravity proceeded from that observation. Darwin was in his twenties when he embarked on the *Beagle*; that voyage resulted directly in his *Origin of Species*. Marconi at 21 was conducting successful experiments in wireless telegraphy. Of Albert Einstein, one of the topmost really great, truly successful men in all history, George E. Harrison wrote: "Most of what he did, woven into the mesh of all future civilization, came about from the long, long thoughts of a youth of 26. Like Newton, Einstein finished his greatest work before the age of 30. . . . It was more than youth that gave young Einstein such willingness to plunge on in new directions, to explain phenomena that had defied explanation in previous terms, but youth played a most important part."

And out of that spirit have come the greatest practical inventions. Fulton was 36 when he first succeeded in propelling a boat by steam power. Bell was 29 when he first exhibited his apparatus for transmitting sound, which was the basis of the modern telephone. Edison was 30 when he invented the phonograph, and he gave us the incandescent lamp at 32. Orville Wright was 32 when he made the first successful sustained flight in a power-driven heavier-than-air machine.

Out of that spirit have come great literary and artistic creations. Shakespeare at 36 had written his best dramas, including *Hamlet*. Although *Faust* came much later, Goethe was in the most productive period of his life at 22. Bach was 29 when he was appointed Court Concert-Master to the Duke of Weimar. Mozart was dead at 36, and left behind him a body of music never equaled for beauty, power, variety, or sheer size. At 25, Leonardo da Vinci was sufficiently famed as a painter to receive special patronage from Lorenzo the Magnificent. Raphael had produced many of his finest works before he was 25.

Out of that spirit have come great political acts—including, quite naturally, revolution. Jefferson was 33 when he wrote the Declaration of Independence, which is one of the most stirring single documents in all history. Danton was 32 when he made his moving appeal to the Estates-General for a democratic government. Lenin wrote many of his theoretical works in his twenties; at 35 he was leader of the Bolsheviks. Mao Tse-tung was at the head of the Chinese Communists while in his early thirties.

The spirit of youth is strong indeed, and for a time seems capable of conquering all; but it is subject to all the ills that may infect the human spirit anywhere. The prime spiritual ill, responsible for most of the others, is fear; and ours is an age in which fear has become almost a condition of life.

And as youth reacts strongly to the hopes and glories of its time, so youth feels the fears of its time more acutely than most. Fear of death, we say, is more a characteristic of old age than of youth; but we are wrong. An awareness of the imminence of death is stronger among the aged; but youth, with more of life to lose, may fear death—either specifically, in a given situation, or generally, in a given world—more than those of us who have lived long enough to resign ourselves to it.

Our own age is terrorized by weapons of mass destruction, the greatest of them the hydrogen bomb. Our own country is thoroughly involved in a cold war with the most formidable foe it has ever faced—communism, championed by two powerful countries that contain or control half the earth's population. Symbols and rumors of this tense situation abound: rockets and missiles, selective service, diplomatic conferences, small wars, limited wars, police actions. No young American male is exempt from registration for military service. War, or the possibility of war, is camped on our doorstep; and war affects the young most of all.

The world that has produced these dangers has also produced changes in man's inner being. During the past half-century, the generally optimistic outlook of statesmen, artists, teachers, businessmen, has been replaced by a fearful pessimism. The young man of today finds little solid philosophical ground on which to base a cheerful view of the world, or of his own life. Religion and morality are in decline; science has led to secularism; the synthetic substances of materialism and skepticism have replaced the more durable elements of idealism and faith. In the present climate of declining virtues and shifting values, it is hard for youth to find a respected authority, a solid basis for thought and action.

As if this were not enough, young people find themselves woefully confounded by the double standard of the adult world. At home, in school, in church, they have been taught to obey the Ten Commandments and to follow the Golden Rule. When they start their careers they discover that their elders have added an eleventh commandment which nullifies the original ten: "Thou shalt not be found out." Instead of doing unto others as you would have them do unto you, it is quite respectable for you to do them out of as much as you can, as long as it's within the law.

Angelo Patri puts it bluntly: "A good deal of the trouble we are having with our young people we can lay at our own door. We, by active example, contribute to their confusion so they scarcely know right from wrong. . . . When a youth enters the business world he sees people who buy things they don't pay for, run up bills and pile up debts they don't pay, don't intend to pay. He hears a businessman make promises he knows he cannot make good. He sees another taking an unfair advantage of someone who trusted him. In civic life, he listens to a politician promising things he knows his audience approves, and then he sees him after election, forgetting all about these promises, do what he said he would not do, and not do what he said he would do. Cheating, isn't it? Soon, youth is disillusioned."

So in the bright lexicon of today's youth there *are* such words as failure, despair, deceit. And words engender feelings; many of our young people are far too ready to "adapt": to give into the fears and neuroses of the age, to heed the voices of doom, to assume that since we are all liable to lose everything at any moment, the only course of action is selfishness, the acquisition of goods and the enjoyment of pleasures by any means at hand—even immoral or illegal means. And the sum of all these failures and feelings of failure, of all these panicky gropings after self-satisfaction, is quite simply the failure of faith.

For youth to be distressed, even depressed, by the sorrows of mankind is no new phenomenon. Young people have always been tempted to follow—without fully understanding—the ancient hedonistic dictum, "Eat, drink, and be merry, for tomorrow we die." Yielding to that temptation is not simply the blind and irrational adoption of a cynically fatalistic attitude toward life; there are real causes for it, and in our own age they seem to be more compelling than ever before.

There is another contributing factor, perhaps specific to our time. There are many more older people in this country today than there have ever been before. The "population curve" stays high for much longer. Youth is outnumbered and outvoted; the accession of youth to positions of responsibility and policy-making is delayed. Youth finds its opinions undervalued, or indeed ignored. And yet we live in a world where more and more of our actions are controlled, or at least suggested, by the government or the cultural climate. The result is a feeling of oppression on the part of youth. Education is better and faster, marriage takes place earlier, young people assume the responsibilities of soldiering and taxpaying and voting; yet they have no voice in public affairs. Their elders, while making hash of world affairs and human relations, are "keeping them in their place." Whether or not the younger folk would do better is, for the purposes of this discussion, unimportant; the youngsters feel, quite rightly, that their influence over their own world—which is in a bad state—is kept to a minimum. Small wonder that resentment, turning to cynicism, turning to fatalism, is bred!

The nature of youth has not changed appreciably during the history of the human race. The qualities and capacities of youth have changed only in the specific terms of the opportunities available, the state of civilization at the given moment. Lately the chances of the human being for a longer and healthier life have been changed markedly for the better.

Yet young people seem to have changed. They seem to have lost faith in the one possession of which they cannot be deprived: their youth itself. They have, in a way, become spiritually old before their time. They have been enticed by the temptations, or frightened by the terrors, of our pleasure-intoxicated and bomb-shadowed world. They have forgotten that it should not be their destiny *to be changed by the world*—to be forced to adapt, and to lose their individuality; it is rather their destiny *to change the world*, to shape it to the requirements of their own vigorous, compassionate, and perceptive natures. As the Prophet put it:

"Your young men shall see visions, and your old men dream dreams." Dreaming of "a better day," or a "Golden Age," is a pastime for the elderly. The young must see the future and find a way to build it.

The spirit of youth in its original essence—independent and idealistic, adventurous, aggressive, confident, courageous—is still with us. It seems now and then to have been abjured by this generation, but it is only dormant. In itself, it is still challenging, exciting, creative, fearless. The real danger is not that it will disappear—it could never do so—but that it will be dampened deliberately by youth, for the sake of acquiescence and safety.

The only people who really fail in their youth are those who reject youth and its spirit. In doing so they are rejecting their potential for success in the future. They are training themselves early to give up individuality for the sake of personality. They have forgotten that the great failure in life is he who has failed to dare, not he who has dared to fail.

A great expression of this spirit of youth, in words of inspired wisdom, was given by Louis Pasteur at the end of the nineteenth century. In its way, that time was much like ours, plagued by disillusionment and doubt, the traditional foundations of morality and religion cracking, the heavy pillars of established economics and politics crumbling. Pasteur was speaking at a celebration of his own seventieth birthday, in the theater of the Sorbonne in Paris.

Almost immobilized by the paralysis that had crippled him in the prime of his life, his voice reduced almost to a whisper by the intensity of his emotion, aware that he was close to the edge of eternity, he suddenly stopped and looked up at a group of young students in the galleries. "Young men," he cried, with added strength and conviction, "whatever your careers may be, do not let yourselves be discouraged by the sadness of certain hours which pass over nations. . . . Live in the serene peace of laboratories and libraries. Say to yourselves first, 'What have I done for my instruction?' and as you gradually advance, 'What have I done for my country?' until the time comes when you may have the immense happiness of thinking that you have contributed in some way to the progress and the good of humanity. But whether our efforts are or are not favored by life, let us be able to say when we come near the great goal, 'I have done what I could.' "

The most tragic figures to enter my study are young people who have lost the basic virtue of youth: faith. Their eyes are weary—and wary—with the look that ordinarily comes only with experience. Their bodies sag under a weight of discouragement and depression. Their speech is bitter and cynical, far beyond the mild and intelligent bitterness and cynicism of some mature minds.

Many of them have no love or respect for their parents. They find no value or purpose in religion. They scoff at ethics and morality. They point out to me the injustices of our economies and the inequalities that mar our democracy. They dwell on the hypocrisy and iniquity that mark the maneuverings of nations on the international chessboard. They see no good in the present and no hope for the future.

What fragrance is to a flower, faith is to youth. Whatever their advantages and talents, if young people do not breathe forth faith, then they have already lost much of their value as individuals. Young people who enter college, a business, a profession, with a deprecatory skepticism, questioning and even denying the value of the subjects they study or the work they do, manifesting no confidence in their activities or objectives and no enthusiasm for the purposes and people they serve, making no sacrifices for a cause they consider right or an ideal they regard as holy—these young people may have all the appearances of glowing life, but there is an aura of premature death about them.

Faith involves a reverence for life; and when that is lost, all is lost. Let a young man lose everything else, if necessary, but let him keep faith: faith in the world, whatever it may be in his generation; faith in his fellow man, of all natures; faith in himself, regardless of his fears and failures; faith in his future, how-

202

ever difficult it may appear. Let him feel toward life—his own, as well as the lives of all men on earth, as did the Roman Tribune Rienzi, who in youth heard the voice of a mystic Pythia whispering to his soul, "Thou shalt be great," and who thenceforth directed his life toward the fulfillment of the prophecy.

Someone has pointed out that the depressions of college students—and more and more American youth goes to college each year—are ostensibly associated with a variety of causes—difficulties in scholastic achievement, social dissatisfactions, infrequency of dates with the opposite sex, athletic disappointments, and so on. As is generally true, however, the apparent causes are not sufficient to explain the entire problem. Frequently a student thinks he is blue because he has been cut from the football squad, whereas in reality it was his dispiritedness that caused him to be cut. College students thrive on pep rallies, to show a team that the school as a whole is behind it. Yet many of them are incapable of restoring their own faith in themselves; many of them refuse to try, or to seek advice. They will turn to smoking or drinking or worse in order to cheer themselves, and will forget that they have within them the most powerful and persuasive of all spirit-builders: faith.

Recently Rear-Admiral Lewis L. Strauss, chairman of the United States Atomic Energy Commission, said, "In a world of new forces and new threats, in a world in which a new and terrible ideology has arisen, faith is the ultimate defense. . . . To have confidence in the future, it is not necessary to decry the dangers of the present, but to realize that these dangers are not inherent in the weapons that men may employ. They are inherent in man. . . . Therefore, for the young people who have come to me to ask: 'Why should I go to college? Why should I study? Why should we marry? Or, having married, why risk bringing children into this kind of world?' I do have a response and a philosophy. The response is, 'By all means do pursue a normal life. Acquire an education and if you are gifted, enter a learned

203

profession. . . . Marry—rear children, for they are the hope of the world. And finally, there is a philosophy for our times—it is a philosophy of faith.' "

Young people ought never to be too proud to turn to others for help—*but those who do it habitually have already lost faith in themselves.* During the most difficult days of the depression of the 1930s, Newton D. Baker liked to tell the story of the son of a family friend who came to see him in his office. "What can I do for you?" the Secretary asked, apprehensively.

"I've come to say goodbye, Mr. Baker," the young man said. "I won't be seeing you for a long time."

"Where are you going?"

"Up to Nova Scotia."

"Why?"

"Well, I can't find a job with much of a future in the States, so I'm going to Canada to try fur trapping."

"Do you know anything about fur-bearing animals? Do you know how cold it can get that far north?"

"No, but I'm young and I'm willing to work, and I'd like to make my own way. If others can do it, so can I."

The Secretary rose and shook his visitor's hand, obviously moved. "May I thank you and congratulate you," he said. "Of all the hundreds of young men who have come to see me in the last few years, you're the first person who hasn't asked me for something—a secure job, or a substantial loan, or an outright gift. You're the only one who has gone out on his own; who, in the true spirit of our early pioneers, is prepared to sacrifice and suffer in order to carve out his career; to go anywhere—to the ends of the earth if necessary—but to do it himself. You have restored my faith in American youth."

There is, of course, such a thing as being too independent. Youth is naturally individualistic and isolationist; age is normally collective and co-operative. Youth has the whole world before it, and likes to be self-sufficient and self-reliant. This may be true of peoples as well as individuals; compare the American people, a young nation, with any of the European peoples or nations. Youth likes to go it alone and to have it alone.

I have often thought that the real Paradise for Adam—that Paradise that really made a man of him—was not Eden, from which he was exiled, but the world into which he was thrust, to earn his bread by the sweat of his brow. Too early and too much help for young people is more often a curse than a blessing. It may bring them outer success, but inner failure. It may destroy their spirit of youth—confidence in their ability to get ahead on their own; courage to adventure and experiment; capacity to sacrifice for an ideal. It often deprives them of the joy of knowing that what they pursue and attain is of their own choosing and creating, born of their own desires and dreams, built by their own hands and hearts. Their occupation may be relatively unimportant, their accumulation of goods insignificant, their kudos from the rest of the world nonexistent. But whatever they are and have will be the reward of their own intelligence and abilities.

When a young man, about a year ago, refused to accept an inheritance of $400,000, millions of young people must have believed him literally insane. They could understand, perhaps, that he did not want the money for himself; but why couldn't he accept it and use it for the good of others? But I believe that the young man saw hidden dangers in the bequest, regardless of his use of it. It would be an irresistible temptation to him to stop creating the life he had envisioned for himself, and to start spending a life created by someone else. He would escape the need for struggle; but would that satisfy the hungers within his own spirit? Perhaps he knew that so much money would so change his life that the spirit of youth would die within him.

When his life is determined by agents outside a man, he may have all the obvious satisfactions and fulfillments without the inner ones so necessary to his growth as a human being. The father who insists that his son follow in his own footsteps—who gives him a good job in the father's office, who guarantees steady advancement, who prepares a ready-made career for the boy—may be driving him to the psychiatrist's couch. In trying to spare him conflict with life, he may be creating more serious inner conflict. By assuring his son financial success, he may be destroying the boy's chances for personal, spiritual success. The most poignant dramas in art are those between generations; they are just as meaningful and bitter in real life, when sons and daughters dare to fight their parents for the sake of their own souls. In almost all the cases I have seen where children broke away from their parents, the temporary wounds were later healed; the parents were, in the end, more pleased with the children's independence than they would have been with their acquiescence.

And when the children have refused to fight, I have seen them lapse gradually into an entirely noncreative complacency. I have seen them achieve successful careers, happy marriages, prominent places in the community—but all this without a sparkle in their eyes, a zest in their activities, an excitement in their attainments. They can never forget that they live in houses that their fathers built. They miss the joy that comes with the creation of one's own life.

It is easy enough for young people to drift into a position of dependence upon others, particularly their parents. From "My father gave me life, so he owes me a living," to "I didn't ask to be born, so the world owes me a living," is not a long step. Dependence becomes habitual. And while it starts as financial dependence, it affects the whole character; ultimately the dependence becomes emotional as well, and in rare cases it may lead to neurosis and physical dependence.

I do not mean to imply that accepting help is shameful. It is not only intelligent but often necessary to ask for help from time to time. There are even young people who ought to follow in their fathers' footsteps. But these are the exceptions. What is important is to keep faith in oneself; to ask for help only in the hour of dire need; and to be sure that receiving help does not become a way out of difficulties that should rightfully be conquered by the individual himself. Young people are born with good health and great capacities; they grow into a spirit of adventure; to deny the capacities, to kill the spirit, is to destroy all possibility of independence, creativity, success, and ultimate happiness.

Fortunately in this respect, but unfortunately in another, youth has a strong tendency to disregard advice and condemn experience. Young people are inclined to mistake knowledge for understanding, and a high I.Q. for wisdom. Frequently they plunge ahead when they might better be cautious. Those with genuine ability and drive get where they want to go anyway, but usually at a higher price than they had to pay. They might have gone by a more direct route—or gone farther—if they had paid more attention to the road-signs set up by age and experience.

It is, of course, all too easy for me to say that if I were 21 again I would find out more, from those who preceded me, about the route I wanted to take. I would know that there are warnings by which I might profit; that I could learn a good deal about pacing myself, watching my stride, taking the turns, recovering from a fall. Along every road of life there are watchers ready to offer guidance. Many of them have put their wisdom into books. And all young men and women would do well to consult them without embarrassment. However well you feel you are doing, however far you have gone, you can always add another technique, a touch of style, to make the race smoother and easier. You would gain more in wisdom than you had lost in time.

And yet I am forced to the rueful conclusion that if I were 21 again, I would undoubtedly ignore these words which to me contain much wisdom. There is something in the independent nature of youth that insists on experiencing everything; even the most logical warnings from those who must know fall upon deaf ears. And I am forced to admit that there is virtue in this bullheadedness; it is as though the young knew instinctively that the setbacks they suffer will ultimately—if they can accept responsibility and not lose heart—be of more value to them than any schemes they might accept to avoid setbacks. It is, perhaps, the courage of ignorance; but it is still courage.

Paavo Nurmi, the famous Finnish miler, whose all-around grace and speed remained unsurpassed for years, wore a wristwatch in every race. He checked his time every quarter-mile; it was obvious that he was running his own race, against time and not against competition. When he had broken the tape, it always seemed as though he could have gone on, with the same effortless stride, for hours.

Nurmi was checking himself not only with the watch, but with all the running know-how he had picked up from older runners and from trainers. He was a strong runner; he was also a wise runner, who brought a mature outlook to his efforts. He must have refused many ideas offered him by well-wishers; but he never refused to consider advice. He never decided that he had reached the point where no advice could help him. He is, in a sense, symbolic of the ideal young man of our time; but the ideal is, by definition, rare. He brought to the independence engendered by self-awareness and talent, a humility born of the desire to do better. He was not afraid, as so many young people are, that the watchers, the advisers, were competitors. He knew the real joy experienced by the old pro when he can pass along his hard-earned knowledge to a beginner—or even to a young champion—and he respected that generous spirit. It did him good. He never lost a bit of his ability or character by consulting the old-timers. He knew how to create a balance between the lessons of his elders and the lessons of his own stopwatch. Every race he ran was a new and exciting experience; every day of his active life he learned something. He was talent without arrogance. The overindependent youth is simply arrogance without talent.

Many impatient younger people see youth as only a rather difficult period, full of humiliations and delays, which precedes the moment when they can pronounce themselves mature and cease listening to what they consider corny advice from their elders.

208

This eagerness to "arrive" is deadly. It generally means that five or ten years which should be among the most carefree and happy of life are reduced to unendurable dullness and savage impatience. Youth—and anyone no longer in his youth will bear me out—is a time for enjoyment, as well as preparation. In youth we may occasionally enjoy the luxury of being foolish; the penalties for lack of wisdom increase with age. Puppy love at eighteen is no tragedy; at forty it can be the ruin of a man. Fantastic speculation, or action on the basis of a very tenuous vision, is rarely tragic at eighteen; at forty it can mean permanent defeat. Youth is a time for experiment and variety. Youth is, in short, a time for excitement. The ecstasies and tragedies of youth would be unbearable to older, more settled individuals. And these same ecstasies and tragedies are among the factors that make the child a man.

The surest way to keep the spirit of youth alive is to provide it with the heady wine of pleasure and enthusiasm. Young people who concentrate so seriously on laying foundations for their future that they deny themselves the joy of enthusiasm, will find something lacking in the future when it is upon them. Those who enslave themselves to tomorrow's work will never be free to enjoy the fruits of that work. The crown of success rests easily only on the brow of him who knows how to wear it lightly.

When most older people hark back to the days of their youth, they recall the good times they had and will never have again. There are some who remember only that they never had any fun at all when they were young; they recall life as empty of joy and enthusiasm. "Of all the words of tongue or pen, the saddest are these: 'It might have been.'" Youth is a one-way street; there is no retracing your steps. Even if we retain much of the forceful and optimistic spirit of youth, we must apply it to different objects; and the intensity of emotion is never the same.

And often we are older than we think. A friend of mine, who was enjoying a highly successful medical career and seemed to be in the pink both physically and spiritually, died suddenly.

The community was shocked. The autopsy revealed that at fifty —with the spirit of a much younger man—he had the body of a seventy-year-old. This was a physical development over which he had little control. The striking contrast between the worn state of his body and the bubbling enthusiasm of his spirit was tragic.

The opposite situation is equally tragic, and Oscar Wilde has given us a classic example in *The Picture of Dorian Gray,* which is the story of a man who inherited a handsome face and a strong body, but so quickly and ruthlessly debauched his soul that he died of spiritual old age even though he retained his physical beauty. Most of us inherit bodies and spirits that would enable us to enjoy the best this world has to offer in sensible satisfaction and reasonable happiness—not only in youth, but later on also, if we had the good sense to avoid idiotic excesses. Too many of us imitate Dorian Gray, dissipating our resources and enthusiasms so rapidly that we are dead spiritually before the period of youth has ended.

And the most pathetic creatures in the world are men and women already blasé in their twenties and thirties. They've seen everything; they've done everything; they've known everything. They've been everywhere, and met everybody. There's nothing they haven't tried—and ultimately tainted. They have also lost the quality of enthusiasm; they are jaded; for them there is nothing new under the sun. They feel this way largely because they have never known how to experience anything more than surface enjoyment. Their pleasures have been sensuous, which means that they have consisted chiefly of a series of titillations. There are no more worlds for these people to conquer because they have never known any world fully enough to realize that all other worlds are different from it. One dish, one vintage, one woman, because they perceived it shallowly, seemed much like any other to them; and ultimately they lose the power even to distinguish between various *kinds* of pleasure. There is no joy in the present, for the jaded; and the future is a vision of horror and boredom.

Many of them worry seriously about their condition, but they tend to react as did St. Augustine, who revealed in his *Confessions* that when his young conscience troubled him over his mistresses, he prayed, "Give me chastity and continence—only not yet!" The blasé promise themselves that some day they will settle down, and see if the serious pursuit of maturity and a full life offers as much pleasure as the fleeting pursuit of sensation—only not yet. The desperate search for the new, the extraordinary, the super-titillating, must go on.

In one of his letters Gustave Flaubert wrote this way about the younger generation in his France: "Each vies with the other as to who shall look the palest and most convincingly say, 'I am blasé.' Blasé! What a sorry thing! Blasé at 18! Is there no longer such a thing as love or glory or work? Is everything finished? Does nature no longer exist for youth, nor flowers? Let's have no more of this."

Part of the danger is that the blasé youth is ill-equipped to handle what success may come his way later on. Early success is always dangerous; it is even worse when it comes to one who has no sense of lasting values. In general, slow and steady success makes for a firmer character and more personal happiness; inwardly, we feel that it is more legitimate, and outwardly, we see that it lasts longer.

John Marquand's *Sincerely, Willis Wayde* is a bitter success story. At one point Marquand has this to say: "The next few months of his life were the busiest and happiest Willis had ever known, since there was nothing so exhilarating as one's first taste of success and achievement. He only realized later that success had its dangerous aspects, especially early success. . . . Bright young men who come along too fast. They were tired because of premature effort, or else overconfidence had made them arrogant. At best, the cards were stacked against someone who was too good too young." *

* From *Sincerely, Willis Wayde* by John Marquand; published by Little, Brown & Company.

211

This may be true in other areas, too. I believe that one of the fundamental causes for the increase in the divorce rate is the widespread tendency for young people to go at marriage too soon, too hard, and too fast. And one of the causes of the unhappy family is that people have too many children before they are ready to be good parents.

Possibly it is the nervousness of the times that makes young people hurry so. But we must beware of impatience. Success is unlike a train; success has no fixed schedule, and we can never say that at this time, in this place, we will board it. More important than when and where we board it is recognizing it when we see it.

And don't worry about the scoffers; let them wonder about you, let them criticize if they must. When you have reached your goal, they'll be in the same spot, criticizing someone else. The impatient ones sometimes don't make it at all, and wear themselves out in the process. Better for your friends to say, "There's Charley, late," than "There's the late Charley." Avoid the situation of the actress of whom Sam Goldwyn is reported to have said, "I'll make her a star overnight, if it takes me a year."

In the twilight of his days, Robert Louis Stevenson wrote, "All my old opinions were only stages on the way to the ones I now hold, as itself is only a stage on the way to something else. I am no more ashamed at having been a red-hot socialist, with a panacea of my own, then at having been a sucking infant. Doubtless the world is quite right in a million ways, but you have to be kicked about a little to convince you of the fact. In the meanwhile you must do something, be something, believe something. It is not possible to keep the mind in a state of accurate balance and blank. Even in quite intermediate stages, a dash of enthusiasm is not a thing to be ashamed of in retrospect. If St. Paul had not been a very zealous Pharisee, he would have been a colder Christian."

Someone has said, "It is good to have been young in youth and,

212

as years go on, to grow older. Many are already old before they are through their teens; but to travel deliberately through one's ages is to get the heart of a liberal education. Times change, opinions vary to their opposite, and still this world appears a brave gymnasium full of sea-bathing and horse-exercise and bracing manly virtues. . . . Our affections and beliefs are wiser than we; the best that is in us is better than we can understand; for it is grounded beyond experience and guides us blindfolded but safe from one age to another."

There are, of course, young people who cannot enjoy their youth because of the burdens placed upon them by others, or because of handicaps inherited at birth. Even before they have completed what is now considered the necessary minimum of education, they have been forced to go to work to help support the family. Or when they are about to respond enthusiastically to the call of adventure or love or art or ideas, or to simple wanderlust, they are balked by a puritanical parent, by the sickness of a relative, by the conservative standards of the family or the community, by the lack of means.

Youth should be able to bounce back vigorously from denial or defeat, but this elasticity does not necessarily come naturally. When youth takes a beating, youth takes it hard. But the ability to snap back is not one which is easily learned later in life. Youth is the time for it. To stand up against the slings and arrows of outrageous fortune as a youth, and to learn to endure them, even to build on them, is to win half the battle of life.

In one of his wise letters the late William Allen White wrote, "In this world of sin and sorrow, Charlie, every man has to take a good many hard knocks. One of the hardest knocks to take is a dose which you are passing through. When I was a young man about nineteen years old, I had a sufficiency of that sort of delicacy. I used to contemplate murder and suicide as minor misdemeanors which I would gladly embrace as a way out of my difficulty. Every man who is much of a man has to take once or twice in his life that kind of horrible jolt. I have a notion that when the Lord gives it to him, he gives it as some sort of a test. If the man stands up under it, the Lord knows that his shoulders are broad enough to stand greater burdens and greater responsibilities which will bring him a capacity for greater usefulness in life. No man in the world ever gets his back broadened except by some weary sorrow. All you have to do during the next ten years is to be a man. Keep clean. Do not get sour and keep at work."

Plants without roots, or brittle plants, are notoriously weak in storms. So it is with people. Those who have their roots in human realities, those who have the suppleness and flexibility to ride out a disaster, are like the reeds, which survive; the others are either uprooted and blown away, or—being inflexible—broken forever. Storms leave wreckage; and the most important act for any of us, after a storm, is not to discover what caused it or where it came from, but to get out and clean up the debris. Later there will be time for thought and discussion, and for preparation against the next disaster.

Here, experience counts. Many of the most unhappy people I know had only a very brief acquaintance with trouble and suffering when they were young. And some of the happiest people I know went through years of early misery. These latter learned how to take a beating and bounce back. They learned that disaster is not spiritually permanent unless we allow it to be so. Setbacks were nothing strange to them; they could stand up under adversity, and move forward when adversity was conquered.

The others were like many young people these days: they went to great lengths to avoid sorrow. Children nowadays seem loath even to sit with their parents during a bout of illness. They make no effort to share the family's difficulties; the idea of doing odd jobs after hours is fantastic. They resent society for not supplying them with luxuries, jobs, glory. They don't realize that trouble is an education in itself, and one which will do them as much good later on as their formal schooling.

To play hooky from trouble is only to postpone to an age when they will be more painful certain lessons essential to the making of an individual and the forging of a career. Troubles are like childhood diseases; when you get them young they don't hurt, and you learn what to do about them, and you develop some immunity to them; but when you get them old, they hurt badly, and it's hard to take them in stride.

Avoiding trouble leads to the short cut, the "angle"; and this in turn leads to an attitude toward life and work that stresses the ease of acquisition rather than the pleasure of performance. Assignments—or marriages—are treated lightly, skimmed over; and credit for the rare good performance generally goes to luck or cleverness, not to the individual himself. One of the great lessons of history is lost: that true value lies in the doing of the task, not in the winning of praise. Success in life depends on conquering difficulties and accepting responsibilities; not on sneaking around the former and rejecting the latter.

In the *Diary of Moreau de St.-Méry's American Journey,* written between 1793 and 1798, are these significant observations—still largely true—on American youth:

Judging from the lack of foresight which seems to be the outstanding characteristic of American sailors, they rely on luck more than on anything else in making a voyage. They fear neither fatigue nor danger; the care necessary to prevent accidents, especially desirable in a calling where everything is hazardous, is practically unknown to them. . . . I shall repeat often that lack of foresight is the most conspicuous trait in the American character. Instead of foreseeing a thousand little annoyances caused by lack of care aboard ship, whether it be the breaking of dishes by the rolling, or the loss of provisions, or a thousand other incidents of this nature, they wait for the accident to occur; then hunt, sometimes in vain, for a way to remedy it. The lesson of today is lost for tomorrow, as was yesterday's for today.

Moreau was probably paying unconscious tribute to the American genius for improvisation, which is certainly part of what he calls a reliance on luck; but his point is well taken nevertheless.

Too many young Americans never learn to come to grips with a problem. Too few of them are aware that early problems are a blessing because they give us early experience in fortitude and persistence. And no cleverness, no luck, no genius for improvisation, will ever replace toughness of character: the courage to meet tragedy and defeat it. Sweet are the uses of adversity; and this, I think, is the sweetest.

In his definition of maturity, Dr. G. B. Chisholm, says, among other things, "Maturity is a quality of personality that is made up of a number of elements. It is a stick-to-it-iveness, the ability to stick to a job, to work on it, and to struggle through until it is finished, or until one has given all one has in the endeavor. It is the quality or the capacity of giving more than is asked or required in a given situation. It is this characteristic that enables others to count on one; thus it is reliability. Persistence is one aspect of maturity, persistence to carry out a goal in the face of difficulties. . . . Maturity includes determination, a will to achieve and succeed, a will to live."

One of the sure signs of the whole man, the mature man, is this quality of perseverance—of determination to reach a worthwhile goal which one has chosen for himself, and a willingness to stick to it—struggle, sacrifice, suffer, if necessary, in order to attain it. Not too many young people have this quality in sufficient degree. They may have it at moments; they may feel the need for it always; but they cannot always meet the need. It is the rare young man or woman who—in college, in business, in the family or the community—is prepared to stay with a job to the end, to concentrate on it regardless of the cost or the temptation to quit, allowing no interference and no interruption. This single-mindedness can be carried too far, but its value in the completion of any given job of work is inestimable. This is a part of maturity: to be so resolved that no diversion, no criticism, no persuasion, can sway you from the course that leads to your goal.

One of the most remarkable revelations of maturity in a young man is one which I read only a short while ago:

216

The proud son of an African tribal chief has surmounted another ob-
stacle in a saga of high purpose, adventure, and perseverance. It may
not sound too impressive that Udo Nikamare of Nigeria is passing
every subject in his first semester at Stanford University. But Hercules
taking on the labors of Greek mythology could hardly have felt a
greater sense of achievement than this man who lives to return to his
people as a doctor. It took Udo years of labor, planning and saving
just to make it to the United States. His first four months of adjustment in a strange land have been hard indeed. Ahead at least lie seven
or eight difficult years of intense study and scraping for money before
he can win an M.D. degree, and Udo is 26 now. "But I should be
living only half a man, if I did not go on," he says.

The only comparable intensity of effort I have recently observed in this country was on the part of the six-year-old son of
one of my friends, who expressed his ambition to be a ship's captain.

"It takes a while to learn how," he was told.

"That's all right," he said. "I'll do it." He paused, and looked
up with a kind of apprehensive determination. "How long?" he
asked. "Two hundred years?"

Bonsai, to change both the continent and the metaphor, has
been practiced by the Japanese for centuries. It is the art of
dwarfing trees into living miniatures. An expert in this art takes
a three- or four-year-old sapling, trims back its roots and branches,
and pots it. As new growth appears, he trims the tree to a desired
shape. Every few years he repots the plant and trims back the
roots. It requires many years for one tree to be fashioned to one
or another of an infinity of fascinating forms. The most exqui-
sitely beautiful of these trees have been watched and tended
for a century.

This kind of persistence and attention to detail is the mark of
the artist, and what the Japanese can bring to Bonsai young people can learn to bring into their lives. Maturity, like Bonsai, requires self-discipline, as well as knowledge and experience. It requires unstinting work. Many of the operations of the Bonsai

217

artist appear inconsequential; without them the goal would never be reached. It is a readiness to devote time and energy to the apprenticeship of everyday life that creates the conditions necessary to future happiness.

There was a time, and not long ago, when men had to put in years as apprentices to their trade before they were trusted to perform on their own. They began, naturally enough, at the bottom. They executed the most menial tasks—scrubbing floors, running errands, carrying tools, cleaning equipment, copying passages—and progressed step by step to more serious responsibilities. Part of the value of this early period was in simple familiarization; by doing the dirty work, an apprentice came to know his way around the shop, and to understand the functions of the various departments. But there was another lesson taught, more subtle and perhaps more important: that every job in the shop has its own value, and that apparently trivial or minute details contributed to the work done.

The art of concentrating on details, of taking pains with trivia, applies to life in general. Guidance counselors have been fighting for years against sloppy dress and sleazy manners, and the issue is still in doubt. Young men and women find it hard to believe that for want of a nail a battle can be lost. Men apply for jobs with uncombed hair and no ties, unshined shoes and dirty hands. Women apply for jobs—or entertain unexpected and interested young friends—in unpressed dresses, hair in curlers. It just doesn't seem worth it to take any trouble; but it is.

(Life is full of paradoxes and surprises. About a year ago in Chicago two young men were invited to luncheon at a Loop hotel to receive citations for their heroic rescue of a number of people, adults and children, from a blazing hotel fire in their run-down tenement neighborhood. The two young men were naturally slicked up and dressed to kill. They started out early, but arrived late. The police had picked them up for questioning: there had been a robbery in the slum neighborhood the night before, and any well-dressed man was obviously a suspect!)

218

What is true of dress is also true of manners. Manners are considered a hangover from the nineteenth century, or the Middle Ages, or some such irrelevant epoch. Why should the twentieth-century male bother to tip his hat? Or rise for a lady who is making more money than he is? Or mind his table manners in a world full of cafeterias and dog wagons? Or show respect for his elders, who have seemingly run the world so far downhill that manners have no value anyway?

The answer, or answers, should be obvious. For one thing, the man who shows no respect for others is not likely to have much for himself, or to receive much from his associates. For another, as carelessness in dress is physical sloppiness, so carelessness in manners is social sloppiness, which is in itself offensive to others; and it is generally felt that one sloppiness leads to another—which means that the man who finds manners too much for him is not likely to inspire confidence in others. For a third, disrespect for others often becomes contempt for others, and the man who is contemptuous of his fellow man is quite simply living in the wrong world.

Two other traits considered trivial by youth but important by the mature are humility and piety. Let us admit immediately that the words have an archaic ring. Let us concede also that the spirit of youth hardly accommodates much of either. The problem is not so much that society demands humility and piety of its youth; the problem is that the brashness of youth is irritating enough when some remnants of those virtues still exist; it is positively intolerable when they have vanished.

Two stories, one for each virtue, illustrate the point. The first is about one of the most universally disliked young men in a small town, who was a sophomore at Harvard. With characteristic brilliance and brashness, he wrote a scholarly treatise on birth control. When the news reached his friends and relatives, the universal opinion was, "What a pity his mother hadn't read it before he was born." The other story is of a Hollywood starlet who was throwing her weight around on the set, prompting a veteran to remark, "Whenever I see a youngster so carried away with herself, I remember the fly riding on a wagon, who looked back, shook his head in admiration, and said, 'Man, look at the dust I'm kickin' up.'"

Humility and piety sound archaic precisely because they are among man's oldest and noblest qualities. They are the keys to an open mind and heart; without them there is no learning, there is no love of life. True, both have been corrupted from time to time by self-seekers. There is a vast difference between an artificial humility, currying favor, and a natural humility, searching for knowledge. There is a vast difference between ritualistic piety, worshiping blindly, and righteous piety, working bravely for the creation of a better world for man and God. The Bible is admonishing the young, and not the mature, when it says, "Better it is to be of a lowly spirit with the humble, than to divide the spoil with the proud. . . . Better is little with the fear of the Lord than great treasure and turmoil therewith."

The Talmud teaches that a man's inner life should be like his outer, and his outer like his inner. Neither should belie the other; each should reflect the other. In short, the whole man should be a gentleman. Young people must realize that the outer man is an introduction to the inner; those who meet us for the first time judge us primarily by what they see and hear. It is only when they have known us awhile that they learn to appreciate our intelligence and character. And a great majority of people never do get to know us that well. They judge entirely by appearances; they think of us essentially in terms of how we look and what we say. Among them are those who make decisions about us; and among those decisions are many which, however inconsequential they may seem at the time, will affect the future.

Well, what can young people do to help themselves steer clear of failure? They can:

1. Hold on to the spirit of youth. Consider it a natural resource,

irreplaceable when wasted. Refuse to let the world corrupt or change it; use it rather to help change the world.

2. Keep faith in the world—its value and purpose—and in others as well as in themselves. Resist those who would convert them to a deprecatory skepticism or a deadly cynicism. Remain optimistic.

3. Rely on themselves more than on others; ask and expect more of themselves than of others. Be independent; feel the joy of creating their own successes and fashioning their own futures.

4. Be willing to accept assistance and advice when necessary. Not be too proud to ask questions and take suggestions from the more experienced.

5. Have fun in their youth; it will never come their way again. Remember that youth is a preparation, but also that it is a time to be lived to the full. But relate their pleasure to permanent values; otherwise it may become pleasure for its own sake; they themselves will turn blasé, and lose heart.

6. Stick to the job, whatever it is at the given moment; let nothing distract or discourage them. Concentrate; refuse to let it go half-finished. And do it well.

7. Learn how to take it. Learn to live wisely with disappointments and hopefully with sorrows. Remember that hard knocks are a part of the business of growing up; future blows will be easier to bear after a little tough early experience.

8. Be attentive to detail. Be sure not to overlook even the most trivial aspects of study and work. Learn to be thorough in the small tasks, and discover that the larger tasks will then be less imposing.

9. Watch their appearance: consider dress and manner important enough to affect their future. Courtesy is as effortless as rudeness, and makes the world a better place in which to live.

10. Cultivate the virtues of humility and piety, not as empty or mechanical devices, but as gateways to sharper perception and higher wisdom. Remember that they bring one closer to one's fellow man and to God.

THE

POWERS

OF

AGE

Chapter Ten

As you are old and reverend,
you should be wise.
—SHAKESPEARE

There is a passage in the Talmud much like Shakespeare's better
known "Seven Ages of Man." It reads: "At birth, a child is
pampered like a king. At two or three, he wallows in the mud
like a swine. At ten, he frisks like a goat. At twenty, making love,
he preens himself and neighs like a horse. He weds and has to
work like an ass. Begetting children and seeking their sustenance,
he becomes fierce as a dog. In old age, he dodders like an ape.
But if he be a man of learning, old age, with its majesty, brings
back his initial kingship."

During the past two decades, the oldster has come to the fore-
ground. A new science—geriatrics—has been born: it is the study
of the problems of old age. People are living longer, but the
world has so little experience of longevity that older people are

not always healthy and happy in modern society. We know that we must develop techniques of success and happiness for the twilight years. We dare not—and need not—let old age fail; it should be the time of mellow happiness to which men have traditionally looked forward.

The years between, when man is no longer young but not yet old, most often determine the character of old age; generally speaking these are the years between forty and sixty. It is the adult in this age group who can most easily be defeated by elements of confusion, and even chaos, over which he seems to have no control. The frustrations of the present are exacerbated by the shadow of past failure and fear for the future. Regrets and apprehensions swirl about this group; at this age a man can be so thrown off by his constant tendency to look backward with bitterness, and forward with foreboding, that he will lose his sense of life's direction. He sometimes loses even the will to go on living.

During this time the fear of failure has its most serious effects. Suddenly, a man faces himself, and cries out with Cecil Rhodes (who, after building an empire in Africa, died in his middle years): "So much to do, so young to die!" Somehow, he feels, the best years of his life have slipped away, and he is still far from the specific goals he had set for himself in the enthusiasm of youth. There is little time left to reach them; his strength and purpose are faltering. The years ahead, morever, are uncertain. He is reminded of this sobering truth often, as his contemporaries begin to lose their grip, or indeed to come to the end of their lives.

He becomes increasingly conscious of physical decline. His body can't take it; his legs tire; his step has lost its bounce. Strenuous exercise is taboo; he must consider his heart. His hair is going or gone. His eyes stumble over fine print. His work potential seems to be decreasing. And of course he will feel, in the light of these other symptoms, that his sexual power is diminishing, which is a direct attack on his feeling of strength and manliness.

He feels, too, that he is slipping mentally. His memory fails him at times; names and faces seem to blur. Learning comes harder; his quickness of comprehension and decisiveness in action are not what they were. He can't seem to remember whether or not this was always so; he is reluctant to admit to himself that age is catching up with him. But he is worried; if there are differences even now, how will it be in five or ten years?

Emotionally, he is not as stable as he was. He is more sensitive to criticism, more easily irritated. He resents remarks that previously he let pass. Problems that were once a challenge to his ingenuity have now become a burden he would be glad to shift to someone else. He angers more quickly, sulks more easily. As a result, he is more moody altogether, more often oppressed by doubt and despair.

This constant concern about deteriorating physical abilities and diminishing mental and emotional capacities adds, of course, to the difficulty of the period. A man may lose touch with his work and his family; he finds himself bored, not sure that it would be worth it to continue in the same old routine. He is not happy at home, and feels conscience-stricken away from home. He is not sure what to do with his leisure time. Is his desire for more ease and pleasure a sign of the deterioration taking place, or is it normal and natural? What balance must he strike between what he puts into life and what he gets out of it?

Questions that he once considered peripheral now become central. Other questions that he once considered answered for good, are now raised again, and more urgently. If he has decided to remain a bachelor, the question of marriage comes up. If he is married, with a family, doubts of his own and their affection rise. If his parents are alive, he begins to feel that every moment he gives to them is stolen from his own life. And of course, he doubts his success. He hears news of high school or college classmates, who have made more money and become more prominent than he. Should he change his business? Should he quit altogether, retire, enjoy himself? Should he risk everything in a last

224

fling for love and power and fame? Will he, before he dies, ever answer any of the eternal questions about life and death, truth, beauty, the direction of mankind?

Those last questions are primarily spiritual, and it is in the realm of the spiritual that he suffers most. Whatever he may have of happiness, success, serenity, he finds that the spirit of defeat and frustration is stronger. And guilt weighs heavily upon him, for his sins, or imagined sins, of commission or omission; for the betrayals of trust, the cynicism, the skepticism that have marred his relations with his fellow man; for his inaction when action might have brought wealth or glory. With all these chains of frustration and fear fastened about him, small wonder that he has little taste for the years to come.

Life does not begin at forty; but neither does it end there. The man of forty, forty-five, fifty, is a complex being, compounded of the ineradicable past and the unpredictable future, and suffering under a lively awareness of both. He is becoming acutely aware that the past cannot be recaptured, and he is afraid that the future cannot be controlled. It has been well suggested that we need a new science—"mediatrics," the study of middle age—as a prelude to geriatrics. Mediatrics would help us to discover new approaches for youth; it would help us to prepare for old age.

Well, what is old age? Edwin Markham, the American poet, expressed one side of the argument very lucidly when he was eighty-three: "Of course there is no complete defense against the declining years, but even at 100 one is old only if he thinks he is old. Man's useless period is when he begins to live in the past, to sink into anecdotage, to shuffle his feet instead of walk, to whine and complain. No man is old as long as his brain is alert, his eye bright, his courage remains to look life squarely in the face."

But this and similar expressions are perhaps more poetic and optimistic than typical. Most of us feel quite otherwise, like the woman in Robert Nathan's "The Married Look," who reflected: "As I went upstairs to wash, I thought how much of our lives as we grow older in spirit is merely getting along with things—without much joy, without much resentment. The in-difference of friends and politicians, the egotism of strangers, the cynicism of poets, the cold dislike of tax-collectors—the malig-nancy of children, the cooling off of love. And how little by little the electric currents of our being wane, and joy and grief and anger give off a milder glow—until at last, the glow fades out altogether in the dark. To find the secret of the current—to grow young again, to burn with the old bright flame—how many men have sought the secret with runes and galleons and alembics and scorpion eggs." *

The late Howard Vincent O'Brien, after spending a few weeks of his last illness at a hotel in Pasadena, wrote a column called, "How to Approach Old Age." In it he said, "In a hotel lobby, one learns some useful things about the art of growing old. The trouble is, most of us fail to study this art until it is too late. The study of it really should begin in early childhood. Grow-ing old is a grim business at best. The body doesn't improve in time nor does interest in others remain at its youthful intensity. The mental muscles stiffen and there is a resistance to face new situations. There is a tendency to stick in a polished groove of habit and to compare unfavorably with the past. Loneliness is the inevitable portion of old age unless there are new friends to replace those who have gone. And for the active career of youth and middle age must be substituted new interests and hobbies.

"This apparently is the only way," he concludes, "to ease the increasing burden of years. Old people pay too much attention to such troublesome organs as heart and kidneys—too little to the most troublesome organ of all—the tongue. To be blunt about it, they tend to be garrulous. If they listened more and talked less,

---

* From *The Married Look* by Robert Nathan; published by Alfred A. Knopf, Inc.

226

they would have more companions among both young and old. I know a woman who is in her late eighties, but also is as popular as any debutante. One reason is that she is always asking questions, always interested in hearing other people's opinions—especially those of her grandchildren and friends. She is that rarity, an interested person. And because of this she has done a marvelous job of time. Nobody even thinks of her as being old."

We can't grow young again. We can't stop our growing old. We can hold back the moment of death, but we can't prevent the process of aging. It is scientifically quite well established that aging is an endogenous process inherent in all living things. Disease and stress may appreciably accelerate the aging process, but they are not basically responsible for it.

We must accept some basic facts, and bear in mind some basic prescriptions. First, the only way to avoid old age is to die during the middle years. Second, old age has been, is, and can be for many a wonderful time of life. Third, we can learn the art of growing old gracefully. Fourth, we can make the last period of life a blessing not only for ourselves but for all those around us. And fifth, we can prepare to leave this life with a smile, happy memories, and high hopes, rather than with sorrowful regrets, wailing, and despair.

Despite the fact that the prospect of old age is not generally a pleasant one, yet we find no evidence of a general desire to avoid it. Very few individuals deliberately accept death as a preferable alternative to old age. Similarly, very few faithful believers in the doctrine of the immortality of the soul and the eternal happiness that awaits the righteous in heaven, rush eagerly into death in order to receive the rewards of the hereafter. Practically all men and women prefer to take their chances with old age. Why not, then, accept it gracefully and consider it optimistically?

The attitudes of society toward old age are in constant but slow evolution. The evolution is not regular; looking about us at other cultures we find a sharply differing treatment of the aged.

In many primitive societies old age was simply a nuisance, a burden, and the sooner the aged were removed from the scene, the better for all concerned. Dr. Ralph Ginzberg, in his article, "The Aging and the Aged," tells us that primitive people's callousness toward the aged is clear and outspoken, as their treatment of the weak and invalid is openly cruel. He reports that various methods of extermination were used, depending on climatic and economic conditions and cultural traditions. In the main, there were three methods: starvation, abandonment, and outright killing (murder or suicide).

He tells of an old Hottentot woman found in a desert, who explained her position realistically, in complete resignation: "Yes, my own children, three sons and two daughters, are gone to yonder blue mountains and have left me to die. . . . I am very old, you see, and am not able to serve them. When they kill game, I am too feeble to help carry home the flesh. I am not able to gather wood and make fire, and I cannot carry the children on my back as I used to. . . ."

In citing the cruelest examples, he reports the explanation given by a tribesman of the Chukchi tribe, in Siberia, in praise of a son who killed his aged mother: "Why should not the old woman die? Aged and feeble, weary of life and a burden to herself and others, she no longer desired to encumber the earth, and claimed of him who owned next relationship the friendly stroke which should let her cut the scanty remnant of her existence."

Among more civilized peoples, old age has generally been regarded as a special mark of God's (or the gods') favor. Mere seniority, in some areas, establishes supremacy in the family and the community.

Among the ancient Hebrews, for example, respect for old age was a divine command in the Sacred Writings. They taught "Thou shalt rise up before the hoary head and honor the face of the old man," and "The hoary head is a crown of glory," and

228

"Despise not thy mother when she is old." Of a certain famous teacher it was reported that he rose whenever he saw even an ignorant old man, "For," said he, "the very fact that he has grown old must be due to some merit." Another renowned teacher always rose before an aged heathen, because, as he said, "of the sufferings the heathen must have endured in the course of a long life." And the sages said, "Respect even the old man who has lost learning, for there were placed in the Ark of the Covenant not only two perfect tablets of the Lord, but also the fragments of the tablets that Moses had shattered when he saw the people dancing before the Golden Calf." One basic principle of the Essenes was "to honor the old and provide for them."

Some years ago, returning from a trip to the Orient, I chatted often with one of my delightful fellow passengers, a highly intelligent Japanese lady. Married to a Caucasian American, she was on her way to our country with him and her son to establish permanent residence. I asked whether she was looking forward to great happiness in a new land and a new culture. "Oh, yes," she answered with enthusiasm. Yet, just as earnestly, she added, "But I don't want to grow old in America. From what I hear and read I find that the aged receive more care and respect, and enjoy greater dignity and devotion among my own people than among yours. I shall go back to Japan to die."

I was reminded of her words when I read, in Pearl Buck's *My Several Worlds*, "China was the ideal country for the old; a pleasant place where one achieved honor merely by growing old. How often had I come on a village anywhere in China to find sitting outside the door on a bench on the edge of the threshing floor a comfortably dressed old man or woman dozing in the sun, pipe in hand, idle without reproach, loved and cared for and made much of, merely because he or she was old. When an aged one spoke, the others listened, eager for the wisdom of his accumulated years.

"It has been a shock to discover how differently the old are treated in my own country and how pathetically they try to hide the number of their years and pretend themselves as strong and able to do a full day's work. Worse almost than the injury to homeless children was it to see white-haired parents and grandparents in old people's homes and even in mental institutions, often without mental illness beyond the gentle and harmless decay of age. I suppose that the uncertainty of economic life and the insecurity of the individual alone in his struggle to maintain himself, his wife and children, make thoughtful tenderness too rare between young and old in our country. The aging feel their children's dread and they try to care for themselves, are guilty if they cannot, and so the generations fall apart in a mutual fear which stifles natural love."

So in our modern world, the pendulum of attitude and action swings to neither extreme. Old age is not an object of inhuman cruelty, nor does it enjoy the privileges of monarchy. In different nations and communities and families, the pendulum oscillates in accordance with their specific cultural heritages and social attitudes. In general, the position of the aged is difficult without being hopeless, and encouraging without being pleasant.

What's wrong, in American society, with our attitudes toward old age? Ours is essentially a Judaeo-Christian civilization; the moral virtues, ethical values, and spiritual visions we claim to cherish spring out of the Old and New Testaments. They teach lasting affection and devotion in all human relationships. They demand respect for every individual. They plead with us not to cast out or neglect our aged. Yet the late Martin Gumpert asserted, with reason, that as a nation, with all our remarkable discoveries and inventions, "we have also lost, or perhaps not yet acquired, a respect for oldness in objects and in people. We do not realize that both, and especially people, can gain in value through the actual process of aging."

One of the things that are wrong—this must be faced frankly—is that our religion (not in profession, but in practice) no longer carries the divine authority or commands the steady obedience of past generations. Scriptures still teach, pastors still preach, the old

230

lessons: care for the aged, respect for the old; but younger ears hardly listen, and younger hearts hardly respond. When the problem arises, we no longer ask, "What is God's will?" but "What is the most practical way?"

This springs partially from the new freedom of children: their right to lead their own lives, without responsibility to their parents. Under this "progressive" dispensation they receive more and more and give less and less. They learn to justify the exorbitant demands they make upon their parents (and often upon society), and to rationalize their own denials of parental requests. The attitude is of course habit-forming, and the younger generation feels no psychological upset when their elders become a "problem," when a "practical solution" must be found.

To put it briefly, family life is decaying. Someone has said, "The solution of the modern problem of old age will not be found in the gentle philosophy of Confucius, nor in the classic exhortations of Cicero, because we are no longer a patriarchal or a rural people. The rocking chair on the farmhouse porch in which Grandpa would drowse away his honored last years with satisfaction to all, is vanishing. But Grandpa is not. The result is that at a time when there were never so many old people, there were never so few of them living with their families."

After all, we have old age pensions and Social Security. Old people enjoy a new freedom too. They no longer depend upon their children's bounty for sustenance, even comfort, even a little luxury. This, however, often works to their disadvantage. Freed from financial obligation, children tend to seek release from other obligations—those of simple inquiry about the old folks' welfare, of visiting in time of health as well as sickness, of sharing joyous occasions, of making manifest their devotion and gratitude in small deeds and simple words.

Then there is the rapid increase of the elderly population, about which a bit more in a moment. This increase magnifies the seriousness of the problem and at the same time emphasizes the importance of a speedy solution. The degree of increase—and

231

of expected further increase—implies a radical change in the economic and social structure of the nation. That change, brought on by old age, promises to be as significant as the one brought on by the machine age.

Up to now, sixty-five has been the almost universally accepted age of retirement in our national economy; let us assume that there are good reasons for this, and let us arbitrarily select sixty-five as the beginning of old age. When you reach it, whatever your feelings or wishes, old age has come to stay. You may still put in a fourteen-hour day; your tennis game may be as good as it was ten years ago. Your creative drives and desires may be as strong as ever. But you have passed a milestone all the same.

(If it makes you feel better, call it the fourth stage of life, rather than "old age." The first is your childhood, through the nineteenth year. The second, your youth, from nineteen to thirty-nine. The third, the middle years, from forty to sixty-five. The fourth is the rest, be it one year or thirty.)

Now that science is steadily lengthening life expectancy, more and more of us will live longer than we had expected in our youth. We have come a long way from that day three hundred years ago when the French philosopher Montaigne wrote: "To die of old age is a death rare, extraordinary, and singular, and therefore so much less natural than the others. 'Tis the last and extremest sort of dying and the more remote, the less to be hoped for. . . . And therefore my opinion is that when one is forty years old we should concede it as an age at which very few arrive; for seeing that men do not usually proceed so far, it is a sign that we are pretty well advanced. And since we have exceeded the ordinary bounds which make the just measure of life, we might not expect to go much further."

In 1850, one out of 38 Americans was over sixty-five. In 1900, it was about one out of 25. In 1950, it was one out of 13. In absolute numbers, those sixty-five or over have practically quadrupled during the last half-century, from 3,080,000 in 1900 to

232

11,514,000 in 1950. Statistical studies indicate that by 1980 we shall have about 20,000,000 citizens over the age of sixty-five. This development parallels the lengthening of our life expectancy, which was about 40 years in 1850, 48 in 1900, 60 in 1930, 70 in 1955, and which has in one area of our population (white female) gone definitely beyond the Biblical promise of three score and ten. And the end is not yet in sight.

The lengthening of average life expectancy is of course largely due to the fantastic decrease in infant mortality. But the lengthening process takes place more and more now at the end of the line. The miracles of medicine are delaying the approach of death, and making late years healthier and happier. As reputable scientists state that the natural life span of man, when he is finally delivered from the dangers of disease, should be between 115 and 125 years, we may some day mourn the centenarian as having been taken before his time.

One of the consequences of this general increase in the proportion of the aged within our population will be a revision of the concept of old age. One hundred years ago, when Abraham Lincoln, aged 52, was leaving his home in Springfield to assume the Presidency in Washington, he said sadly in his Farewell Address, "I am an old man." He believed that he was approaching the close of his life, and that he would probably never see his friends again. Today, a man in his early fifties feels that he is in the middle of his middle years, at the peak of his powers. At 65, he may be persuaded to slow down. But he is not prepared to stop. He is told that since he has crossed 60, he can count on reaching 80. Then he may think about being old. In his eightieth year Dan Beard said, "Age? I make no such weak admissions."

Soon, a great part of our population will be living into the seventies; many of us into the eighties; and an appreciable number into the nineties. Therefore, the problem of growing old is no longer just a question of what to do with and for our parents and grandparents; the question becomes more and more,

What shall we do with and for ourselves? Our concern with geriatrics is not merely a gracious concession to our elders, but of vital importance to ourselves.

Thomas Wolfe wrote, in one of his letters, "I will not be vain enough to suggest it is growth, but at any rate I was a young man when I wrote *Look Homeward, Angel*. I am approaching middle age now. I think I know more about life, more about living, more about people now than I did then. I know that I have a deeper understanding, more sympathy, more compassion, than I had ten years ago. I hope it is reflected in what I do." * That last sentence is the key to the letter. Men and women middle-aged and older do know more about life and living, more about people; do have a deeper understanding of themselves and others. The tragedy is that what they know is not always reflected in what they do. They are preoccupied with worries about what they no longer have, and what they are in the process of losing; as a result, they fail to use the abundant resources left to them, which can still bring them a wealth of peace and happiness.

The famous naturalist William T. Hornaday said, "Uncountable millions inherit rigorous and disintegrating occupations from which they never escape, which lead to early graves. But with intelligence and honest effort, much can be done toward making old age mean 80 or 90, instead of 60 or 70. Today, at 80, I am elderly but not old. My faculties are in first-class working condition, my face is unlined, my relish for food would shame a wolf. I sleep like a boy. As 'old age' goes, I'll not be through even at 90. At that age I will still be able to fight with my pen, if not with my fists."

In his middle years and old age a man knows that life is a complex of victory and defeat, success and failure, joy and sorrow. He knows this wisdom, from the Book of Proverbs: "The soul of the

* From *The Letters of Thomas Wolfe*, collected and edited by Elizabeth Nowell; published by Charles Scribner's Sons.

sluggard desireth and hath nothing; but the soul of the diligent shall be abundantly gratified. . . . Righteousness guardeth him that is upright in the way; but wickedness overthroweth the sinner. . . . There is he that pretendeth himself rich, yet hath nothing; there is he that pretendeth himself poor, yet hath great wealth. . . . By pride cometh only contention; but with the well-advised is wisdom. . . . Good understanding giveth grace; but the way of the faithless is harsh."

He can distinguish between right and wrong, good and evil, as they are interpreted in the mores of the community in which he dwells. He should be able to discern the difference between the superficial and the essential, between the passing and the permanent, between the shoddy and the real. He should be able to profit by the mistakes of the past and plan to avoid them in the future. He should be able to absorb past disappointments and defeats, and to strengthen his virtues and values. He should be able to see life steadily and see it whole.

In another letter Thomas Wolfe wrote, "There has been a good deal of talk about the 'lost generation,' meaning the young men who came up during and after the last war, but I wonder if the real lost generation is not these men of middle or advanced middle-age who keep saying the old phrases, trying to whoop it up in the old way over something that is gone forever. It made me think of a pep meeting at a morgue, a cheering squad of ghosts. And in the name of God what are these men going to do? They have only one language, one set of values."

This passage points up another danger of middle and old age. Some of us try to hold on to the past, and thus become its prisoner. It is bad enough when, like the Bourbons, we forget nothing that is old and remember nothing that is new. But it is far worse when we seek to impose the old dead world upon the new living one. We become ghosts, haunting the present and spoiling the future. We spin out the webs of our destiny in a cold morgue. We are corpses before our time.

It is not easy for a middle-aged man to envision his remaining years as full of promise for happiness. Few of us are mature enough to assert, with Robert Browning:

> For thence—a paradox
>   Which comforts while it mocks—
> Shall life succeed in that it seems to fail;
>   What I aspire to be,
> And was not, comforts me;
>   A brute I might have been, but would not
> Sink in the scale. . . .

And even fewer are ready to join him in this:

> Grow old along with me!
> The best is yet to be,
>   The last of life, for which the first was made:
> Our times are in His hand
>   Who saith, "A whole I planned,
> Youth shows but half; trust God: see
>   All, nor be afraid!"

The average man is not conscious of the aging process, but he does not like the idea of growing old. George Bernard Shaw was one of the most conspicuous of the twentieth-century artists who came to terms with age—he seemed somehow to have been very old all his life. Shaw went even further; he seemed proud and happy with his old age. He wrote his first play when he was thirty-nine, and began a fifty-five-year-long career of creation. Shortly before he died, a young British journalist was sent down to his home in Ayot St. Lawrence to persuade him to contribute an article on "How to Grow Old Gracefully." At first Shaw demurred brusquely. Then, with a humorous glint in his eye, he said, "I know you are only trying to carry out a ludicrous assignment. To keep you from going away empty-handed I'll tell you how I happened to settle in this little town. I was here on a visit, and in the course of my long walks alone, happily I came upon a graveyard. One of the tombstones bore an inscription that ran something like this: 'Mary Ann Southworth—born 1815—died 1895. May her soul rest in peace! Her time was too short.' That settled it! I decided that if eighty years was the village's idea of a short life, Ayot St. Lawrence was the place for me."

Shaw lived to be 94. Perhaps part of his longevity was due to spending his declining years in that small and peaceful village, under its influences of ease and grace. I suspect, though, that much of it can be attributed to the philosophical spirit he developed during the early years of his exciting career in the great city of London. When he was 78, still writing and producing plays that startled and shocked the world with their sharp sarcasms, their thunderbolts of criticism, a newspaperman asked him, "How old is old?"

"Why bother about one's age?" he retorted. "I'm not distinguished by having birthdays. At 22 a man is too old for sprint-racing, and in England too young to be Chancellor of the Exchequer. At 70, a woman is too old to have a baby, but young enough to run a village post office. Man is a complex of parts, no two of which reach their prime on the same date. All simple questions about age are therefore unanswerable."

But far too many of us try to answer them; and finding them unanswerable, assume that we have failed, that our lives are finished, that there is nothing more to be said or done. We have accepted the common definitions of "what should be accomplished" or "what we should leave behind us," and if we reach sixty-five without living up to those definitions, we give up. Or we try to escape by denying our age and accomplishments.

The fundamental failure of the older person is a refusal to accept the fact about his age and then to act his age. He cannot change the fact that he is no longer young, that he may not live many years more. He must stop trying to prove that he is as good as he ever was, particularly in the physical area, work or play or sexual activity. He must get over that There's-so-little-time-left

237

feeling. He can leave that uncertainty to God, and simply be sure to live each day as well as he can. His days may still be long upon this earth, particularly in our generation; and what greater tragedy is there than that of the man who gives up at the age of 65, and spends the next thirty years just waiting? If he has not attained the successes of which he dreamed, then let him enjoy those he did attain. He must stop competing with what-might-have-been; he must learn to live with what is.

In one of her poems, Carolyn Wells observes:

> *Youth is a silly vapid state;*
> *Old age with fears and ills is rife;*
> *This simple boon I beg of fate—*
> *A thousand years of middle life.*

Most psychiatrists, especially experts in geriatrics, agree that middle age can be a man's most productive period; when, because he has greater economic security and personal maturity, he can concentrate on specific objectives. And the significant shift in our times is toward a longer middle period—ultimately up to seventy or eighty or even ninety—so that all we say here about the middle years will be more and more applicable to old age as well.

Let the middle-aged man, or the old man, take a good look at himself before he yields to self-pity and quiescence. He is not, after all, suffering a breakdown, or preparing for death; he is having a thoroughly natural experience, passing from one age to another. If he is to do it gracefully, exercising all his talents and making the most of his past, he must see himself as he is.

Seeing himself as he is is the first step in preparation for the journey into old age. In his youth, after all, he looked forward to the future as the continuation, and not the conclusion, of the present. He was trained and helped to make the transitions between childhood and adolescence, adolescence and maturity. Now, with the later years upon him, it is even more essential that he live gracefully and purposefully. If there is loneliness, for example, the mind has knowledge, the heart has desires, the soul has sources of peace and inspiration; he can draw upon all these in his time of need. He can make new friends; re-examine old opinions; attach himself to new causes. He must look ahead with interest, even delight, and not with loathing; the real joy of a journey is in the traveling, and not in the destination. (Returning from one of her many trips to postwar Europe, Anne O'Hare McCormick said, "One of the worst tragedies in Europe is the five-year-old people who look like seventy because they have seen things no child should ever see." To my mind equally tragic is the seventy-year-old who talks and behaves like a child of five, because of the things he has failed to see and think and feel during his lifetime. For him, age is tragic because he never prepared for it in his youth.)

First, self-knowledge and preparation. Then, an awareness that the advantages, and not the deficiences, of old age must be emphasized. Two thousand years ago Cicero wrote, in his *De Senectute*, "I find four reasons why old age appears to be unhappy: First, that it withdraws us from active pursuits; that it makes the body weaker; that it deprives us of almost all bodily pleasures; fourth, that it is not far removed from death." He then goes on to prove all four reasons invalid, and that there are compensations offered by age which are far more valuable than the advantages of youth. We, of course, can modify his reasons until they lose all force. Old age no longer keeps us from active pursuits; the body does not weaken anywhere near as much in these days of miracle drugs; the popularization of sports has given us a wide range of physical pleasures that Cicero never knew; and death is farther removed every day in our society.

Edward Osgood Brown, commenting on *De Senectute*, asserts: "I believe that you will come to see, if you will only accept it, that there is a wisdom which comes with old age—a better sense of proportion than the hotheadedness of youth or the midsummer madness that middle age has. For brightness of the eyes it gives a deeper knowledge of the heart; for gaiety and gladness, an understanding sympathy. We see and understand what younger eyes have missed. The counsels of the old are merciful. We are freed from narrow and intolerant enthusiasm; from fanatic partisanship, from opinions which, because of environment and fostered prejudices, had almost become obsessions. . . . We gain the intellectual power to weigh and measure the influences which play on the intellect. The old man sympathizes with both saint and sinner. Life seems less tragic to him than to the young, because it is less intense. He knows that all sorrows subside, that the disappointed lover will find some other girl, and the defeated candidate another activity. . . . Is there not in all this, compensation for even diminished mental energy? For the glow of contending effort, age has the calmer joy of repose and the remembrance of races run, goals reached, and prizes won."

Even when these lessons have been absorbed, there is another danger: boredom. If active habits have been formed through the years, boredom is already defeated; for some, an extraordinary effort is required to remain active. But activity is indispensable. Gladstone at 80 was busy studying Greek; Franklin Delano Roosevelt found Justice Oliver Wendell Holmes, at 90, reading Plato "to improve my mind."

Why burden others? Busy yourself instead with their concerns and cares. You will forget your own problem in the search for solutions to theirs. A busy life is as good a cure for the tensions and trials of old age as for those of youth.

And when all this is accomplished, frame this "Prayer for the Aged" somewhere in your home:

> *Most prayers are for the young, O Lord,*
> *But this do for the aged,*
> *Grant them growth of spirit*
> *To compensate for other things they miss*
> *And give them newer vision for the merit*
> *Of gratitude—Let them enjoy each day*

That comes as fresh to age as youth arose,
    Unfolding to maturity, the way.
The sunset paints the sky before it goes;
    Give them some task that only they can do,
A niche to fill as long as life shall last,
    The strength of mind to trade old thoughts for new,
And yet a time for dreaming of the past—
    And more important, Lord, than all of these,
Someone who will love them dearly, please.

IN

QUEST

OF

WISDOM

Chapter Eleven

> There is a teaching: A man must
> not say, "I will study so as to be
> called a wise man, or Rabbi, or
> elder, or to have a seat in the col-
> lege," but he must study from love
> —the honor will come of itself.
> —THE TALMUD

"Civilization," said H. G. Wells a generation ago, "is a race between catastrophe and education."

I was reminded of that sententious remark when I recently
read this, in the introduction to one of the *World Perspective
Series:* "The modern world imagined itself on the threshold of
Utopia but awakened to find itself on the very edge of an abyss."

The overriding paradox of modern civilization is that man's
extraordinary success in the search for knowledge, which enabled
him to unearth the secret of the atom, has also taught him the

secret of absolute self-destruction. All scientists are haunted by the ever-growing realization that education which promises man more abundant life may bring him absolute death.

This is not a new discovery. The peoples of antiquity knew it well, particularly the Hebrews, Greeks, and Romans, whose records reveal a monumental concern with education. The learned Rabbis who guided the life of the Jewish people said, "The very foundations of the world rest on the breath of the schoolchildren." They tell of a renowned sage who, upon meeting a friend with a cloth bound carelessly about his head as he hurried his child off to school, asked, "Why such haste? Why do you leave your house in such unseemly attire?" "Because," his friend replied, "every other consideration must give way to that of getting children to school." From that moment on the sage himself would partake of no food until he had taken his son to school.

There is a warning in the Talmud: "A community that neglects to establish schools for children is bound to perish; its well-being, its moral and social life must needs be endangered, and it falls prey to the enemy when men of constant faith cease to exist therein." A passage in the Midrash tells: "If you wish to destroy the Jews, said the wise Oenomous of Gadara to Israel's foes, you must first destroy their synagogues and schools. For as long as the voices of their children continue to chirp in the schools and they are taught the word of God, all the world will not prevail against them."

What is education? The word derives from the Latin *educere*, which means to draw or lead out; this implies that education is the development of intelligence and emotional capacities already present within the individual. Funk & Wagnalls' New Standard Dictionary defines it as, "The systematic development of the normal powers of the intellect, feeling, and conduct so as to render them efficient in some particular form of living or for life in general." Gibbon says, "Education is the harmonious development of all our faculties. It begins in the nursery and goes on at school but does not end there. It continues through life whether we will it or not. Every person has two educations, one which he receives from others, and one more important, which he gives himself."

The mystic philosopher Martin Buber, a gifted educator of our time, sees education as a dual process—a combination of the skills and rewards of a gardener and a sculptor. The one provides the proper environmental conditions and removes the obstacles, so that the potential within the seed may come to fulfillment. The other fixes an image, fashions a mold, and shapes the original material to the optimum, preconceived, outer form. The one opens the best path; the other follows it to the best destination.

I like to think of education as a kind of photosynthetic process —the continued absorption of elements outside the individual by the developing potential within him; a constant exchange between the growing individual and the world about him which contributes to his growth. There can, I believe, be no real education without "induction." The world, like the sculptor, shapes the clay of the individual to a form; but the nature of the clay—and therefore the limitations to the form—is inherent in the individual. Education is interaction: absorption of, and contribution to, the external world by the developing internal world.

The developing individual: the child is father to the man. This is another way of saying, "As youth goes, so goes the nation"; education determines the destiny of a person and also of a people. Next to creation, education, in its broadest sense, is the most important force in human society. Creation gives man life. But it is education that helps him to live well—physically, mentally, emotionally, spiritually.

When we think of ancient Greece, there first comes to mind Athens, the city of culture, the home of a great doctrine that has never yet—save in ancient China and among the ancient Jews— been put into practice: that the reins of government should be entrusted to the great minds, the trained teachers, the well-educated. Second is Sparta, where physical education taught man his own limitations, so that when the time called for it, he could surpass them. But Greece means first, last, and always Socrates, who gave his life, in a sense, for education.

Socrates was more than educated; he was wise. True wisdom is rare; and perhaps the wise man alone may be said to be truly educated. A Socrates! A Moses! A Jesus! A Buddha! A Gandhi! These were great men, almost symbols now, symbols of what man can be. But the great mass of humanity—you and I—still spend our years in a slow and laborious climb toward wisdom. We are content to reach its outermost edge. We are limited, and we are aware of our limitations; we must work together if we are to create any happiness, any greatness, while we are on earth. We must work together to pass along to future generations the experience and hope of the past. We must work together for the sake of our own children.

They tell of a group of itinerant almoners who came to the gates of a certain city and asked to see its guardians. For a moment the sentries were nonplused; then they brought forth the elected officials of the community. "These are not your guardians," said the almoners. Next they brought forth the tycoons, masters of the community's economic life. "These are not your guardians," said the almoners. Now they brought forth the aristocrats of the community, the best families. "These are not your guardians," said the almoners. The sentries threw up their hands: "If none of these be the guardians of the city, then tell us who they may be."

"Go get your teachers," said the almoners, "the teachers of your children. They are the guardians of the city."

The ancient Rabbis, who saw learning as a primary purpose of life (Jews are, in fact, the only people who ever taught that the duty to learn was a divine command; "Thou shalt know" is a phrase that occurs over and over again in the sacred lore), saw education in three dimensions. There were three different words for it, and a special group dedicated to it was called *Chabad,* a

Hebrew word fashioned of the first letters of the three different words.

First, there was *Daath,* which is knowledge, i.e., the acquisition of information, the accumulation of facts. Knowledge alone was not education. A man who possesses knowledge is undoubtedly informed but not necessarily educated. He may be like that famous teacher who, upon his death, was described by his colleagues as "a basketful of books."

Second, there was *Bee-Nawh,* which is understanding, i.e., the capacity to distinguish between bits of knowledge and to perceive the relationships among them. There are many students who assimilate information easily but never acquire understanding. In tape-recorder fashion, they can feed back accurate facts, exact information. They cannot, however, analyze and explain the meanings, the values, the purposes of the facts, or the place of those facts in reference to life in general.

Third, there was *Chauchmauh,* which is wisdom, i.e., something more than the acquisition of information or the analysis and explanation of that information. This is the distillation of knowledge and understanding into their mature application to the problems of human life. This is the apex of education; the summit from which the human spirit, now master of all that it surveys, can behold life in all its fullness. Wisdom is the crown of knowledge and understanding; its attainment is the climax of a process that began at birth and will end at death. "But wisdom, where shall it be found?" Job asks. "Man knoweth not the price thereof." Then he affirms, "Yea, the price of wisdom is above rubies. The topaz of Ethiopia shall not equal it. Neither shall it be valued with pure gold."

The teachers classified their pupils into four types. The first was compared with a funnel, which lets water run straight through, and retains nothing which it has received. The second, to a sponge, that mops up good and bad liquid and holds everything it happens to absorb, without discrimination or selection. The third, to a sieve that sifts the good from the bad; it gets rid of the

246

bad but does nothing with the good. The fourth, to a strainer, which retains the lees, and passes the good wine.

The first type does not even reach the first rung on education's ladder. Knowledge is imparted to him but not implanted within him. The second type stands on the first rung. He has knowledge, an accumulation of facts, useless or valuable, harmful or helpful. But he has not learned to select, to differentiate between the sweet and the sour.

The third has reached the second rung; he now not only knows, but also understands what he knows. He discards that which is of little or no value, but holds fast to that which is useful and helpful. The fourth has attained the highest rung. He has not only stripped himself of all that is trivial, but he has learned to apply his wide knowledge and deep understanding to the major needs and issues of life. He is the truly wise man; he is genuinely educated.

Strange as it may seem, the most pressing educational problem of our time is to be found at the bottom of the ladder, not at its summit. It is the problem of fundamental knowledge, the transmission of the *ABC*s of information and the teaching of the three *R*s. Johnny doesn't seem to be able to read and write and figure the way he used to—not only in the grade schools, but even in the great universities. Knowledge, which was once the cornerstone of education, may soon be serving as its headstone.

The old commandment, "Thou shalt know," is being replaced by a new question, "Whom dost thou know?" Personality and popularity have become more important than independence and individuality; as a result, influence has become more important than knowledge. A command of angles enables a man to go further than a grasp of facts. Few people remember, or care about, Francis Bacon's dictum: "Knowledge is power." After all, with power they can buy knowledge.

Just a few years ago, the factual knowledge of freshmen entering one of America's largest state universities was carefully studied and analyzed. The revelations were startling: 40 per cent of the entrants had no mathematics beyond arithmetic; many of them were unable to complete a problem in long division. One third had no training at all in grammar, even English grammar. Less than half could spell many words in common English usage. Four out of ten could not read quickly or accurately, or write correctly a single paragraph that made real sense. Is it any wonder that a college graduate has been described as a "four-year loaf that comes out half-baked"? Mark Twain once defined a cauliflower as only a cabbage with a college education. Even after graduation, many college people are still no more than cabbages.

In any discussion of the crisis in education (a perennial; like the poor, it is always with us), criticism is leveled at the schools and the teachers. But the fundamental fault is always traced back to the homes and the parents. And rightly so. Yes, we have too few schools and they are inadequately equipped and staffed. Yes, our teachers are often ill-educated, unprepared; they are surely underpaid. Of course we should build more and better schools, have smaller classes, richer curricula, more progressive programs. Our teachers should have higher pay, better status, more secure tenure. Knowledge should be considered an end in itself, and not a means toward a material end—earning more money or making a "good" marriage. The pursuit of education should be its own reward. All these values should be affirmed; all these ideals should be achieved. But they are not, and will not be in the foreseeable future. Why?

A clue to the answer is in a passage I have never forgotten, from a novel of almost a generation ago, *The Plastic Age*, by the late Percy Marks. In it college students were expressing deep disappointment with college life. Where they had hoped to find noble souls and high ideals, they had found only pettiness, narrowness, meanness, baseness. Their old professor listened patiently, and smiled sympathetically. "Of course men grow coarse while they are in college," he said. "But that doesn't mean that they wouldn't grow coarser if they were not in college. It isn't college that coarsens a man and destroys his illusions. It is life.

248

Don't think you can grow to manhood and retain your pretty dreams. You have become disillusioned about college. That's the price of living. The average college graduate has loftier ideals and is less materialistic than the man who has not gone to college. I wish I could believe that the college gives him those ideals. I can't, however. The colleges draw the best that society has to offer." *

Our schools and colleges can draw only the best that our homes and communities have to offer, not only in the quality of mind, but in the quality of attitude and ambition, desire and dream. It is not simply a question of the buildings and equipment offered by the community; it is also a question of the standards and mores which the community supports and promotes. If parents and citizens show clearly that they prize knowledge, that they will pay a proper price for it, that they respect its possessors and transmitters, the first battle will be won, and there will be reason to hope that learning can be restored to the high place it once occupied in the hearts of men.

Perhaps this story will encourage those embattled warriors now fighting for better schools and teachers; it bears repeating to politicians. An emperor of ancient Rome invited an Oriental potentate to visit the Eternal City. A special feast day was proclaimed in honor of his arrival, and on that day the entire population participated in a mass celebration: parades, pageantry, games of skill, high revelry. At the height of the day's activities, the emperor drove his distinguished guest to the summit of the highest of the seven hills. "Tell me," he asked, as they gazed out at the grandeur before them, "wherein do you think lies the secret of Rome's strength?"

The Eastern monarch reflected. "Surely," he answered, "Rome's strength is in her mighty army, which conquers all that it surveys."

* From *The Plastic Age* by Percy Marks; published by Appleton-Century-Crofts, Inc.

"No," said the emperor. "It is not in her army."

"Then it must be in the great wealth gathered through victories over many nations."

"No. It is not in her wealth."

"Then it must be in those massive walls which render the city impregnable."

"No. It is not in those walls. If you would behold the secret of Rome's strength, look down into those playing fields at the foot of the hill." The emperor pointed to thousands of boys and girls participating in the sports and games. "There," he said, "is the strength of Rome. All that we are, or hope to become, lies within the lives of our children."

Biologists suggest that it is for the purpose of education that man has been given a longer period of infancy, proportionately, than all other animals. Man has more to learn, if he is to be adequately equipped to cope with a complex environment, to survive its rigors and pressures. But the educating process does not end with adolescence, or indeed at any given point. Human beings have no choice; they go on being educated all their lives. No isolation can prevent it; let a man sit, like Simeon Stylites, atop a stone pillar in an oasis in a vast desert, all the days of his life; let no wayfarer approach him; he will still absorb education. There is a constant interplay of hereditary capacities and environmental reactions. Immanuel Kant and Henry David Thoreau are recognized as highly educated men; yet Kant is said never to have traveled more than sixteen miles from his home town of Königsberg, and Thoreau spent all his creative years in the neighborhood of Walden Pond.

Robert Maynard Hutchins and Mortimer Adler are two of our foremost proponents of the doctrine that education is a lifetime process. They have insisted that schools and colleges do not educate man; institutions simply equip him with basic tools, the tools he will need to go on educating himself. Yet for most young people, graduation is an end to education; obviously, it should be the beginning. They regard the diploma as a license to leave off learning. A sheepskin can cover a number of sins, and two of them are laziness and ignorance.

One of the understandable reasons for this sudden halt in the learning process is a preoccupation into which many people are forced, the preoccupation with the demands of simple material existence. But these demands lessen every year, and the opportunities for purposeful learning increase every year. Today the basic trouble is that by and large we have little respect for purposeful learning. Often the process of withdrawal from the life of the mind begins in schools and colleges, when men and women should be most alert, most grateful for instruction. When he was president of Princeton University, Woodrow Wilson once observed that colleges had become circuses, where too much attention was paid to the sideshows and not enough to the main tent. A professor in a football-mad university complained that there was too much stadium and too little studium. Some years ago an Oriental student at one of our large Midwestern universities described it as an athletic club where facilities for study for the physically unfit were also provided.

An American tourist visiting the University of Stockholm, Sweden, tells that he came upon a mob of wildly shouting students swarming around a fair-headed, ruddy-faced young man. A wreath of green leaves about his shoulders, he was being pelted with roses as the campus rang loud with cries of, "Rah, rah, Carl!"

"This must be some exceptional athlete in one of the major sports," the American hazarded.

"No, no," was the reply. "He's graduating as the honor student of his class."

"Well!" exclaimed the American. "This is the first time I ever saw so much wild excitement over scholarship."

Quickly the astonished question came back, "For what purpose, then, does your country build schools?"

The question is still valid. Even when knowledge is stressed the results are sometimes baffling. Within the past two years we have witnessed extraordinary displays of memory, of retained knowledge, on the television quiz programs. The winners have exhibited a remarkable grasp of facts; but very few of them have at the same time impressed us with a corresponding understanding of their knowledge: its meanings, relationships, values, purposes.

This is a truly discouraging aspect of modern education: that even where the buildings and staff are adequate, education does not lead to a rounded understanding. Much of our learning is superficial, without depth. Rarely do facts sink into the soul, where they may mingle with basic learning, sensitive feeling, lofty dreaming. If occasionally they do go deep, rarely do they come up again as part of a greater comprehension, a broader vision.

Jokes that run the rounds may illustrate this failing better than any number of theoretical statements. The following two brief essays are said to have been written for examinations in American history. The facts in them are certainly accurate. The first read, "Benjamin Franklin was a poor boy. He went around the streets of Philadelphia, carrying a loaf of bread. He became a printer. He married a red-headed woman. Then, he discovered electricity." The second read, "Patrick Henry was a very smart boy. He studied law. He became a great orator. He was elected to the State Legislature of Virginia. He married a very rich widow. Then he cried, 'Give me liberty or give me death!'"

They say of George Lyman Kittredge, the great American Shakespearean scholar, that while walking through Harvard Yard one day he pointed to the Widener Library and said, "Every Harvard building but that one could burn to the ground and we would still have a university." A great university, of course, must have a great library. It must offer its students access to the knowledge and art of the centuries, to the ideas of the great minds of the human species. But a great university must also have a great faculty, a group of inspired teachers, without whose fire and enthusiasm and compassionate understanding, students might learn nothing of value from any library.

This is the second great problem in modern education: that Johnny must not only be able to read the books and absorb the facts; he must also learn to see meanings and relationships and values. Johnny needs great teachers, men and women dedicated to the task of creating educated human beings. Men and women for whom the transmission of bare knowledge is not enough; men and women who will not be content until what they have taught is understood, assimilated to the mind and heart of the student. As knowledge is the first step in education, so understanding is the second. Wisdom, the third step, the goal, cannot, perhaps, be taught; but without understanding none of us will ever have the capacity to attain the ultimate wisdom.

We have referred several times to the fully educated man; now we shall try to find out what he is, and how he becomes what he is. "The real distinction between educated and uneducated persons," says Edward C. Lindeman, "is not to be found in such superficial criteria as academic degrees, formal study, or accumulation of facts; indeed, formal learning may and often does lead people into narrow scholarship and out of life. Educated persons find their satisfaction in bringing knowledge to bear upon experience. And the best informed person is still ignorant if his knowing is not also a lively ingredient of his living. . . . To be educated is not to be informed, but to find illumination in informed living."

Cardinal Newman's definition of an educated intellect was "that it have a connected view of old and new, past and present, far and near, and an insight into the influence of all these on one another without which there is no whole, no center. Mere 'men of information' lacking that center are not really educated; they see the tapestry of life on the wrong side and it tells no story." President William Rainey Harper, in an address to freshmen entering the University of Chicago, once said, "Young gentlemen, an educated man is a man who by the time he is twenty-five has a clear theory formed in the light of human experience down the ages—of what constitutes a satisfying, a significant life—and who by the age of thirty has a moral philosophy consonant with racial significance. If a man reaches these ages without having arrived at such a theory, such a philosophy, then no matter how many facts he has learned or how many processes he has mastered —that man is an ignoramus and a fool, unhappy, probably dangerous."

Perhaps the most truly educated man of all time, Socrates, asked, "Whom then do I call educated? First, those who manage well the circumstances which they encounter day by day and those who possess a judgment which is accurate in meeting occasions as they arise and rarely misses the expedient course of action. Next, those who are decent and honorable in their intercourse with all men, bearing easily and good-naturedly what is unpleasant and offensive in others, and being as agreeable and reasonable to their associates as it is humanly possible to be. Furthermore, those who hold their pleasures always under control and are not ultimately overcome by their misfortunes, bearing up under them bravely and in a manner worthy of our common nature. Finally, and most important of all, those who are not spoiled by their successes, who do not desert their true selves, but hold their ground steadfastly as wise and sober-minded men, rejoicing no more in the good things that have come to them through chance than in those which, through their own nature and intelligence, are theirs since birth. Those who have a character which is in accord, not with one of these things, but with all of them—these I maintain are educated and whole men possessed of all the virtues of a man."

Whenever I search my mind for a sharp distinction between the educated and the uneducated man, my memory reaches back to a story told by Irvin Cobb. A Texas oil tycoon, whose wealth far exceeded his wisdom, was persuaded that there were places outside the borders of his own fabulous state that were nevertheless worth visiting. So he went off to Europe. Carefully following his Baedeker, he visited one cathedral after another. One afternoon, while he was dutifully viewing the Canterbury Cathedral, a pink-cheeked clergyman came out of a side door and asked whether he was an American tourist. "Yessir," he answered proudly. "I hail from the great state of Texas." Just then the cathedral chimes began to ring, playing a sacred hymn. With an ecstatic look on his face the clergyman sighed, "Isn't that music heavenly?"

Bending his head low, the tall Texan asked, "What did you say?"

Raising his voice a little, the clergyman answered, "Do not the notes of those chimes sound like the tongues of angels?"

Cupping his hand to his ear, the Texan yelled, "What did you say?"

Meekly the clergyman pleaded, "Don't you feel that God is actually speaking to you through those chimes?"

Shaking his head in despair, the Texan roared, "Sorry, Pahson, but them bells is makin' so much noise I can't hear a word you're sayin'."

To me that story illustrates the difference. The soul of the educated man is sensitive to the world about him. It responds knowingly, discerningly, appreciatively, and sympathetically to every nuance of human observation, experience, and association. Like the thirsty soil, eagerly drinking in the rain, or the flower turning its face to the sun, it reaches out and takes into itself all that life has to offer, absorbing it thoroughly, and growing by so much. It has learned to see life maturely, and to love it for what it is, even if it often falls short of the ideal.

The soul of the uneducated man is dull, insensitive, and unresponsive. The rain of life's variegated wonders, in all their changing forms and colors, can pour down upon it and the sun of life's infinite treasures of beauty and love and joy can shine upon it and the soul cannot absorb them. Without them, the soul does not just cease to progress, to grow; without them the soul withers, the spirit becomes as dust. Without them, man is less than man; the divine spark is dead, and man has wandered from the divine way.

My favorite definition of the educated man is that of the late Reverend Joseph Fort Newton. "When is a man educated?" he asked. "When he can look out upon the Universe, now lucid and lovely, now dark and terrible, with a sense of his own littleness in the great scheme of things, and yet with unfaltering faith and courage. When he knows how to make friends and keep them, above all, when he can keep friends with himself. When he can be happy alone and high-minded amid the drudgeries of life. When he can look into a wayside puddle and see something besides mud, and into the face of the most forlorn mortal and see something beyond sin. When he knows how to live, how to love, how to hope, how to pray—glad to live and not afraid to die, in his hands a sword for evil, and in his heart a bit of lifting song."

There is a story about a candidate for a Rabbinical degree who one day told his teachers that he was ready for the final examinations. They asked about his preparation: had he carefully studied the Bible, Mishnah, Midrash, and Talmud? "Yes," was his answer. "I have gone through them all—all the books and sections—five times."

"Splendid," they smiled. "But what we want to find out is whether they have gone through you. Have the Divine Commandments been written on the tablets of your heart? Have the holy words of the Sacred Scriptures and the Rabbis' teachings been woven into the warp and woof of your spirit? Have they become part of your soul?"

The ancient sages taught, "An ignorant man cannot be pious." By that, they meant not that knowledge necessarily made for piety but that learning was essential to piety. Learning is more than preparation for a livelihood; more than cultivation of the mind or spirit; more than the harmonious development of one's native abilities. Learning is never really yours until it has gone through you, become a part of you, whether it is a book or a piece of music, or a work of art, or an idea. The next time you go through a book, ask yourself before you set it down whether or not it has gone through you. When you go through a museum, consider whether the paintings have gone through you. If the answer is no, go back; go back again; make it yours.

Think of this story: On a lonely island a man came upon a group of sages sitting around a table, studying the Holy Law. On their faces he beheld a radiant look of such beatific happiness that he cried out, "They must be in Paradise!"

"No," his companion answered, "they are not in Paradise. Paradise is in them."

When learning becomes part of a man, he shines with its glow. His learning makes his spirit sparkle; his soul takes on a new life. Charles Darwin, toward the end of his life, when he was world-famed, once mused, "If I had my life to live over again, I would make it a rule to read some poetry and listen to some music at least once a week; for perhaps parts of my brain now atrophied would thus have been kept active through use. The loss of these tastes is a loss of happiness and may possibly be injurious to the intellect and more possibly to the moral character, by enfeebling the emotional part of our nature."

Schools have concerned themselves primarily—almost exclusively—with factual education. They have concentrated on the task of filling minds with much information and little inspiration. Poetry and painting, music and sculpture, are often extracurricular, if present at all. The arts that move men—that affect their emotions directly, that become the true culture of an age by influencing men's souls, and not their bodies—are relegated to a secondary position, and often to oblivion. Yet the development of character—surely important to the school—is a process in which the heart plays as great a part as the head. Self-respect, fair play, the values of decency and integrity, are, with luck, absorbed in school; they are rarely taught directly, and most teachers seem to feel that they are out of the province of the educator. Nothing is more certainly within that province. The education of the heart should not be entrusted exclusively to homes and churches; children may come to feel that the heart should be permitted to influence them only at home or in church. Character training should be in every public school curriculum. Without it, a child is only half-educated. Without it, a child never learns to control and use his emotions. Very early in life, he should begin to know what it means "to do justly, to love mercy, and to walk humbly. . . ." The sages used to say, "He in whom the fear of sin comes before his knowledge, his knowledge will endure. But he in whom his knowledge comes before the fear of sin, his knowledge will not endure."

Someone has defined the word "sympathy" as "your pain in my heart." Sympathy and compassion are two of the virtues of the heart; one of the great ills of our generation is that we understand so little of either. In good times we tend to let them atrophy; traditionally, the benighted or oppressed have known their full value. Some years ago, before the Supreme Court's desegregation decision, the School Board (its membership was of course entirely white) of a small town in the Deep South called local Negro leaders to a meeting. They proposed a joint campaign for a public bond issue necessary to build additional schools, and suggested that the division would be 50–50. After the campaign had been under way for a month and seemed to be on the way to success the School Board called a second meeting and suggested that perhaps the division should be 60 per cent for the whites and 40 per cent for the Negroes. When the campaign was six months old, and its success was assured, a third meeting was called, and it was then suggested that the division should be 80 per cent for the whites and 20 per cent for the Negroes. When the Chairman of the Board saw the look of deep disappointment on the faces of the Negro leaders, he asked whether they felt that the proposal was unfair. The answer was, "Well, no. The longer this goes on, the more it looks as though you white people need more education than we Negroes do."

Both the intellect and the heart must be educated; and that

258

education must itself be directed to the service of others as well as self. John Dewey, who brought the philosophy of pragmatism into the field of education, described a truly educated man as one who had learned to be socially efficient, to serve well the needs of his fellow men. He knew, as Bertrand Russell had insisted, that self-sufficiency must come before social efficiency. But he contended that in order to become one's best self, one must be carefully taught how best to serve society.

Epictetus, the most famous of the Grecian slaves owned by Roman masters, once rebuked the members of the Senate by defiantly asserting, "It hath been said that only the free can be educated. But I say unto you that only the educated can be free." Free from bondage to the natural passions and normal urges of man's animal nature. Free from slavery to selfish desires. This is the freedom that enables man to live as a dignified being among other dignified beings. Freedom *from* is not enough; there must also be freedom *for*. For self-improvement and self-enrichment, for service to the peace and welfare of one's fellow man. Freedom for the fashioning of a personal character, for the sincere pursuit of the noble, the ideal, the divine. Man must become free enough to feel that he is a partner of God in the everlasting work of creation.

So we must also make certain that education is not only for this world, not only for the control of finite matter, but also for the understanding of infinite spirit. The man who has only the worldly approach to life does not truly live. And one of the most significant changes taking place today in college life is the renewed emphasis on religion. It is not only that many universities sponsor an annual religious emphasis week, during which they seek to expose the students to religious influences and inspiration; more important, the divinity schools in such great universities as Harvard are being accorded greater prominence and higher status. Religion has once again become a topic for serious discussion rather than skeptical dismissal in classrooms and bull sessions. God is coming back to the campus.

And the campus needs Him, as the world needs Him. The

tycoon and the teacher are responsible to the same Master. One Sunday morning, they say, two members of a village church were praying in neighboring pews. One was the town's business tycoon, the other its most venerable teacher. The tycoon was praying, "O Lord, I thank Thee for the great wealth I have accumulated, and for the high position I have attained in this community. They have filled me with joy and pride. I thank Thee that it is my munificent contributions that have built this church, have made it possible to pray in this holy place, have given this preacher the opportunity to speak Thy Word. I thank Thee that if it were not for me this sanctuary would not be here."

The teacher heard him, and prayed, "O Lord, forgive me, a miserable sinner. I was that man's teacher."

IN

QUEST

OF

GOD

Chapter Twelve

> *Let a man love God with a perfect love whether it go well with him or ill.*
>
> —RABBINICAL SAYING

Religion has come full circle in our time. In twentieth-century America religion has returned to the point from which it began in the primitive world. Decades of research on the earliest forms of religion among the peoples of antiquity have demonstrated that the service of God—or gods—was offered in return for worldly success. Religion was a means, a technique, whereby man might "get things"—satisfy his desires, calm his fears, fulfill his dreams. It had little or nothing to do with faith, morals, or spiritual growth.

In the beginning man lived in a universe that was an utter mystery. It comprised thousands of perplexing phenomena, threatening terrors, agonizing experiences, with which man could not cope and for which he could find no adequate explanation. There were the stars moving eternally in their fixed courses, the seasons changing endlessly and regularly, the friendly days alternating with the hostile nights. There were lightning, thunder, earthquake, and flood. There were hunger, pain, disease, and death. Just to remain alive in such a universe—much less to consider success and happiness—was a supreme task.

At first man put his faith in magic and miracles; through his shamans and fetishes he sought to subdue the seemingly malevolent forces, to compel them to do his bidding. Ages rolled by, and the capricious "powers" continued to perform arbitrarily, regardless of man's demands; and man began to see that his tactics were futile. Slowly, painfully, he entered the period of religion.

"But later," writes Lewis Browne in *This Believing World,* "when he got it through his head that not even with his shamans and fetishes would he unfailingly coerce the rain, he tried instead to cajole it into falling. And only when that happened, did religion really begin. So long as man was naïve enough to believe that by the possession of some fetish or the utterance of some spell, he could force the spirits to do his will, man had not yet advanced beyond unqualified faith in magic. Not until the sharp bludgeoning of repeated failure rendered him a meeker and wiser man, did he begin to put his faith in what may be strictly termed religion. Not until he had grown up sufficiently to suspect that some attempts at coercing the spirits were doomed inevitably to failure did he begin to try to persuade them instead." *

Man had changed the means; but the end remained the same. Now it was persuasion instead of coercion, but the purpose was still to secure certain worldly results that would make human life bearable, successful, peaceful. Rich harvests; large flocks; many

* From *This Believing World* by Lewis Browne; copyright 1941. Used by permission of the publisher, The Macmillan Company.

children; protection against enemies (demonic as well as human) and suffering, and death; the admiration and esteem of one's fellow man; and, above all, favor in the eyes of the Divine.

The description of a deeply religious and highly successful man in the first chapter of the Book of Job is very significant: "There was a man in the land of Uz whose name was Job, and that man was wholehearted and upright and one that feared God and shunned evil. And there were born unto him seven sons and three daughters. His possessions also were 7,000 sheep and 3,000 camels and 500 yoke of oxen and 500 she-asses, and a very great household, so that this man was the greatest of all the children of the East."

You served God so that God would serve you. You were good so that God would be good to you. You sacrificed—i.e., gave some of your possessions to God—so that He would give you more in return. It was almost a pure business proposition: piety at bargain rates. You hearkened unto Him so that He would hearken unto you. *Quid pro quo;* tit-for-tat. Religion was a technique in using God for your own purposes—not in finding out how God might use you for His purposes. It was for your will, and not His, to be done.

But the higher wisdom was there. It was latent, for the most part. Yet there is a magnificent early expression of it in the final chapter of that same Book of Job (in this sense, the Book of Job is almost a complete history of the development of religion): "Then Job answered the Lord and said: I know that Thou canst do everything and that no purpose can be withholden from Thee. Who is this that hides counsel without knowledge? Therefore have I uttered that which I understood not; things too wonderful for me which I knew not. I had heard of Thee by the hearing of the ear; but now mine eyes see Thee."

It took many centuries for religion to reach that peak of wisdom. Or this one, from Isaiah, Ch. 58 (read regularly on the Day of Atonement): "Is such the fast that I have chosen? The day for a man to afflict his soul? Is it to bow down his head as a bullrush and to spread sackcloth and ashes under him? Wilt thou call this a fast and an acceptable day to the Lord? Is not this the fast that I have chosen? To loose the fetters of wickedness, to undo the bands of the yoke and to let the oppressed go free and that ye break every yoke? Is it not to deal thy bread to the hungry and that thou bring the poor that are cast out to thy house? When thou seest the naked, that thou cover him and that thou hide not thyself from thine own flesh?"

Those two passages are among the highest and holiest expressions of religion. There are others like them, in both the Old and New Testaments, and in the sacred writings of other religions. This is religion expressed as a success of the inner spirit—in terms of love and morality, faith and humility. This is religion as made manifest in the famous prayer attributed to St. Francis of Assisi: "Lord, make me an instrument of Your peace; where there is hatred, let me sow love; where there is injury, pardon; where there is doubt, faith; where there is despair, hope; where there is darkness, light; where there is sadness, joy. O Divine Master, grant that I may not so much seek to be consoled as to console; to be understood, as to understand; to be loved as to love; for it is in giving that we receive; it is in pardoning that we are pardoned; and it is in dying that we are born to eternal life."

The true religious feeling has survived until our own time. Vincent B. Silliman expresses it when he writes:

Let religion be thus a recurring challenge to the best we have and may be; let it be a trumpet call to action that is utterly generous. Let religion be to us the dissatisfaction with things that are, which bids us serve more eagerly the true and the right. Let religion be the sorrow that opens for us the way of sympathy, understanding, and service to humanity. Let religion be to us the wonder and the lure of that which is only partly known and understood. . . . Let religion be to us ideals that are true and right; yet ever beyond our finest achievement. Let religion be to us security and serenity because of its truth and beauty. . . . Let religion be to us hope and purpose, discovering for us opportunities to express our best through daily tasks and associations, uniting us in fellowship with all that is admirable in human beings everywhere, and holding before our eyes the prospects for a nobler life for all mankind.

As these lines are written I am preparing to celebrate the Passover Festival, which recalls the redemption of my ancestors from slavery and the birth of their freedom. My Christian neighbor is making ready for his Easter devotion, a Holy Day that recalls the resurrection of his Saviour, who died for his salvation. Synagogues and churches will be crowded with worshipers thinking of religion in its highest, rather than lowest, terms: as a difficult path leading to redemption, and not as an easy road to success. Both sacred days emphasize the crisis of surrender, one to the will of the Lord, the other to the way of the Saviour.

Both days remind us that through religion we may find the light—the light of faith and love and hope to illuminate the darkness of solitude, lack of meaning, and purposelessness that fill the lives of so many millions. Both days reassure us that through religion we may look upward and outward to the universe, that we may catch a clearer vision of God's everlasting might and mercy, which are an eternal source of strength and solace. Through religion we may also learn to look inward, to find within ourselves the Kingdom of Heaven: Zusya, at his best.

The Day of Atonement and Christmas are two other Holy Days when houses of worship are full, when the devout glimpse the spirit of religion at its most high. But the rest of the year, regular services are, as a rule, infrequently and indifferently attended by both Jews and Christians. Consequently, the religion they absorb and honor is that of the marketplace and the movies, the slick magazines and the best-selling books: religion at its crassest, "modern" religion.

Five years ago it was announced that while only one American in ten was a churchman when the first Federal census was taken in 1790, the latest showed a church membership of 59 per cent. A Gallup Poll estimate indicated that since 1950, when those figures were gathered, church membership has climbed to 79 per cent of all adults. In 1953 the cost of new Sanctuary buildings went above $600,000,000. It is estimated that Americans give to their houses of worship over three billion dollars a year.

There are other signs indicative of an unusual upsurge in religion. The Bible remains the annual best-seller. Inspirational books dealing with various aspects of religion have been high on the best-seller lists for over a decade, some of them achieving phenomenal sales. Hardly an issue of any popular magazine, highbrow or lowbrow, fails to carry at least one article on religion. Clergymen have become syndicated columnists, radio commentators, television stars, delivering daily and weekly religious messages.

The Congress of the United States has a Prayer Room. Also the United Nations. Meetings of the President's Cabinet are reported to open with prayers. Written prayers are served with meals in the dining cars of *de luxe* trains. They say that in the Southwest, football games are started with prayers. Once in Dallas, Texas, a bathing beauty queen was selected under such divine guidance. Religious themes are more and more frequent in the plots of stage, radio, and television shows. Hollywood could almost be called militantly religious. The newspapers carry many columns of religious notes and information.

A few years ago President Eisenhower, while installing a predominantly business government, spearheaded a "Back to God" movement. Its openly avowed purpose was to play Pied Piper; to lure all God's children, at least once a week, back into America's thousands of houses of worship. It frankly faced one of the best-known secrets in American religious life—the increasing emptiness of the pews, almost in inverse proportion to the rising membership rolls.

A paradox, obviously. A grave contradiction. Seventy-nine per cent of the adult population is enrolled; the very airwaves are saturated with religion; yet it was felt, and urgently, that a Back to God movement was necessary.

266

There is, in fact, a serious danger that our churches and synagogues will in time suffer the fate of those in Soviet Russia—will become museums, or mausoleums, or monuments, preserving the memory of a religion that was once alive and is now dead. They tell the story of a new minister in a small Oklahoma town who had this problem on the local level. Practically everybody in town was a church member, but nobody ever went to church. The young man spent the first four days desperately calling on the membership, begging them to come to his first services. He failed, as they had said he would.

He considered his plight. Then he placed a notice in the local newspaper, stating that as the church was dead, it was his duty to give it a decent Christian burial. The funeral would be held the following Sunday afternoon. Morbidly curious, the whole town turned out. In front of the pulpit they saw a huge coffin, smothered in flowers. The minister read the obituary and delivered a eulogy; he then invited his congregation to step forward and pay their respects to the dearly beloved who had departed. The long queue filed by; each mourner peeped into the coffin and turned away with a guilty look. In the coffin, tilted at the correct angle, was a large mirror.

So in spite of the boom in construction and enrollment, we are a bust in devout prayer and regular worship. Religion is experiencing an inflation of the flesh and a recession of the spirit. Congregations contain more and more families, but fewer and fewer who are faithful; more *pay*-ers but fewer *pray*-ers. The attitude of the American church- or synagogue-goer seems to be a reversal of the old spiritual: "It's my brother, it's my sister, but it's *not me, O* Lord, standin' in the need of prayer."

Some years ago *Fortune* Magazine, which caters particularly to successful businessmen, published an article called "Businessmen on Their Knees." The burden of its message was that since the end of World War II there had been a reconversion not only of machinery, but also of men in the industrial and financial worlds: a return to religion, a rebirth of faith in God and His word. Brushing aside a few skeptical or cynical dissenters, the article insisted that this return was not just another public relations gimmick, like the exploitation of Christ and Christmas, or the feeling that religion was a good investment for one's conscience, or excellent insurance against communism. This return, the article concluded, was a genuine expression of an acknowledgment of the truth Woodrow Wilson had uttered at the close of World War I: "The world cannot be saved materially, unless it be redeemed spiritually."

I was quoted, in that article, as one of the dissenting voices. To me, there is a difference between lip service to religion and life sacrifice to God. "Everybody talkin' about Heaven ain't goin' there." Belonging to a church may have nothing to do with belief. Recently an American tourist visiting Nazareth asked a Moslem religious leader if the spirit of Jesus Christ was still to be found in this ancient Palestinian village that had been his birthplace. The Moslem replied, "Many enter churches, but few recognize the truth of Christ. Many kneel but few pray. Not all who worship know Christ."

A World Congress of Faith was held in London just before the outbreak of World War II. Among the Far Eastern delegates were two Tibetan monks, representing Buddhism. They had come to the Congress in response to an urgent invitation, and had accepted on condition that they decide what they wanted to be shown, and that they be permitted to return home whenever they wished. After two weeks, they suddenly announced, in the middle of important deliberations, that they must leave for Tibet at once. Leaders of the Congress begged them to stay, but they were adamant. At least, the leaders pleaded, they might give their reasons for going. "There is no God in England," they explained.

"What? Haven't you seen Westminster Abbey, St. Paul's Cathedral, our hundreds of houses of worship?"

"Yes," the monks replied. "But these cathedrals and churches are either shut or empty most of the week, and open one day a

268

week, and even on that day few people go to them. Your banks are always full of worshipers; they are open and crowded a whole week, closed only one day a week; we see that here in the West there is no God but money." And the Tibetan monks went home.

The worship of money is nothing new; we have already referred to it often in this book. The worship of money is as old as the Golden Calf that broke Moses' heart. The possession of money in large quantities frequently stands in the way of any other worship. Ernest Renan, a scholarly non-Jewish historian of the Jewish people, discussing the ancient Sadducees, an aristocratic and powerful sect who rejected belief in immortality, observed cynically, "A rich Jew needs no Heaven." That observation applies with equal force to Christian and Jew today. Too many of our moneyed members of churches and synagogues are so busy accumulating and enjoying the pleasures of earth that they have little concern for the treasures of Heaven.

The worship of money is not new; *what is new is a reversion to the use of religious worship as a means to make money.* Man has fallen back three thousand years; he is again seeking to bend God to his will; he has lost all notion of bending himself to God's will. Religion has become a kind of mutual fund; careful observance of a few rules will guarantee good standing and an annual six per cent. Moses, Jesus, Buddha, Lao-tze, Gandhi, Baeck, Schweitzer were never interested in mutual funds; they have sought, through the ages, to make of religion a guide, a spiritual way, through which man might learn to serve God, not to coerce or persuade God to serve him.

I have read somewhere, in a recent report on Soviet Russia, that when the word "God" was printed with a capital letter in a school text, the initial was changed to lower-case in each of a million copies before the edition was released. This is what Americans are doing today: using God in lower case. When William James coined the phrase "the bitch goddess success," he may have had some inkling of what was coming to pass in America: that God would become a tool, religion a technique; that the

269

recitation of prayers and the reading of verses would be urged as a positive way to achieve one's ambition in life—to find a good job, come into money, make a hit at the office, be popular, win a husband, heal illness, ward off death.

The most famous evangelistic preacher of our day tells us that prayer brought him the last portion of $25,000 he needed to launch his first important radio program. The widow of one of the best-known ministers of our generation and authoress of a best-selling inspirational book on his life tells us of a friend who succeeded in acquiring a much-needed pastry cook and dishwasher for her seaside inn through this informal prayer: "I haven't the least idea where to find this help, Lord. This hotel is your business as well as mine. Will you please lead me to a dishwasher and pastry cook?" After the prayer she rose, dressed, went out in the car to the main street, and found two men—one a pastry cook and the other a dishwasher—waiting at the bus stop. They served the entire season and proved to be the best help she ever had.

God is not only a mutual fund; He is a banker, and an employment agency. We have, in our own overweening vanity, made the Almighty a maid of all work.

Perhaps the most famous inspirational author of our time tells us in an early chaper of his best-selling book—it sold over a million copies—of a man who, facing a probable business failure, succeeded by repeating this Biblical verse, "I can do all things through Christ Which strengtheneth me" (Philippians 4:13), several times upon retiring, three times before arising, and three additional times on the way to his crucial appointment. "It seems incredible," the elated man subsequently reported to the author, "that a few words from the Bible would do so much for a person."

He was right. It is not only incredible, but impossible; not only doubtful, but dangerous. (It is, by the way, a striking example of rendering unto Caesar the things that are God's!) It is a throwback to the primitive concept of religion. The bludgeoning of God for favors is not as open and direct, of course, as it once was.

It is all done in a more civilized—we might even say, a ruthlessly refined—manner. But the technique is basically the same, and so is the goal. If one could really count on this technique to reach this goal, then we might all be wise to practice what is implied in the injunction: "And why are ye anxious concerning raiment? Consider the lilies of the field, how they grow, they toil not, neither do they spin." (Matthew 6:28.)

The difference between earlier and later forms of celestial bribery may be seen in the traditional difference between the Japanese and the American manner of giving presents. The Japanese will present a gift with the definite expectation that you will, at the proper time, return the favor; when he is ready for it, he will let you know without blushing. The American presents the gift apparently with no strings attached; but with it goes the understanding that some day the recipient will express his gratitude in equally concrete form.

On a little higher level this new ancient religion is what the late Paul Hutchinson called "the cult of reassurance." In an article entitled "Have We a New Religion?" he asked, "What is this cult of reassurance? It is a flocking to religion especially in the middle-class circles for a renewal of confidence and optimism when they are in short supply. It is a turning to the Priest for encouragement to believe despite everything that has happened in this dismaying century, the world is good, life is good, the human story makes sense and comes out where we want it to come out. . . . It is a cult of affirmation (positive thinking) and a rejection of all contemporary cults of denial.

"Naturally it makes its greatest appeal to middle-brow Americans who are at odds with themselves and their lives. This is a huge class and it has been growing ever since Sinclair Lewis' bewildered Babbitt found himself staring into his shaving mirror and wondered what his high-geared life was all about. The nation is full of confused persons who feel that there is something wrong, something deeply unsatisfying, about the lives they are living, but would have trouble saying what it is and even more trouble

271

in discovering what to do about it. These are the people who are not yet badly enough disturbed (or wealthy enough) to be ready for a psychoanalyst, but they are frustrated, depressed, and have a feeling that they are victimized by life, and some of them are on the way to a crack-up."

This modern cult of reassurance was initiated by the publication of the late Rabbi Joshua Liebman's surprise success, *Peace of Mind*. That book was succeeded by a spate of others, following in general the same formula, promising to resolve modern man's mental and emotional problems, to help him overcome worry and anxiety, relieve him of any sense of guilt and fill him with confidence and courage. Up to now it has reached its peak in Dr. Norman Vincent Peale's *The Power of Positive Thinking*.

In justice to the memory of Rabbi Liebman (I knew him and his philosophy well) it must be said that his "peace of mind" was never intended as a pleasant soporific, or a mild anesthetic, to make men and women insensitive to the sorrows of human life; or as an aid to acquisition, a success formula that would guarantee success with built-in happiness. To him, peace of mind was not a sedative; neither was it a tranquilizer. Peace of mind did not mean absolute rest, permanent release from the constant struggle against tension and temptation; rather it was a kind of inner security from which could spring a righteous discontent with things as they are, and a restless, relentless drive to make them what they ought to be. It meant mature understanding, intelligent adjustment without sacrifice of individuality. It meant wisdom in attitude and action. Basically, this book is in harmony with his views. "Ours is a money culture," he wrote. "There is no doubt about it . . . and there are large numbers of people in this culture who make acquisition rather than enjoyment their goal in life. They literally kill themselves in the greedy pursuit of more and more wealth. The idolatry of material success has infected all classes in our American society, and the inevitable failure of the vast majority of people to obtain luxury and great wealth is responsible for the gnawing sense of insecurity and self-disdain."

272

In general, however, the perceptive criticism leveled at inspirational books—and at the ministers who preach this regressive religion—by Dr. Eugene Carson Blake, Stated Clerk of the Presbyterian church in the United States, is justified. Dr. Blake has charged that the books and ministers in question were superficial in their interpretations and misleading in their presentations; that they were omitting or glossing over some of the most profound and vital teachings of the Jewish and Christian religions. "Church leaders are concerned," he said, "that people with a new religious interest may attempt to turn that religion into magic—that is, to try to use God for their own purposes rather than to serve God and find His purposes. To try to use God for any purpose, however noble, is wrong."

Dean James A. Pike of the New York Cathedral (St. John the Divine) has warned, "In the realm of personal religion there is a tendency to seek to use God as one of a number of resources to enable us to get what we want and enjoy life as we would. Much modern religion sees God as a means to an end, keeping us first and placing God second. Thus, God is seen as helping us sleep better, calming our anxieties, making us more attractive to people, and making us more successful. Our anxieties can be a means of grace. It is true that if God is put into the center of things lives usually work out better. But true religion puts God first and us second.

"In the public realm," he continued, "the same tendency is seen. We are told that we should return to religion to strengthen us against communism. Of course, we are against communism. And if as a people we were truly devoted to God we would be secure and nothing would disturb our peace. But to seek to use God, who is everlasting, as a means to attain something that is earthbound, something that is part of the passing show, i.e., our particular national interest, is to turn things completely around."

A poll of our nation's undergraduates on their religious interests and habits has revealed that though they have jumped aboard the bandwagon of religious revival, their church attendance has not increased (it has, in fact, declined); that the teachings of Dr. Peale, very popular in the general revival of interest, are not popular on campus. Barnard College girls term one inspirational writer "a religious Dorothy Dix," and have asserted that he distorts Christianity; is, indeed, successful because he knows how to package wares slickly. An undergraduate at New York University declared, "Once religion promised pie in the sky. Now we have the inspirational boys who promise pie in the penthouse."

In fairness to Dr. Peale and his confreres, it must be pointed out that despite their distortions of the deeper values and purposes of religion and their extravagant claims for the "power of positive thinking," of vocalizing prayer, of Bible reading, of religious pep talks, they have nevertheless given religion in our time a new lift, as well as a new look. They have made religion more respectable in high places; they have reminded us that religion is primarily concerned with problems of the soul, and not with social problems; they have encouraged the use of the dynamic insights of psychiatry and psychoanalysis as aids to religion; they have imbued Americans with a temporary, and perhaps artificial, but still helpful, spirit of confidence and optimism, at a time when men might well be expected to give way to pessimism and despair.

There is a great void in our age; it is where real religion ought to exist and does not. Here again I turn to the late Paul Hutchinson: "For what today's cult of reassurance most lacks—and indeed disavows—is a sense of life's inevitable failures. Here is the point at which it stands in starkest contrast to the teachings of America's most searching contemporary theologian, Reinhold Niebuhr. Many say they find Niebuhr hard to understand, but there is one central idea in his writing which should be easy to grasp, for it is validated by universal experience. This is the contention: that all human effort, however noble, after achieving, contains within it an element of failure. Perhaps one reason Americans say they cannot understand Niebuhr is because their minds simply will not harbor this fact, that all success is dogged by failure. We Americans must succeed. We cannot appreciate life with any other expectation. But Christianity, in the most profound sense, is a religion of failure."

So is Judaism. So are all great religions. Read carefully the writings of the Prophets and Psalmists in the Old Testament and the teachings of Jesus and preachings of Paul in the New, and you will understand what Dr. Hutchinson means when he says that religion is for failure. It is for those who are aware that much of life is fear, frustration, loneliness, denial, defeat, despair, death. And who among us is not occasionally, if not frequently, aware of this? We have discussed the issue throughout this book; and we ought to see by now that some ambitions, some areas, some associations in our lives will be failures.

As I write these lines, on the eve of Easter, I have before me a profoundly true excerpt from a magazine editorial of two years ago—even truer now than when it was printed: "Easter A.D. 1955 finds men's lives touched also with a universal sense of hunger, of some great lack which makes material gains seem to crumble even in the getting and makes men grope for a greater spiritual content and meaning to their lives. The statistics of their gropings are all about us—hardly a day passes without a new expression of it." Anne Morrow Lindbergh goes away by herself, seeking in solitude a way out of the "torn-to-pieces-hood" of mechanized life that makes modern woman feel like a telephone exchange or a laundromat. In *Gift from the Sea* she tells that those long hours of inward searching make her feel "melted into the universe, lost in it as one is lost in a canticle of praise, swelling from an unknown crowd in a cathedral. We must turn inward for strength, for the Kingdom of Heaven is within." Thomas Merton, in *No Man Is an Island,* speaks of every man's need for "full discovery of who he himself really is."

Today's new success religion is also for failure, but for failure in material wishes, physical health, emotional balance. It is not far from Dr. Coué's technique: Repetition of the phrase "Every day in every way I'm getting better and better" was the equivalent thirty years ago of today's cult of reassurance. A loaf of optimism, a jug of prayers (preferably short, snappy prayers), a mouthful of quotations from the Bible, and an occasional nod from Thou —and I can conquer all. I can be a success.

How often, through the years of my ministry, have tortured souls wandered into my study begging for just such a Little Dandy Instant Cure-All! Couldn't I recommend prayers, Scriptural passages, specific rituals that would do the trick quickly? Can't religion show them how to convert their failures into successes—professional, marital, social? Isn't there some key phrase, some new idea, that will cast out hate and fear? Perfect love casteth out both; but perfect love is not so simple to find. With deep regret, I have had to confess that my religion had no simple answers, no slick formulas, no set rules (success guaranteed or your money back), no absolute assurances.

Sometimes I tell them this story: Once a little boy was playing hide-and-seek with his friends. At one point in the game, when it was his turn to hide, they quit playing, and went on home, without telling him. When he knew what had happened he broke into tears. His grandfather came out to comfort him: "Do not weep, my son," he said, "because your friends left and did not come to find you. There is a lesson in this. All of life is like a game between God and man. But it is God who weeps, because man does not play the game fairly. God is waiting to be found, and man has gone off to search after other things."

God is always waiting to be found. But he must be sought in the right spirit: with faith and honesty and high purpose. If man is willing to play the game properly—to serve God, and not demand that God serve him; to give himself to God, and not demand gifts from Him; to submit to God's will, and not demand that God submit to man's—then God will not hide His face forever.

"Seek ye the Lord while he may be found," cried Isaiah. "Call ye upon Him while He is near." Seek God—not gifts from His hand. Call upon God to be near Him; do not command

Him to be near you. True religion means finding God and filling your life with His spirit; learning to understand His word, to perceive His will, to follow His way. That way is the path which the "I" of the individual must take to the "Thou" of the universe, in order to become one with Him, and thus to become Zusya.

Théophile Gautier once tried to define real love: "To renounce your individuality, to see with another's eyes, to hear with another's ears, to be two and yet be one, to so melt and mingle that you no longer know whether you are you or another. To absorb continually, to radiate constantly, to reduce earth, sea, sky, and all that is in them, to a single being, to give yourself to that being so wholly that nothing whatever is withheld, to be prepared at any moment for sacrifice, to double your personality in bestowing it. That is love." And that is the path and purpose of true religion.

The philosopher Albert North Whitehead once defined religion as "what a man does with his solitariness." Yes, it is a way of dealing with one's aloneness; but it is also a way of dealing with others—one's family and friends and fellow men. And it is a way of dealing with the universe itself—its implacable forces, its insoluble mysteries. Religion is the path to man's best self; and the discovery of his best self is man's only meaningful success.

Moses, in herding his flock through the wilderness of Sinai after years of loneliness, looking inward and outward at once as the bitter memories of the past and confused dreams of the future tore at his spirit, became himself when he finally faced himself under the Divine scrutiny in the burning bush. So it was with Gandhi, who left a successful law practice and a high place in the community, chose the solitariness of principle, poverty, and prison, long fasts, lonely vigils of faith, and became himself by confronting his God, facing himself under the Divine scrutiny. And so with Schweitzer, philosopher, theologian, musician, doctor, who rejected the paths of fame and eminence and went to face himself under the Divine scrutiny at a jungle post in Lambaréné. Yes, religion is what a man does with his solitariness.

Yet measured by the standards most of us apply to ourselves, all these men, and Jesus too, were failures. Today they are regarded as successes; but mankind has adopted a very convenient double standard, one for itself and one for its heroes, who by accepting the greatness within themselves make it unnecessary—we think—for the rest of us to do so. Ultimately we either sanctify or hate our heroes; we cannot bear the thought that the qualities which made them great are qualities which exist latently in all of us, and that it is not they who are exceptional for being heroes, but we who are exceptional in our smugness, self-deceit, hypocrisy, laziness. Moses gave his life to his people; they grumbled and complained and in the end rebelled against him. The disciples of Jesus disobeyed, doubted, and denied Him. Gandhi was revered by millions but resented by other millions; he died at the hands of an assassin. Schweitzer remains a great man, one of the greatest spiritual successes of our time, self-exiled from a civilization that is eager to honor him. Yet I often wonder whether he remains in such high repute because the world has found it unnecessary to pay any attention to what he believes and says.

I thought of all these remarkable figures when I read George Edward Woodberry's evaluation of Cervantes' *Don Quixote*. "Don Quixote," he writes, "achieves the ideal of his soul, however badly he fares with fortune in the outer world. He is complete in true knighthood and when his madness leaves him, it cannot take away the nobility of nature which it brought the gentleman whom it found nameless and unoccupied on his little estate and made one of the world's heroes. The vocabulary of moral praise cannot explain his virtues. He is brave, resolute, courteous, wise, kind, gentle, patient. What tenacity there is in his resolution, what recklessness in his courage, what fatalistic senselessness in his resignation, what endurance in a land of lost causes, what sadness of defeat accepted in the quiet of adversity."

Matthew Arnold once defined religion as "morality tinged with emotion." There can be no enduring morality without reli-

278

gion; but there can be no religion without a vital morality. One of the fundamental causes of the failure of religion in our time is the general decline of morality, coupled with an increasing tendency to divorce it from religion.

Not long ago I lunched with a distinguished member of my congregation. Within the last decade the man has won spectacular successes in the business world; he is in the forefront of a very small and admirable group of dynamic civic leaders. I was seeking to enlist his more personal and generous interest in the activities of our temple; I wanted not only material support, but a more regular attendance at Sabbath worship.

He set forth apologetic reasons for his negligence in the past and his reluctance to involve himself for the future. He gave the usual arguments, and emphasized one which I have referred to before, and which, because of the man's experience and reputation, I could not gloss over: he had discovered too many members, and even leaders, in church and synagogue affairs who publicly professed a profound concern about the truths of religion and the teachings of God, but who privately (in their family relationships and business dealings) violated them at will, barely managing to stay within the conventional and legal limits of modern life.

He then went on to make a very startling statement—startling for a businessman, though it would not have been for a clergyman. With an earnestness of expression and a sincerity of intention that I have rarely caught in a man's face and voice, he asserted that during the thirty-odd years of his contacts with competitors and customers, he had witnessed an appalling decline in the ethical integrity, moral decency, and spiritual nobility of human character. Men and women whose word was really their bond, he had found few and far between; so were those in whom personal honor triumphed always when challenged by a chance for material gain; so were those in whose eyes lying, cheating, and stealing were not simply means to an end but thoroughly degrading sins. Money or its equivalent—power, position, prestige—is, he insisted (not cynically, but regretfully) king in our society; and the getting of money, by fair means (many of which are immoral) if possible, and even by foul means (all of which are immoral) if necessary, is the primary goal of the average American businessman.

As he spoke, I was reminded of a story from the Talmud about the sage Rabbi Jochanan ben Zakkai. This renowned teacher lay on his deathbed, laboriously breathing away his last moments on earth. His grief-stricken disciples begged that he impart one final word of wisdom, before eternity sealed his lips.

With a supreme effort, straining his every nerve, he whispered "May your fear of God be as great as your fear of man." Amazed, the students hurriedly asked, "Master, you must mean rather the contrary: Our fear of man should become as great as our fear of God."

"No, my sons," the Rabbi sighed with a dying gasp. "May you learn to be afraid of doing wrong in the eyes of God Who you think does not see you or in His love will not punish you, at least as much as you are afraid of doing wrong in the eyes of your fellow man, who you suspect may find you out and have you punished under his law."

The Talmud suggests that when a man comes before the Heavenly Court for judgment, he will be asked, "Did you deal fairly in your livelihood?" That is, did you observe the laws of God and not merely the laws of man in making money? Were you as careful when the sums—or temptation—involved were small as when they were great and obvious? Did you stay within the law merely to avoid punishment? Did you examine the sources of that livelihood? At whose expense did they come to you? In all your successful manipulations, was there a man cheated for your benefit? A customer? A competitor? Your company? Your country?

The Heavenly Judge might remind him of a Midrashic story. There was a teacher who earned his livelihood preparing flax at home and taking it to the market for public sale. One day his pupils said to him, "Rabbi, you toil long and hard. It is not good. We will buy you a donkey to ease your burden." They bought a donkey from an Arab, and found a pearl hidden in its saddle. They presented the donkey to their teacher: "Now you need work no longer."

"Why?" he asked.

"We bought a donkey from an Arab and found a pearl in the saddle."

"Does the owner know about the pearl?" asked the Rabbi.

"No."

"Go and give it back to him," said the Rabbi. "Am I a barbarian? No! I would rather hear the Arab exclaim, 'Blessed be Our Lord!' than possess all the riches of the world."

The Heavenly Judge might also quote this rabbinical teaching: "The law, 'Thou shalt not set a stumbling block before the blind,' is extended to mean: you must never hide part of your intention in giving advice to any man. You must not say: sell your field and buy a donkey, when you are really intending to circumvent him, and get his field by buying it from him. Perhaps, in self-defense, you will argue: 'I gave him good advice. It was really to his advantage to sell his field and instead obtain the donkey.' Even so! You must not act thus. There is no actual law against deceitful behavior, but good feeling and the higher justice (the law of God) declare that it must not be done." There is an old couplet that runs: The meanest man I ever saw/Allus kept inside the law.

And I suspect that on Judgment Day the most telling question will be this: Did you always set human values above material gains? Or did you collect income without wondering about its source, about the lives, the conditions, the possible miseries, of those who created it? Were you worried about the bodies and minds and souls of the men about you? Did you see your employer, your employee, your patient, your client, your customer, as a human being or as a source of income?

"Why did the Tower of Babel crumble?" is an old question;

and the answer is still full of meaning. The Tower crumbled because those in charge of the work cared more for the job than for the workers. When a brick fell to earth, they paused to bewail its loss; when a worker fell, they urged the others to work even harder. The brick was more important than the man; so God destroyed the structure.

A few years ago a judge in Toledo, Ohio, ruled that stingy bank officials, who had stayed within the laws of man but ignored the laws of God, were primarily to blame for the embezzlement of $7,541 by their cashier over a period of years up to 1942. Pointing out that the bank had hired the man in 1920 at a yearly salary of $1,080, and had raised him, by 1942, to only $1,900, the judge refused to pass sentence on him. Instead, he said, "If I had the authority, I would sentence the bank officials and board directors to read every year the story of Scrooge at Christmastime."

Rabbi Israel Salanter, a learned and revered teacher of the eighteenth century, was an unusually righteous and pious man. One day he stepped to a full pail of water to wash, and used only a splash of it. His pupils were astonished; their teacher had failed to fulfill properly the commandment to wash his hands thoroughly before eating. Hesitatingly they turned to him: "Please forgive us for questioning you; but we cannot understand why you used so little water."

And the saintly man replied, "I have discovered that the maidservant fetches this water from a distant well. She, poor creature, bends low under the heavy load, with the yoke on her shoulders for so long. I do not think it right to perform a *mitzvah* [religious commandment] at the expense of someone else's shoulders."

What America needs is not men and women on their knees, but men and women on their toes, reaching ever higher to bring the laws of God into the laws of man. What America needs is not so much to draw its citizens into churches and synagogues, but to draw the purposes of churches and synagogues into the hearts and homes of the citizens. We need not so much to put life into religion; we need to bring religion into life. Not to bring the average man back to religion, but to bring God back to every man, into his everyday life—His Word, His Way, His Will.

There is a wise, inspiring passage toward the end of the late Lloyd Douglas' novel, *Invitation to Life*. Actress Sally Lingley is a spoiled, talented darling of the rich. Her egotism, callousness, and cynicism have led her to professional failure. Utterly discouraged, she visits Dean Harcourt in the cathedral, seeking counsel. "I'm not even sure that I believe in God," she cries. "That is not important just now," he smiles. "I mean it isn't quite so urgent at present whether you believe in God as whether God can believe in you. If you will conduct yourself in a manner that might encourage Him to believe in you, in time you may feel that you can return the compliment." *

Matthew Arnold once described God as "a power not ourselves, making for righteousness." That dynamic power, eternally fashioning not only righteousness but beauty, truth, love, and peace, continually challenges our wonder and wisdom. Its mysteries are too deep for us to fathom; its forces too mighty for us to measure; its purposes too veiled for us to penetrate.

We must return to Job and cry out with him: "But wisdom where shall it be found? And where is the place of understanding? Man knoweth not the price thereof; neither is it to be found in the land of the living. . . . Whence then cometh wisdom? And where is the place of understanding? Seeing it is hid from the eyes of all living. And unto man he said: 'Behold the fear of the Lord, that is wisdom; and to depart from evil is understanding.' "

The road to God leads to wisdom; the way of religion to understanding. But in the beginning we must be willing to take the road, travel the way, without any assurance of wisdom and

* From *Invitation to Life* by Lloyd Douglas; published by Houghton Mifflin Company.

understanding at the end. We must step forward with a genuine reverence for the "power" and a true passion for the pursuit of the good: what Immanuel Kant called "the starry heavens above and the moral law within." Then we may achieve spiritual success; we may find happiness and peace at the end of our quest.

In speaking of nature's ministry to men, Ralph Waldo Emerson said, "The stars awaken a certain reverence because though always present they are inaccessible, but all natural objects make a hundred impressions when the mind is open to their influence. Nature never wears a mean appearance. Neither does the wisest man extort her secret and lose his curiosity by finding out all her perfection. . . . Nature in its ministry to man is not only the material, but is also the process and the result. All the parts incessantly work into one another's hands for the benefit of man. . . . We are taught by great actions that the Universe is the property of every individual in it. . . . Nature stretches out her arms to embrace man; only let his thoughts be of equal greatness."

It is through religion that man may learn to muster thoughts, feelings, visions, that may match those of the Divine; that he may not only make himself a partner of God in the creation of good, but also, by putting himself in tune with his Maker, become his best self—Zusya. He must be prepared to make the whole journey. He must do it with faith and courage.

Tolstoi once set down an old legend. Centuries ago there was a saintly man who lived alone on a desert island. One day a group of fishermen landed near his hut; among them was a very old man, so simple-minded that he could hardly communicate, and knew nothing of prayer. Filled with deep compassion, the saint took infinite plans to teach the simpleton the Lord's Prayer. Thanking him humbly, the old man departed with the fishermen. A few hours after the boat had disappeared into the distance, the hermit saw what appeared to be a human shape on the horizon, walking on the water's surface, approaching the island.

284

As the shape took form and set foot on land, the saint recognized his pupil. He ran to meet him.

"Would you help me?" the old man stammered. "I have forgotten the Lord's Prayer."

The embarrassed saint turned away. "You don't have to pray," he answered, and sent him on his way. Striding over the waters, the old man hurried to join his comrades.

IN

QUEST

OF

PEACE

Chapter Thirteen

> *Nothing can bring you peace but the triumph of principle.*
> —EMERSON
> *When a man finds no peace within himself, it is useless to seek it elsewhere.*
> —LA ROCHEFOUCAULD

Some years before the awful destruction of World War II and the awesome invention of the atomic bomb, James Hilton wrote an enchanting and popular novel called *Lost Horizon*. Now it seems not only enchanting but also prophetic. It was, you will recall, the story of an English statesman carried accidentally to an idealized Tibetan city called Shangri-La, "hidden in the heart of the plateau; of what in the full shimmer of moonlight appeared to be the loveliest mountain on earth—an almost perfect cone of snow, simple in outline as if a child had drawn it—impossible to classify as to size, height, or nearness—so radiant, so serenely poised, that he wondered for a moment if it were real at all." It was a place of permanent, perfect peace.

Hugh Conway, the Englishman, was soon brought before the High Lama (now over 200 years old) and informed that he had been chosen to succeed him. Why, asked Conway, should he make this sacrifice, forever exiled from his own great civilization? To what purpose was this valley isolated from the rest of the world? "There is a reason," answered the High Lama, "and a very definite one, indeed. It is the whole reason for this chance-sought colony of strangers living beyond their years. We do not follow an idle experiment, a mere whimsy. We have a dream and a vision. We have come to see that all the loveliest things are transient and perishable, and that war, lust and brutality may some day crush them and there be no more left in the world. We see nations strengthening not in wisdom but in vulgar passions and the will to destroy; we see their machine-power multiplying until a single-weaponed man may match a whole army—a time when men exulting in the techniques of homicide will rage so hotly over the world that every precious thing will be in danger, every book and picture and harmony, every treasure garnered through two millen-niums, the small, the delicate, the defenseless—all will be lost.

". . . And Shangri-La, hidden here in the heart of Tibet, un-known to the so-called civilized world, will escape. We shall, we hope and believe, outlive the doom. Here we shall stay with our books and our music and our meditations, conserving the frail elegancies of a dying age and seeking such wisdom as men will need when their passions are all spent. We have a heritage to cherish and bequeath. I place in your hands, my son, the heritage and destiny of Shangri-La. I believe that you will live through the storms. And after, through the long age of devastation, you may still live, growing older and wiser and more patient. You will conserve the fragrance of our history and add to it the touch of your own mind. You will welcome the stranger and teach him the rule of age and wisdom, and one of these strangers, it may be, will succeed you when you yourself are very old. Beyond that my vision weakens—but I see at a great distance a new world stirring in the ruins, stirring clumsily but in hopefulness, seeking its lost and legendary treasures, and they will all be here, my son, hidden behind the mountains in the valley of the moon, preserved by a miracle for a new Renaissance." *

The source of Shangri-La's permanent peace was not the wisdom of the High Lama, or the way of life that characterized the valley. There have always been wise men who warned of the destruction and death that war brings. There have always been peaceful and happy experiments in community living. Tahitis in fact, as well as Tibets in fiction, have been with us since Adam and Eve were first set down in the perfect peace of an earthly Paradise. The secret seems to be detachment: detachment from, as opposed to involvement in, the civilizations of mankind. The Utopian society is hidden away in a forbidding range of mountains, or on an uncharted island in a vast sea, or in a deep valley lost in a dense forest, or in a closed circle of brotherly communion, like that of the ancient Essene sect in the Dead Sea Desert, or like that of monks and nuns in monasteries and convents. It is almost primitive in its material purposes and achievements, simple in its needs and interests, unhurried in its aims and activities, uncomplicated in its attitudes and associations. The essence of the secret seems to be that if one reduces the number and importance of acquisitions and possessions, and thus eliminates or minimizes the competitive drive for public distinction, outer success, the traditional marks of his superiority over his fellows—if one develops a detachment from worldly objectives and transient pleasures, from urges and dreams that cry painfully for fulfillment, then he can find his Shangri-La, and live always on a plateau of perfect and permanent peace.

Johannes (Meister) Eckhart has described disinterestedness or detachment (*Abgeschiedenheit*) this way: "Perfect detachment is without regard, without either lowliness or loftiness to creatures; it has no mind to be below nor yet to be above; it is minded to be master of itself, loving none and hating none, having neither likeness nor unlikeness, neither this nor that to any creature; the only thing it desires is to be one and the same. For to be either this or that is to want something. He who is this or that is somebody; but detachment wants altogether nothing."

This kind of detachment has often been described as very close to the Buddhist state of nothingness, which at its purest becomes Maya, or nonbeing. A legend among the Zen Buddhists tells that Bodhidharna, the first Zen patriarch in China, came there from India in the sixth century. The Emperor Wu, a pious and studious follower of the Buddhist way of life, invited the patriarch to his court and asked him to explain the highest and holiest truth as set forth in the Mahayana Sutras.

"A vast emptiness and no holiness," answered Bodhidharna.

"Who are you, then," the Emperor demanded, "that stand before me as if there is nothing holy and nothing high in the vast emptiness of ultimate truth?"

"I do not know, Your Majesty," was the answer.

Of course he didn't know; because where there is emptiness, there is nothing: no holiness, no happiness, no sin, no sorrow, not even identity. Where there is true detachment, there can be no dissatisfaction, no dissension, no disturbance. There can be no clash of interests, because there are no interests. When the detachment is absolute, permanent and perfect peace follow; but it is the peace of death, and not of life.

Absolute detachment is impossible. If one can keep his eyes closed to the outside world—even to the slight shifts of light and shadow, the play of sun and wind—he can hardly escape the changing thoughts of his inner world, unless he is in a state of nonbeing—unless, in short, he has ceased to exist.

The peace that mankind has sought for centuries is that of life, not that of death; not the detached peace of a special community, cut off from the world; not the peace of the mystic dream; not the saintly peace of total self-abnegation: but the peace that is wrested out of the very struggle for personal survival on this earth, the peace torn from the very tensions that arise in the conflicts of society, the peace that is found not in seceding from life, but in living it fully, controlling it, fashioning it to accord with the human vision of God's Kingdom.

The peace of life cannot be perfect, and it cannot be permanent. The very essence of living is movement, and movement always encounters resistance, and resistance means conflict. Armed warfare may someday cease—and soon, we hope; but the inner conflicts of humanity will never be totally resolved. Peace on earth in the political sense is a distinct possibility—even, I should say, a necessity—but absolute, permanent, perfect peace of mind for all men everywhere is an illusion, and a dangerous illusion at that.

After long and concentrated perusal of the Bible, the ancient sages recognized the problem. "Great is peace," they taught, "for if beings above, among whom is no jealousy or hate or contention or wrangling or quarrel or strife or envy, need peace—as it is said, 'He maketh peace in His high places' (Job 25:2)—how much more do the beings below, with whom these bad qualities are present, need peace!"

The Bible teaches, "Seek peace and pursue it." The pursuit of peace is a full-time job—and here is a clue to man's dilemma. It is like the pursuit of truth, beauty, justice, love, happiness—the pursuit of any absolute. When Pontius Pilate asked, "What is truth?" he was being philosophical, and not cynical; he was asking a question that has obviously not yet been satisfactorily answered.

Here is the clue, stated bluntly: Because we cannot count on the attainment or permanence of the absolute virtues, *it is in the pursuit of those virtues that man's success lies.* Every virtue has its vice—love has hate, truth has falsity, beauty has ugliness—and we are all compounded of both. To attain either perfect virtue or perfect evil is to cease existing: the goal of man should be not perfect virtue, *but the knowledge that he has lived his life in pursuit of perfect virtue.*

Look back over this book. Nowhere have we demanded perfection in anything; nowhere recommended absolute virtue; nowhere advocated formulas, shibboleths, dogmas of perfect justice, truth, beauty and love. But everywhere we have stressed compassion. And what is compassion, after all, but the capacity to feel that another man's imperfections are matched by my own? That we are all of a mixed nature? That none of us is without failure, sin or shortcomings? *When a man is in search of virtue he may perhaps never forgive himself his own sins, but he must always forgive others theirs.*

In his preface to *Towards a Science of Peace,* Theo F. Lentz points out, "Peace has become a dangerous word. To evade that for which the word should stand, however, is far more dangerous. This book is based upon the twofold assumption that practically speaking the road to peace is not known, but that it can be discovered if enough of us make it our main business to look for it. No blueprint is presented here for peace action. But rather a proposal for peace research action. This is a radical proposal for a new and profound approach to an exceedingly important and baffling problem." *

The teachers in the Talmud were keenly conscious of the importance of the constant pursuit of peace; they said, "Every Israelite must seek to promote peace in Israel even as Aaron sought to promote peace. If a man sits in his place and keeps silent, how can he pursue peace in Israel between man and man? But let him leave the place and roam about in the world and pursue peace in Israel. Seek peace in your own dwelling place and pursue it in

* From the preface to *Towards a Science of Peace* by Theo F. Lentz; published by Bookman Associates.

another place. Be of the disciples of Aaron, loving peace and pursuing peace, loving thy fellow creatures and drawing them near the Torah."

Peace is first of all an individual problem, as the passage from the Talmud indicates, and then an interrelational, universal problem. Those who cannot live in peace with themselves will never live at peace with others. Peace, like charity, begins at home, within a man's own soul.

The pursuit of inner peace has been one of the most vigorous of our time. Ever since Freud postulated the unconscious and helped us peer into its deepest recesses, we have become increasingly aware of the warfare in constant progress within the human personality. We picture the id, the ego, and the superego as a system of checks and balances in constant conflict; often the conflict creates such a high degree of tension that an almost superhuman effort is required to stave off self-destruction. Split personalities are not the only casualties; there are also spoiled personalities, warped, soured on life; and many are the scars which cover unhealed wounds.

In the years of my ministry I have, from time to time, told our Sunday School children that they were little zoos. Inside them, there must be a number of animals; sometimes they growl like dogs, claw like cats, rage like tigers, clown like monkeys, laugh like hyenas, eat like pigs, are stubborn as mules, and behave like jackasses. They must be careful and conscientious zoo-keepers, ever watching those animals, caging them when necessary, in order to function well in human society. I have warned them that they must be the masters of these animals, and not their slaves, and that their primary task is to keep peace among them.

Adults do not need the parable, but they should accept the lesson. Inside all of us are animal instincts, ready at any moment to destroy the human balance we so laboriously build from childhood on; ready, in other words, to destroy the inner peace, the maturity, we have attained. When we have not mastered these instincts, tamed them, assimilated them, learned to recognize them and to control them, we are not masters of ourselves, and we are a long way from being our best selves: Zusya is not Zusya.

An old story, repeated in my book, *The Power of Faith*, tells about a college professor, wearily marking examination papers while his restless eight-year-old son, eager for companionship, tugged away at his sleeve, demanding attention. Finally, in desperation, the professor scattered on the floor the pieces of a jigsaw puzzle of a map of the world. Certain that he had won an hour's respite, he returned to his work; but within ten minutes his boy cried delightedly, "Look, Daddy, it's finished!"

"Impossible," he protested.

"But look, Daddy, there it is."

One glance confirmed the report. "How did you do it so fast?" the professor asked.

"It was easy. There was a picture of a man on the other side. So I put the man together and then the world was together."

Man himself is our most difficult puzzle, and putting him together is our most crucial problem. We must create peace within the individual by bringing him to the truth about himself, his fellow man, his own soul. We must create a world of individuals before we can hope for a world at peace; we must convince men once for all that there is no profit in gaining the whole world, if they must lose their souls in the process.

An English engineer was once sent by his London office to a remote station in Central Africa to supervise an important long-term project. It took him months to assemble his equipment, hire natives, and trek to the site. The day work began he received a cable from his home office ordering him to abandon the project and return immediately, bringing with him the bulk of the equipment. He and his men headed for the Atlantic coast, packing the equipment on their backs and maintaining a stiff pace. After two weeks of forced marches they were within a day of the coast, but they were exhausted. He urged the men forward, but they sat down and refused to move. He begged, pleaded, cajoled, threatened; it was no use. Finally he asked, "Why, after driving

293

yourselves for two weeks, why, now when success is over the hill, do you give up?"

"My master," answered the leader, "we will rest here awhile, to give our souls a chance to catch up with our bodies."

The last few generations have done much for the body of man: strengthened its tissues, lengthened its years, granted it time and energy for more and more of the delights of this earth. But we have done little for the soul of man. It is time now for a rest: time to allow the spiritual capacities of humanity to catch up with its physical progress. There is little danger for us of death by starvation; but there is danger to our souls, exposed to all the strains and tensions of a success-ridden civilization, grievously wounded by the assaults of a materialistic age.

A prayer which Plato, in his *Dialogues,* ascribes to Socrates, runs: "Beloved Pan and all ye gods who haunt this place, give me beauty in the inward soul; and may the outward and inward man be at one. May I reckon the wise to be wealthy; and may I have such a quantity of gold as none but the temperate can carry. Anything more? That prayer, I think, is enough for me."

Man cannot arrive at a state of inner peace unless he trains his body to come to terms with his soul; unless he establishes a balance between the longings of the flesh and the yearnings of the spirit. As he appeases his physical hunger, he must allow time to concentrate on those values which will nourish his soul, which will satisfy his hunger for wisdom and salvation. Neither body nor soul can live happily without the other.

Neither can interrelational peace—brotherhood among men— be perfect and permanent. Again, it is in the search for it that virtue lies. "So great is peace," said the teachers of the Talmud, "that God decreed that His own name, which is written in holiness, may be blotted out in waters to produce peace between a man and his wife."

There was once a Rabbi Meir who knew the priceless value of

294

peace. Every Friday evening he gave a public sermon or an exposition of Scripture in his synagogue. There was a woman who went faithfully to hear him; one evening his sermon was long, and when the woman went home she found that the lamp had gone out, and her husband was angry. He asked where she had been; she told him. He answered, "Never shall you enter this house again until you have spat in the eyes of the preacher," and he turned her out.

Through the Holy Spirit Rabbi Meir saw what had happened, so he announced publicly that he was suffering in his eyes. "Any woman," he pleaded, "who knows how to whisper a spell against pain in the eyes, let her come and whisper it."

The neighbors said to the woman, "The time has come. Pretend that you are going to whisper a spell, and then spit in his eyes."

She went to the Rabbi, who said to her, "Can you whisper a spell?"

In her nervousness she was honest, and answered, "No."

He said, "Spit seven times in my eyes; that will heal them." She did.

He said, "Go now, and tell your husband, 'You ordered me to spit once, and I have spat seven times.' "

Then his disciple said to Rabbi Meir, "Should the Law be thus made contemptible? If you had told us, we could have sent for the man and lashed him with rods till he had made it up with his wife."

And the Rabbi replied, "Shall it not be with the honor of Rabbi Meir as with the honor of his Maker? If the Holy Name may be washed away in water to make peace between a man and his wife, how much more is this true of the honor of Rabbi Meir!"

Furthermore, the sages taught, so great is peace that in the Scriptures are fictitious words, used to make peace between Joseph and his brothers. "For it says: *Thy father commanded before his death, saying, 'Forgive, I pray thee, the trespass of thy brothers'* (Genesis 50:16–17), and we do not find in the Scriptures that

295

Jacob had given such a command. The fictitious words were for the sake of peace—a man should always be eager in increasing peace with his brethren and relatives and with all men, even the heathen in the street, so that he may be beloved above and popular on earth, and acceptable to his fellow creatures." Peace is great, when it is within an individual; it is even greater when it is interrelational.

Brotherhood becomes more difficult as the circle widens beyond the family and into the community; it is just because the ties of brotherhood are so feeble that each year we proclaim a special Brotherhood Week. (They say that there is a marked difference between the caress of a dog and that of a cat: a dog nuzzles out of affection, but when a cat rubs against you, he is not caressing you—he is caressing himself on you. At brotherhood meetings I frequently find people who are simply caressing their own consciences—or vanities—when they express fraternity with others. Being tolerant makes them feel good; but otherwise they are not really concerned. They put on a show, and pat themselves on the back for being such good fellows; they stick their thumbs into the Brotherhood pie, and think, "What a good boy am I!")

Watching the scene in *The King and I* where the brown ruler of Siam and the white English governess waltz together wildly, I thought of the striking difference between the waltz and the minuet. In the minuet the partners come into occasional contact by touching hands; but they keep the proper distance always. In the waltz they come much closer together; they embrace. In the minuet there is a cool, impersonal look in the faces and a stiff formality to the maneuvers. In the waltz, a warm smile flashes from the eyes, and there is an unrestrained sweep to the movements.

Interfaith and interracial meetings are generally minuets. The participants, it is all too often clear, have agreed on the kind of dance, on the tempo; they gesture gracefully and bow graciously; they make slight contact in their movements, they are correct in their approaches. But they do not waltz. They do not embrace their fellow men with ease, much less enthusiasm. And at midnight, so to speak, Cinderella, the minority group, loses her shining glass slipper; her glamorous coach turns back into a pumpkin, her glittering gown turns to rags, and she goes back to the kitchen of the community.

Toward the end of the nineteenth century, when religious and racial tensions were not as explosive as they are now, William James wrote an essay entitled, "On a Certain Blindness in Human Beings." He dealt with the blindness common to us all, because of natural limitations within ourselves: a blindness to the feelings of creatures and peoples other than ourselves. "We are," he said, "practical beings, each of us with limited functions and duties to perform. Each is bound to feel intensely the importance of his own duties and the significance of the situations that call these forth. But this feeling is in each of us a vital secret, for sympathy with which we vainly look to others. The others are too much absorbed in their own vital secrets to take an interest in ours."

The indifference is mutual: Each of us, too absorbed in his own vital secrets to care about others, feels that the others share that egotism. That is the fundamental blindness. I have never forgotten the truism expressed by the great French statesman Edouard Herriot in Paris, to the Sherwood Eddy Seminar Study Group, of which I was a member in the summer of 1937. "There is not a single nation on the face of this earth," he asserted, "that does not want peace. The real difficulty is that every nation is convinced that the other nations do not want peace." And so we stand forever on the brink of war.

There is a song in *The King and I* called, "Getting to Know You." The English governess sings and dances it with the many children of the King of Siam. It is a delightful, lilting expression of man's ability to overcome his blindness through learning and love. Getting to know and appreciate the real "you" of anyone is difficult enough, and more so when it is covered over by a different color, or creed, or class, or country. It is, for that matter, hard to get to know the real you in yourself.

297

At the close of World War II the Emperor of Japan invited Elizabeth Vining, an American Quaker schoolteacher, to become a member of his royal household, not only to teach the Crown Prince English, but, as it was aptly put by the Japanese prime minister, to open for him windows to the Western world. In her book, *Windows for the Crown Prince*, Elizabeth Vining confessed that while she had opened many windows of knowledge and understanding for the Crown Prince, she had found similar windows opening for her, so that her understanding of Oriental beliefs and conduct became much more intelligent and sympathetic. In curing a certain blindness in another, she had eradicated a certain blindness in herself.

A few years ago Dr. Lih Sing Tsai, a professor of psychology at Tulane University, performed a bold experiment with an alley cat and an ordinary rat, in support of his contention that natural enemies may be taught to live peaceably side by side. Before the American Association for the Advancement of Science, he showed how the cat, a confirmed rat-killer, had been educated to co-operate with the rat. He claimed that his experiment laid a biological cornerstone for world peace, and that it put to rest both the Spencerian distortion of Darwin's "survival of the fittest" and the Marxist dogma of class struggle. (It is not commonly known, by the way, that Darwin listed co-operation first among the means of survival, which would seem to indicate that those who best learn to co-operate may best survive. This is a fact often conveniently omitted by those who like to justify their own social egotism by depicting society as a jungle whose inhabitants are constantly at each other's throats, the winners, or the fittest— e.g., those who have sufficient intelligence and leisure time to write books about it!—being obviously superior to all the rest and more deserving of survival. Perhaps the fact that their *books* never survive is significant.) The alley cat, at any rate, was indeed ferocious; he had killed five rats in the laboratory. The cat and the rat were brought together by a series of experiments that made it necessary for them to press a button with their feet simultaneously in order to procure food. Finally, using the same techniques, a dog was brought into the picture. These three natural rivals learned to live together peacefully, and to work together for survival. Dr. Tsai asserted that survival through co-operation can—he might have said "must"—also be achieved among nations in an atomic age.

Atoms, as a distinguished scientist has pointed out, never roam around alone. They are always in combination with other atoms. If you purpose to lure a hydrogen atom away from an oxygen atom, you can only do so by inducing it to unite with something else. It can never be persuaded to go it alone. Atoms, it appears, are incurable joiners. The scientific term for their capacity to join is "valence."

Human beings are not natural enemies. Their instinct is for friendship. Like atoms, they prefer not to roam about alone. Man is, in short, a gregarious animal; but his capacity to unite with others, his valence, varies. The variance is due more to the forces of environment than to any hereditary factors. But the valence is always there, however weak or restricted. (I once heard an undergraduate at a Harvard Club luncheon state that the snobbery of his classmates was so extreme that they considered two of themselves—of "the right kind," of course—to be a crowd!) Many of us restrain the normal urge to be with, and part of, others, and to become, through that union, "more than we are"—in reality, what we were intended to be, what we truly are in our souls. The true individual is not only undivided within himself; he is also undivided from others. He must be part of the lives around him. Without that, lacking the basic human compassion, he remains only a personality.

Many of us, if we do join others, limit our sympathies to certain special groups, similar to ourselves racially or ethnically, religiously, politically, intellectually, socially. Then, like certain atoms when they are grouped together in sufficient numbers, we become explosive: we gang up on other groups and threaten them with humiliation or extinction. Human beings, like atoms, must

299

join in order to function; but the function must be constructive. There is a symbolic parallel here. When the atom is used for its most destructive purposes, the atom loses its identity; it is split, and the elements are transmuted. These transmuted elements become "fall-out," and continue the destruction. So it is with men: When they are transmuted by destructive purposes they become pariahs, and regardless of their original strength, ultimately we consider them dangerous outlaws.

The split Adam is potentially more dangerous than the split atom. The fission of man—his division into different, and mutually suspicious, races, religions, cultures, nations—still remains the most serious menace to world peace. Man united can always control the atom divided. But man as he is today—divided by a thousand cold wars that have rung down iron curtains, bamboo curtains, silken curtains, social curtains of suspicion, fear, resentment, prejudice, hatred—cannot survive.

The problem seems simple: Man may continue divided, and die, or learn to unite, and live. Theo F. Lentz states it graphically: "The paradox of human contradiction has reached an all-time high. With well-nigh universal desire to live, men seem to be making the most elaborate preparations to die. While sick of the sight of slaughter and misery and despair thus far produced by war, the nations of the earth are making their most prodigious preparations for ever greater war. At the stage of man's greatest enlightenment and 'humanitarianism,' the foremost nations of our time pile higher and higher their stock of tools for destruction. This we do for the sake of security and with an assumption of sanity. With the conquest of hunger and despair only partially completed, the resources of the earth are being wasted in human conflict. Behold human ingenuity increasingly dedicated to human frustration and destruction."

The High Lama's prediction seems hauntingly near the truth— except that even Shangri-La will be unable to escape the blazing war that may come, and the split-second destruction made possible by the hydrogen bomb or some unpublicized successor to it. None of the frail elegancies of a dying age will be saved; it is possible that not a single individual, not even the High Lama himself, will survive. Civilization will be left to the cats, dogs, and rats—or perhaps simply to the rats, who have learned to survive underground.

A few years ago during Christmas week I saw a clever animated cartoon, startling in its portrayal of the human destruction that World War III may bring. It depicted a world without man; not a single human survivor remained. Within the ruins of a once-magnificent cathedral a wise old mouse, sitting on a shattered, dusty, cobwebby organ, conducted a Sunday School class, telling the young mice the tragic story of man's failure. The moral lesson he drew was quite clear: With all his genius and greatness, man had failed in his struggle to survive because he had been unable to wage peace as well as he waged war. He had forgotten that he was created in the image of his Maker; and ultimately he had destroyed that image forever.

There are three paths to universal peace: the path of universal love, the path of universal learning, and the path of universal law. They are not mutually exclusive. The love of peace has been everywhere preached and rarely felt. The learning of peace has been everywhere approved and rarely pursued. The law of peace has been everywhere adopted and rarely respected.

Examine the teachings of any people of any age, primitive or advanced, and you will find that they contain, in one form or another, the doctrine of love. The commandment "Love thy neighbor as thyself" is basic not only to the testaments of Judaeo-Christian culture, but to the testaments of all cultures. The Talmudic observation that "hate destroys him who hates as well as him who is hated" was born of bitter human experience. "Man must love his fellow creatures and not hate them," the sages taught. "The men of the generation which was dispersed over the earth (Genesis 11:1–9) loved one another and so God did not destroy them but only scattered them. But the men of Sodom hated one another and so God destroyed them both from this world and from the world to come." And Jesus' Apostle Peter taught, "Love ye one another," as he sought to bring the salvation of God's peace to all mankind.

Apostles of peace have preached and practiced the doctrine of love throughout the ages. They have dreamed and dared and died for it over and over again: an Isaiah, a Buddha, a Jesus, a Gandhi. And millions of men and women have pledged their souls to follow them. But hate, the obverse of love, the shadow inevitably cast by any strong light, seems to spring eternal in the human breast. It takes only one Hitler (who may arise anywhere, in any generation) to unleash it, to send its sweeping destruction over the face of the earth. And for a time all the accumulated love of the ages, stored up and transmitted to men, communities, churches, homes, cannot halt it.

Hate wears many disguises, the most common of which is prejudice. Prejudice is probably born of a desire for security and superiority in the face of an envy or a fear; it is often a reflection of the inadequacy—conscious or unconscious, real or imagined— of its bearer. When prejudice is firmly fixed in the hard core of a group over a period of generations, it is difficult for the waters of love to dissolve it. A fellow clergyman returning from an extended tour of South Africa a few years ago told me this story: He attended a lecture in Johannesburg, where tension over the policy of *apartheid* (firm legal segregation of the colored from the white) was at its height. The speaker, a government official, was expressing great admiration for Gandhi; he said that by his reckoning Gandhi was as great a man as Jan Smuts. This, thought my friend, was high praise indeed from any white South African, particularly from a government official. And then he overheard a white woman, seated behind him, exclaiming, "But how can Gandhi be great? He has a brown skin!"

Yes, hate is strong and has many disguises; to hate Gandhi was to hate love itself.

For generations it was believed that if enough men were shown that war does not pay, that it hurts the victor as well as the vanquished, that its conquests are illusory and temporary, that it sows the seeds of further war—if all this were shown, man would renounce war. We are beginning to understand now that though knowledge is power, it is never a deterrent to the use of power. Learning—that is, learning the lessons of war—is not sufficient by itself to bring about the establishment of peace. There will always be those, both learned and ignorant, who believe that God is on the side of the biggest battalions and bombs. There will be that handful of power-corrupted men willing to risk destruction on the chance of becoming another Alexander the Great.

And there will be those who refuse to study the lessons of the past. There will be those who are incapable, mentally and emotionally, of distilling wisdom from experience. There will be those who are morally callous or spiritually obtuse. There will be the cynics: those who have learned all the lessons but are still so tempted by the prizes of war—deceptively proffered to the multitudes in gaudy wrappings and handsome labels like "Freedom," "Honor," "Equality," "Independence," "Security," "Self-defense"— that they will not hesitate to plunge mankind into the blood-bath once again.

Learning is necessary; but not, apparently, the kind of learning that consists of an examination of history. Rather, it must be an inner education, compound of experience, inner peace, respect for all life, and love of God. The goal of this learning is not a fact or a theory; the goal of this learning is Zusya.

However well, however properly, an individual loves and respects his fellow man and himself, he cannot achieve true peace unless he submits his existence to specific laws of belief and behavior. Whatever knowledge individuals acquire, however forcefully they break through the barriers of color, religion, culture, country, class, they cannot maintain peace unless all subject themselves to laws that are impartially and inexorably enforced.

The American Negro, for example, has been struggling for almost a century to achieve a full measure of liberty, equality and fraternity under our democracy. Since his emancipation—even before, in many quarters—men of religion have insisted that God's perfect love includes us all, and that the Commandment "Love thy neighbor as thyself" admits of no exceptions. Respectable educators have long known that there is no inherent difference in capacity or character between the Negro and the white; all educated Americans have at least been exposed to the truth about race. Yet not until the Supreme Court declared desegregation the law of the land, did our country really bestir itself to make democracy more than a word. Love had been preached; learning had been available; but it was law that made the difference. During the bus boycott in Montgomery, Alabama, in protest against segregation, someone asked an elderly Negro woman whether her feet didn't get tired, walking so many miles each day. "Yes," she answered, "my feet get tired. But I'm happier than I've been in years. You see, before this boycott, my feet were never tired but my soul was. Now that my soul is no longer tired, I hardly feel it in my feet." A short time later it was possible for her to ride again; a law decreed desegration on the buses. What is true for individuals, groups, and communities is also true for nations.

Of course, you can't simply legislate peace into being, any more than you can love it or learn it into being. Passing a law never solves a problem unless there is an agency for enforcement; and enforcement becomes easier in proportion to the love and understanding brought to the problem by the public. The Supreme Court's decree did not solve the problem of segregation, or the problem of race; the problems will be solved by proper enforcement, backed by generosity and understanding among men. The Supreme Court established a goal and a direction; it is now up to the public to make progress.

Similarly, the passing of resolutions in the United Nations will not solve the problems of world peace unless there is a power for enforcement behind them. There must, of course, be law before enforcement; the United Nations, like the Supreme Court, has set a goal and a direction.

Dr. Albert Einstein, a great physicist and a greater man, once described his feelings about the old League of Nations. "I am rarely enthusiastic," he said, "about what the League of Nations has done or has not done. But I am always thankful that it exists." When, despite the fact that President Wilson had created it and pleaded for it, the United States refused to join the League, an Englishman remarked, "The Americans are a strange people. They established the World Court and wouldn't be a part of it. They created the League of Nations and refused to join it. And they invented the cocktail and then made it illegal to drink it."

I shall always believe that our failure to join the League helped pave the way for World War II. The League, without the strongest single world power, deteriorated to a debating society; without our strength and full participation, there was no world law. And why did we refuse? We were afraid to yield any of our sovereignty because, as the French statesman put it, we were certain that our own great nation wanted peace, but we were equally certain that none of the others did.

Victory has given us a second chance; it may be the last. We not only helped to create, but eagerly took our place in, the United Nations. We established it on the soil of our own country; we have stayed with it through crisis after crisis; we strengthened it immeasurably by our leadership and sacrifice in the police action in Korea—the first common effort on the part of free nations to enforce world law. We know that the United Nations is our best hope for world peace. Its laws and resolutions may be momentarily ineffective; but in time we shall find a way to enforce them.

The struggle of nations toward peace may be likened to the struggle of mountain-climbers toward a peak. To provide each with the maximum safety, they bind themselves together on one rope. When one slips, the joint effort of the others saves him. When one has reached the peak, he can pull the others after him. Each remains an individual; yet they share danger and success together.

The United Nations has barely begun its climb. Some of its members are slow in starting; others stumble and slip; still others seem to do nothing but impede progress. Effective machinery to govern conduct, to enforce rules, has not yet been created. But the rope binding the nations together must not be broken. The alternative, in an age of hydrogen bombs, is too horrible to contemplate. It is now the United Nations or, very likely, nothing.

Shortly before his death, Woodrow Wilson told Josephus Daniels that he was not discouraged at the failure of the United States to accept his idea of collective security as embodied in the League of Nations. "It is a good idea and good ideas prevail in the end. I will even give Providence this chance:" he added, "they may think of a better way." There is only one way, essentially: each nation must give up some of its sovereignty in return for greater security. Of what value is total and egotistical sovereignty —national or personal—if its cost is eternal conflict? Shall young men bleed and die for an abstract political ideal never truly realized in all man's history and which, if it were realized, could be destroyed by one nuclear bomb; which, if it were realized, would be an abomination unto the Lord? Honor and freedom are human ideals, worthy and necessary in the sight of God, worth struggling for and even dying for; but absolute sovereignty is an impossible political abstraction; for an individual, absolute sovereignty would mean total isolation and the death of the spirit.

To be a real individual, a man cannot be alone. Each of us has his own goals: he must reconcile himself to life, find inner peace for himself. But the life he lives, the peace he seeks, exist in a world of human beings—as, for a nation, they exist in a world of other nations—and cannot be divorced from that world. In his *The White Tower,* James Ramsey Ullman told the symbolic story of six mountain-climbers representing six nations, bound together by their rope, each working toward the summit of a high mountain. One of them said, "Each of us is alone—despite the fact that each is tied to the others by the common needs of life." In a sense this is certainly true; each of us stands alone before his Maker. But we are all bound to others by the common needs of life, and those needs become more pressing every day. None of us

306

will reach the peak of individual peace unless those to whom we are tied also reach it.

The internationally known mountain-climber Mallory, who died in the attempt to conquer Everest, was once asked what it was that drove him constantly back to the assault on that highest peak. His answer is famous; he thought for a moment, and then said, "I suppose just because it's there." Because Everest was there, a challenge, and because responding to the challenge was part of Mallory's nature. Well, peace is there, too. It is not a fictional Shangri-La. We see it dimly through a mist of shattered hopes and broken dreams; but it is real. It is the sum of all the peace within individuals, all the love, all the wisdom, all the law, all the compassion that man has tried to live by for centuries. Peace is a challenge to all of us, a challenge that none of us can meet alone. We need each other; we need the blessings of God to do His work. Together we may strive for the universal good, and find the peace sought in all ages. Then we shall be Zusya; then we shall be man in all his glory; then we shall be the true children of God.

ABOUT THE AUTHOR

For twenty years Dr. Louis Binstock has been Rabbi of Temple Sholom, The Temple on the Lake, in Chicago, one of the largest Jewish congregations in the country. Here, as well as in his earlier pulpits in Baltimore, Charleston (West Virginia), and New Orleans, he has had a large and devoted following from all races and creeds. As spiritual counselor and adviser, he has helped countless people to solve their personal, marital, family, and religious problems. This book is based on a lifetime of helping other people.

In addition to his ministerial responsibilities, Dr. Binstock has been active in civic causes, serving as president of the New Orleans Rotary Club and the Chicago Urban League. He has lectured over the radio and on platforms across the country. His first book, The Power of Faith, *was published in 1952.*